The
Viking
World

The
Viking
World

James Graham-Campbell

Foreword by David M Wilson

Ticknor
& Fields

New Haven
·
New York

The Viking World
Chapters 1-2, 4-7, 10, text © James Graham-Campbell 1980
Chapters 3, 8-9, text © Frances Lincoln Publishers Limited 1980
Artwork © Frances Lincoln Publishers Limited 1980

First published in the USA in 1980 by
Ticknor & Fields

Published in Great Britain by
Frances Lincoln Publishers Limited

Library of Congress Cataloging in Publication Data

Graham-Campbell, James.
   The Viking World.
   Bibliography: p. 214
   Includes index.
   1. Northmen. I. Title.
DL65.G63 1980   948.02   79-21521
ISBN 0-89919-005-7

Filmset by Keyspools Limited Golborne Lancashire England
Colour separations by Newsele Litho Limited Italy
Printed by L.E.G.O. Vicenza Italy

Contents

IN MEMORIAM
TOM DELANEY
(1947-1979)

e cannot *die* without using a Norse word, we cannot go to *law*, or eat an *egg*. Familiar place-names of history and geography – Naseby, Whitby, Longford, Lundy, Anglesey – were given by Scandinavian settlers. Yorkshire Ridings, the Manx Tynwald, English earldoms, Irish trading towns have roots deep in Scandinavian administration and thought. The English-speaking peoples are bound by ties to a colourful and mixed past in which one of the more gaudy elements is Viking.

The Vikings, who were excoriated by their contemporaries as brutal and bloody, have become objects of uncritical admiration because of their adventurous spirit and gifts of improvisation. And with reason. Out of nowhere they burst on to a comparatively stable society to shake its complacency: they colonized new lands, traded over seemingly impossible distances, fought bravely and with spirit and established themselves inland and built a whole confederation of states which survive today, more stable and less bombastic than most. Their medieval descendants recorded some of the Viking deeds in a romanticized Christian form in stories that belong with the great literature of the world – the Norse sagas. In the north lay a genius which Mr Graham-Campbell and the various contributors to this book record with care, attention and enthusiasm.

The most easily understandable symbol of the Vikings is the ship and Sean McGrail's chapter here is the first account in many years of Viking Age sea-faring in English by one who is both a master mariner and a PhD in Archaeology. New ships are discovered year by year and our knowledge of this aspect of the period has increased immeasurably. During 1979, for example, *Odin's Raven* made an epic voyage from Norway to the Isle of Man, enabling scholars and practical seamen to understand and clarify many obscurities in our general knowledge of ships and seafaring a thousand years ago. Also in 1979 at Hedeby, in what was once Denmark, one of the most elaborate excavations of recent years has uncovered within the gently shelving harbour of this famous Viking town fragments of a Viking warship, with almost non-existent keel and timbers of such beautiful detail that it can only be challenged in craftsmanship by the great ship found in the burial mound at Gokstad, Norway, which is so familiar a symbol of the Viking Age.

Year by year archaeology discloses more and more of the material culture of the Viking Age. New studies of the material reveal new knowledge, new interpretations of their coinage and economy, of their political organization and of their health and housing. New finds tell of new (sometimes rather technical) aspects of their culture which add to the over-all picture. Excavations at Vorbasse in Denmark have not only revealed a true village composed of farm complexes, but also houses with byres at one end and living quarters at the other. A honeymooner in the south of England finds quite casually a gold arm-ring; while hard-working grind by Norwegian excavators at Westness in Orkney uncovers the first properly excavated Scottish Viking Age graves for many a year.

But archaeology, while glamorous and potentially the richest mine for future knowledge of the material culture of the north, is deeply illuminated by the study of contemporary and later literature concerning the Vikings. There is a splendid immediacy in reading a runic inscription of the eleventh century from Sweden to a man who died in England in the city of Bath. Was he buried perhaps in the grand abbey which a few years earlier had seen the coronation of one of the greatest Anglo-Saxon kings, Edgar? The chapters by Dr Page and Miss Fell on the more literary elements of this tale should be read with attention, particularly as the illustrations in this book are rich and lush and might draw the mind away from an understanding of it against the background of poverty in which the people lived. We cannot but be moved by beautiful pictures of vertical landscape taken in the best light of day in Sweden and Norway by skilful photographers. But imagine yourself in those self-same places on a February night, hardly able to stand in the wind, soaked to the skin with rain, wearing inadequate or smelly clothing with only the prospect of a smoky fire and an earth floor to return to. Then one can perhaps understand better the longing for other lands where the living was easier and where the pickings were rich. This is surely one of the reasons for the Viking Age. One of the most remarkable features of the period, however, is the way in which the human spirit achieved new heights. It is the intention of this book to explain, or at least investigate, this phenomenon.

David M. Wilson

Pagan People & Their Lands

Norway's mountains rise abruptly from its western fjords, leaving little space suitable for human habitation and turning its sparse population to the sea. From these shores, in the late 8th century, Norsemen launched the first raids on Britain and Ireland that marked the beginning of the Viking Age in the West.

Background to the Viking Age

The period known as the Viking Age extended from the ninth to the eleventh centuries. This was the time of the Viking movements overseas, when Viking ships sailed from Scandinavia, at the heart of the Viking world, out across the northern hemisphere, on voyages of piracy and invasion, and journeys of commerce, exploration and settlement.

The world of the Vikings consisted of a loose grouping of the Scandinavian homelands and new overseas colonies, linked by sea routes that reached across the Baltic and the North Sea, spanning even the Atlantic. Viking settlements were to be encountered from Newfoundland to Novgorod and from the North Cape of Norway to Normandy in the Frankish Empire. Viking ships sailed the northern waters from the Labrador to the White Seas; they harried the Atlantic coasts of Europe to the Straits of Gibraltar, even penetrating the western Mediterranean. The rivers of the British Isles and the Continent carried their warships deep into the heart of Western Europe; the Dnieper and the Volga brought their merchant craft to the Black Sea and the Caspian and so into direct contact with the worlds of Byzantium and Islam.

To be a Viking was strictly to be a pirate, for the Old Norse noun *viking* meant piracy or a pirate raid, and *víkingr*, a pirate or raider. It is misleading to describe three centuries of northern history as an age of raiders – for by no means all Scandinavians were. But the usage is too convenient and long-established to be abandoned, and will be applied here to all those of Scandinavian blood, whatever their occupation or intent, unless they are further identified by nationality – as Danes, Swedes, Norse (from Norway), Icelanders or whatever the case might be. Often such identification is impossible, for the European and Islamic sources frequently refer to their Viking assailants and to Scandinavian merchants only by general terms, such as Northmen or pagans.

The beginning of the Viking Age in the West was marked by an outburst of Scandinavian sea-piracy during the last couple of decades of the eighth century, when Vikings raided Western Europe for the first time. Their early targets included many monasteries, and this direct assault on Christendom brought horror and terror to all who lay within reach of their attentions. The increasing number of raids during the ninth century, and their frequency in the tenth, makes the term Viking Age, in its literal meaning, appropriate for this period in the West. During the eleventh century the attacks gradually diminished in number and intensity. At the same time the pagan peoples of Scandinavia came to accept Christianity, and Norway, Sweden and Denmark emerged as nation-states comparable to many of those in the rest of Europe, whose civilization they now embraced.

By about 1100 the Viking Age was over throughout the Viking world: in many areas the Viking settlers and merchants had become absorbed into the local populations; in others, such as Iceland, their heritage lived on, as it does today.

Throughout these three centuries of Viking adventure, there remained at home in Scandinavia farmers, hunters, fishermen and trappers who led the same lives as their forebears. It was those who stayed at home who provided the resources that made the voyages practicable. The ships had to be built, equipped and provisioned. Supplies had to be accumulated for the winter months, and so had the commodities required to make up the cargoes of the traders. No true picture of the Vikings and their achievements can be gained without some understanding of their economic background in Scandinavia, and so of the very different landscapes of their separate homelands.

Denmark

Denmark today comprises the peninsula of Jutland and the large islands of Fyn and Sjælland, together with nearly 500 smaller

Women enjoyed a good position in Viking society – both in theory and in practice. This Swedish pendant (enlarged) depicts a Viking woman wearing typical Scandinavian dress.

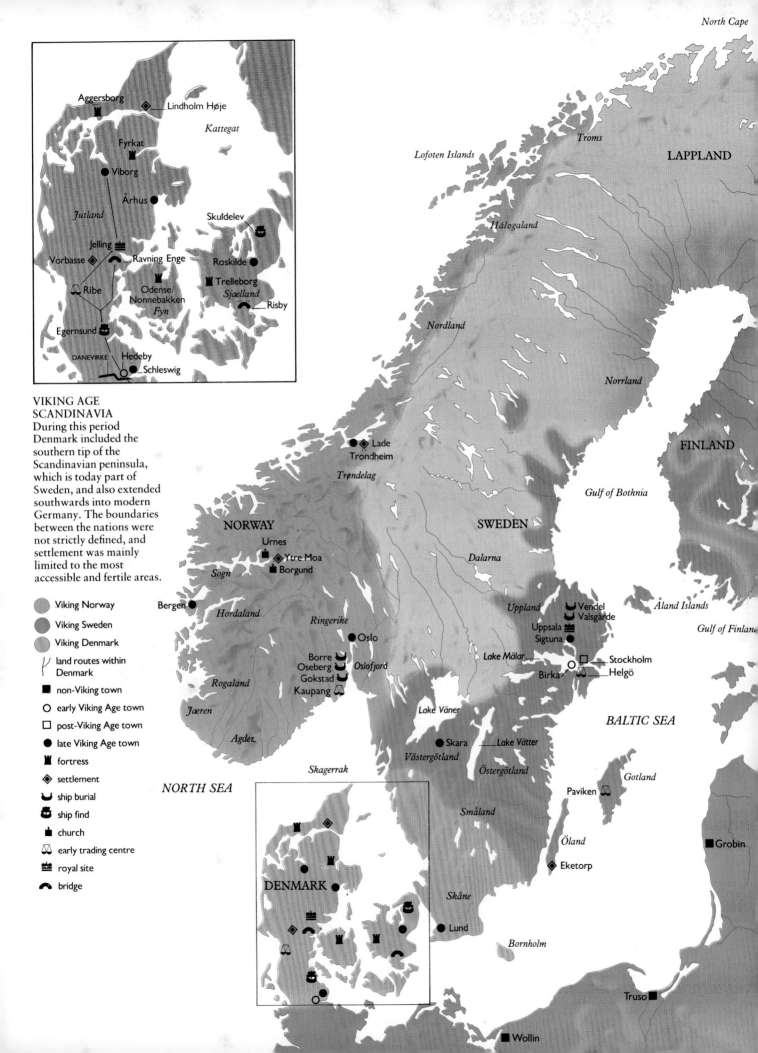

North Cape

Aggersborg
Lindholm Høje
Kattegat

Fyrkat

Viborg

Århus

Skuldelev

Jutland

Jelling
Roskilde
Vorbasse
Ravning Enge
Trelleborg
Ribe
Sjælland
Odense/
Nonnebakken
Risby
Fyn

Egernsund

DANEVIRKE
Hedeby
Schleswig

VIKING AGE SCANDINAVIA

During this period Denmark included the southern tip of the Scandinavian peninsula, which is today part of Sweden, and also extended southwards into modern Germany. The boundaries between the nations were not strictly defined, and settlement was mainly limited to the most accessible and fertile areas.

- Viking Norway
- Viking Sweden
- Viking Denmark
- Ⓨ land routes within Denmark
- ■ non-Viking town
- O early Viking Age town
- ☐ post-Viking Age town
- ● late Viking Age town
- fortress
- ◈ settlement
- ship burial
- ship find
- church
- early trading centre
- royal site
- bridge

LAPPLAND

Lofoten Islands

Troms

Hålogaland

Nørdland

FINLAND

Norrland

Lade
Trondheim

Trøndelag

Gulf of Bothnia

SWEDEN

Urnes
Ytre Moa
Borgund
Dalarna

Sogn

NORWAY

Åland Islands

Uppland
Vendel
Valsgärde
Uppsala
Sigtuna
Gulf of Finland

Bergen
Hordaland
Ringerike

Lake Mälar
Stockholm
Birka
Helgö

Oslo

Borre
Oseberg
Gokstad
Kaupang
Oslofjord

Rogaland

Lake Väner

BALTIC SEA

Jæren

Agder

Lake Vätter

Skara
Västergötland

Östergötland

NORTH SEA

Skagerrak

Gotland

Paviken

Småland

Öland

Eketorp

Grobin

DENMARK

Skåne

Lund

Bornholm

Truso

Wollin

Lake Mälar in central Sweden provides a direct route from the Baltic into the heart of the well-forested and fertile region of Uppland. Here, on the island of Björkö, there flourished the Viking town of Birka.

islands, including Bornholm in the Baltic, well to the east of the rest of Denmark. However, during the Viking Age Danish territory was considerably more extensive, for the southern Swedish provinces of Skåne, Halland and Blekinge also formed part of the Danish realm. At the base of the Jutland peninsula, the Danish frontier lay further to the south than its modern counterpart, in the region of the river Eider. It was defended by a series of earthworks, known as the Danevirke, in which a single gap was left for the so-called *Hærvej* (Army Road). This great route ran south from Viborg in northern Jutland to Holstein, a frontier region where Danes, Saxons, Frisians and Wends met and mingled. There it linked with the routes that traversed

the North European Plain from which Denmark projects like a flat thumb. More than half of Denmark is less than 100ft (30m) above sea level, and Denmark's highest point attains only 568ft (173m), in dramatic contrast to Norway's 8,400ft (2,560m).

The German cleric Adam of Bremen, who had had long conversations with the Danish King Svein Estridsson (1047–74), described eleventh-century Jutland thus:

And whilst the whole land of Germany is frightful with thick forests, Jutland is still more frightful, where the land is shunned on account of the poverty of its produce and the sea on account of the infestation of pirates. Cultivation is found hardly anywhere, hardly any

The Limfjord bisects the flat landscape of northern Jutland, linking the North Sea to the Kattegat at the mouth of the Baltic. Traces of the ploughed-out rampart of the Viking fortress of Aggersborg may be seen in the field in the foreground as a ring of lighter soil.

brought them their wealth. In the south, the narrow base of the Jutland peninsula provided the shortest and safest route for trade between Western Europe and the lands around the Baltic – a source of wealth developed by the Viking Age town of Hedeby. Control of the ship-passages between the North Sea and the Baltic also lay in Danish hands, for all the routes passed through the archipelago between Jutland and Skåne.

Sweden

The wide variations in soil, climate and relief throughout its thousand-mile length mean that Sweden has a diverse mantle of vegetation. To the north of Skåne, the low plateau of Småland with its thin and poor soils was sparsely populated except for certain valleys, and so formed a natural boundary with Viking Age Denmark. The central lowlands of Sweden divided into two well-forested and fertile regions, that of the *Svear* (who were to give their name to the whole country) and that of the *Götar*. The *Svear*, centred on the province of Uppland, with their royal seat at Old Uppsala, dominated the tribes living

place exists suitable for human habitation, but wherever there are arms of the sea, there the country has very large settlements.

Denmark during the Viking Age was extensively wooded with oak and beech; of the remainder of its gently undulating landscape much was wasteland, sand dunes and heaths. However, the soils of some of the islands were fertile and Adam of Bremen noted of Sjælland, where the seat of eleventh-century Danish kings was situated at Roskilde, that it was 'famous for the valour of its people and for the richness of its produce'.

Nowhere is more than thirty-five miles from the sea, and it was the sea that provided the Danes with much of their livelihood, and

13

This fine head of a 9th-century Norseman was carved on the side of a richly ornamented wagon found in the Oseberg ship burial in Norway – the grave of a wealthy woman, often identified (without certainty) as Queen Åsa of Vestfold.

be practised along the coastal plain, and even there the inhabitants have to contend with long severe winters, when the Gulf of Bothnia is frozen over. The population is as sparse today as it must have been in the Viking Age.

The coast of Sweden has seen considerable changes since the Viking Age for it is still recovering from the heavy weight of ice that once overlay it. In the north the land rises some 40in (100cm) each century, although this rate decreases towards the south and in the extreme south the land level remains constant. Much of the coast is fringed by archipelagos of rocky islands, while parallel to the coast of *Götaland* lies the long narrow island of Öland. Of particular importance and wealth during the Viking Age was the Baltic island of Gotland, consisting of a great limestone mass with good farming land around its coasts and sheltered bays. Its inhabitants exploited to the full its strategic position at the centre of the Baltic and enjoyed an independence of their own.

around the great lakes called Hjälmar and Mälar, and those of the adjacent Baltic coasts. The *Götar* lived in the region on the east of the vast Lake Väner in the provinces of Västergötland and Östergötland. To the west they were cut off from the North Sea by Danish or Norwegian territories – for in the Viking Age the Swedish province of Bohuslän was a Norwegian possession, although occasionally it was dominated by the Danes.

To the north lies Norrland, extending well beyond the Arctic Circle. The land falls away south-eastwards from the high plateau along the Norwegian border, to a coastal plain along the Gulf of Bothnia. Much of the terrain is covered with coniferous forest; a great deal of the rest is bare rock. Agriculture can only

Finland

East of the Baltic, Swedes had by the beginning of the Viking Age begun to settle in Finland. Its surface is pockmarked by some 55,000 interconnected lakes, many surrounded by bog and fen. No other country in the world has so high a proportion of its area under forest. There is, however, a narrow plain that extends for fifty or sixty miles along the coast of the Gulf of Bothnia and the Gulf of Finland, which was populated by Finns among whom the Swedes settled; in the far north, as in Sweden and Norway, was the territory of the Lapps. In the south-west the coast is bordered by an archipelago of small islands and reefs, among which the Åland Islands form the largest group.

Norway

Norway's mountains, rising abruptly from its fjord-indented coastline, turn the faces of its sparse population to the sea. If the mainland coast of Norway were measured in a direct

The significance of an enigmatic group of figures carved on one end of the Oseberg wagon is unknown, but provides some evidence of the Vikings' appearance. A woman restrains the arm of a man with his sword raised against a rider with a dog. The pattern below is of interlaced animals.

A pre-Viking helmet from a chieftain's grave at Valsgärde in Uppland, Sweden, is shaped like an iron crash-helmet, with a spectacle-like guard for the eyes and nose; its rich ornament has largely perished. Viking helmets were descended from this type, and did not have horns.

line, it would be about 2,000 miles long; its actual length exceeds 12,500 miles. Even this total excludes the thousands of offshore islets (at least 150,000 in all) that protect Norway's western seaboard and form a sheltered sea route down most of its length – the 'North-way' that gave Norway its name.

The steep-sided fjords are long and narrow; the Sognefjord, for instance, extends for a hundred miles, but is rarely broader than three. Settlement is confined to narrow ledges and small plains at their heads, deposited by the inflowing rivers from the high plateau. More than half the country lies at altitudes above 2,000ft (610m), but there are just a few areas with gentle slopes that are well covered with soil, notably around the Oslofjord, but also in Jæren near the southern edge of the fjord country, and further north in the region of Trøndelag.

The Oslofjord, or *Víkin* (the Inlet) as it used to be called, has two great valley systems draining into it – Østerdal and Gudbrandsdal. From these valleys passes lead northwards to the rich farming area of Trøndelag, a wealthy and important region during Norway's Viking Age, with important contacts east to Sweden, as well as north and south by sea along the 'leads', the routes sheltered by the multitude of offshore islands.

Further to the north, extending in a narrow strip to the North Cape and broadening out to the White Sea, lay the region of *Hálogaland*, meaning perhaps Land of the Aurora. This was a thinly populated area where Norse Vikings took tribute from the Lapps and exploited the rich natural resources by hunting and fishing.

The south-west of Norway, except for the rich farming land of Jæren, is essentially an area of high plateau. Its coast is unprotected by skerries and, being exposed to the south-west, is rocky and dangerous for shipping. The far south also lacks inland routes of importance and so was a remote area in the Viking Age, as it was to remain for many centuries.

Regional differences

These geographical differences in the Scandinavian homelands led to variations in both agricultural and building practices. Stock-raising in Denmark did not require the same amount of labour as in much of the rest of Scandinavia, where the long, hard winters meant that animals had to be housed and fed indoors for several months each year to ensure their survival. So Denmark's exports will have included cattle and horses (largely no doubt in the form of hides), while for Norway and Sweden furs obtained by hunting were much more important. Timber was used for building throughout Scandinavia, but Denmark lacked suitable materials for the drystone techniques that were also in use in the other countries.

Viking movements overseas

The varied landscape of Scandinavia also determined to a great extent the directions of the Viking movements. Norse Vikings looked inevitably to the west, for a short voyage across the North Sea, sailing due westwards from the main area of population, brought almost certain landfall in Shetland, Orkney, or on the Scottish mainland. The Northern Isles served as stepping stones to the Hebrides, Ireland, the Isle of Man, and north-west England – or westwards to the Faeroes and Iceland. In turn the Icelanders settled Greenland, and the Greenlanders went on to explore part of the North American coastline.

Sweden looked eastwards, as in part did the Danes, and already before the Viking Age there were Scandinavian communities established on the southern and eastern coasts of the Baltic, created or developed with a view to trade. For Sweden the beginning of the Viking Age was marked by the establishment of regular contacts with the East, in particular with the eastern part of the Islamic Empire in western Asia, reached via the river Volga.

The Danes, although involved with the Swedes along the south Baltic shores, looked mainly to the west along the southern coast of the North Sea – the territory of the Frisians. The Frisians were renowned as merchants in the eighth century, and at that time they established commercial contacts with Scandinavia, as the development of Ribe on the west coast of Denmark demonstrates; Frisian coins have been found among the workshop sites and deep deposits of cow dung that form its earliest levels. There also seems to have been a Frisian element in the earliest settlement of the town of Hedeby on the east side of the peninsula, with direct access to the Baltic. In the ninth century, however, the wealth of the Frisian merchants provided rich targets for Viking raiders and their chief port of Dorestad was repeatedly plundered. Danish Vikings continued their westward movement through the English Channel to raid France and southern England, continuing even further to become involved in affairs in Ireland. But their main area for overseas settlement was provided by the conquest of eastern England.

The reasons behind the great outpouring of people from Scandinavia that marked the Viking Age are unknown. The search for wealth, whether in the form of goods or land, is the most apparent, while population pressures at home may have provided the stimulus that sent people abroad. Dynastic strife and the growing imposition of royal

A gilt-bronze bridle-mount, also from Valsgärde in Sweden, illustrates the Scandinavian tradition of stylized animal ornament from which Viking art sprang. It is decorated with a pair of barely recognizable creatures, with intertwining, ribbon-like bodies and large, round eyes.

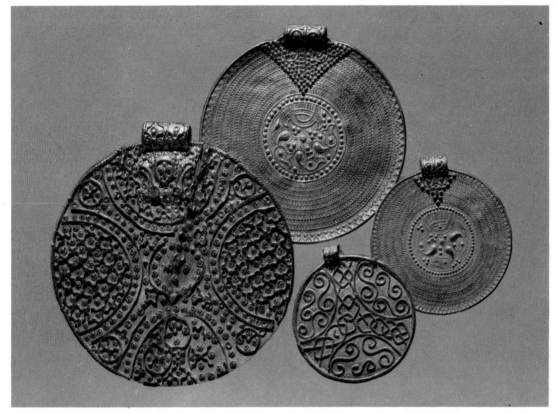

Pendants from Gotland represent a tradition of Scandinavian goldsmiths' work that stretches back to the 5th century, when such ornaments were first made. Originally these copied Roman coins and medals, although they are no longer recognizable as such by the Viking Age.

power drove some to seek new lands. Above all we must remember the quality of their ships, which, for the first time, made such expeditions possible.

Commerce

The beginning of the Viking Age was almost certainly a less sudden event than it is often depicted; dramatic emphasis is generally placed on the first recorded raids, but one should also take into account the more elusive process of the opening up of Scandinavia to the rest of Europe, and to the worlds of Byzantium and Islam, by the establishment of regular commercial networks with West and East.

Within Scandinavia a number of small trading and manufacturing centres flourished during the eighth century, among them Ribe, which has already been mentioned, Paviken on Gotland and Helgö in Sweden. Helgö, which is situated on Lake Mälar, consists of several groups of houses, including the workshops of smiths, bronze-workers and

bead-makers, that flourished particularly in the fifth and sixth centuries. Helgö continued in occupation into the Viking Age, although it was then eclipsed by the nearby town of Birka. The iron and ornaments produced by its craftsmen were traded locally and some were also exported. Its imports came in return mostly from around the Baltic, but its raw materials of precious metals, bronze and glass originated in both Western and Eastern Europe. Two remarkable finds are quite contrasted in their ultimate origins – a bronze figure of Buddha from northern India, Kashmir, or Afghanistan, and an inlaid bronze mount made in Ireland that may be a crozier-head (see page 91).

Helgö lay at the centre of the kingdom of the *Svear*, not far from Old Uppsala where there stands an impressive group of burial mounds of its pre-Viking kings. Helgö's wealth and trading contacts, maybe even its products, are also reflected elsewhere in Uppland in the rich boat graves of Vendel and

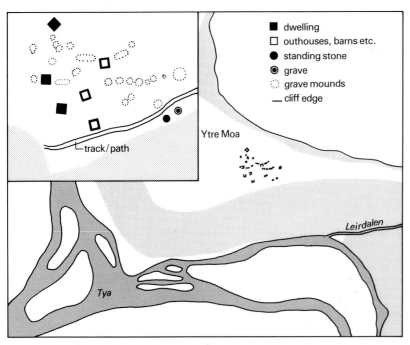

Few Viking Age farmsteads have been excavated in Norway. That at Ytre Moa in Sogn occupied a small plateau above a river. The farm dwellings and outhouses were surrounded by the family graves.

Valsgärde – the cemeteries of two families who, judging from their possessions and the lavishness of their burial rites, must have been local chieftains. In both cemeteries, which continued in use into the Viking Age, there appear to have been deposited in each generation one major ship burial, containing a warrior equipped with fine-quality weapons and highly ornamented equipment, and sometimes his horses and imported luxuries such as drinking glasses. The ornamented bridle-mounts are covered with designs created from the bodies of stylized animals. These designs had originally been borrowed from the naturalistic art of the provincial Roman Empire, but had then undergone a continuous process of modification in Scandinavia from the fifth century, remaining in use in one form or another to form the basis of various styles of Viking art.

The structure of society

The chieftains' graves at Vendel and Valsgärde introduce us to the aristocratic level of Scandinavian society in the centuries before and during the Viking Age. At the apex of that society, of course, were the kings and princes.

Viking Age royalty will be making regular appearances in the course of this narrative. Although we do not know of their graves in Sweden, the ship burials of Oseberg and Gokstad in Vestfold, beside the Oslofjord, and the royal burial place of Jelling in Jutland, provide us with direct archaeological evidence for the status and possessions of certain kings and queens of Norway and Denmark respectively.

The chieftain, or *jarl*, would have had about him a warrior-band drawn from the free men of his region. During the Viking Age Scandinavian kings were successful in establishing their control over the activities of such leaders, depriving them of their independence, and so consolidating their countries into proper kingdoms. The free men, *karlar*, who formed the bulk of society, were generally farmers, although some might be specialists of one kind or another, such as boatbuilders, weapon-makers or goldsmiths.

Farms employed slave labour and the slave, or *þræll*, was generally despised (although he might be of high birth) and had few rights (although slaves might be freed from bondage by gift or purchase). Slavery at this period was a recognized institution in northern Europe and among the Arabs, and the Vikings were to become the greatest slave-traders of their day, supplying the Islamic Empire with a commodity that their piratical activities made readily available, in return for the silver that they so much coveted and that the Arabs possessed in abundance.

Modern archaeology

The greater part of our knowledge of the Vikings in Scandinavia is still derived from the study of grave-goods, for, fortunately for us, a full range of objects from daily life was provided for the pagan dead. Silver ornaments and coins were deposited in graves only in very small numbers, but are found instead in hoards, hidden in safe places for security, and then never recovered. One can only conclude that silver was regarded as family wealth, in the same manner as land, and so not buried with its owner – or that it had conveniently been decided that there was no use for it in the afterlife.

Settlement studies are, however, gradually gaining in importance as more sites are excavated and the finds processed. These sites include towns and trading centres, such as Trondheim and Kaupang in Norway, Hedeby (now in northern Germany), Lund and Löddeköpinge in southern Sweden, and other sites such as the Danish fortresses (for example Fyrkat), and the great pre-Viking stone fort of Eketorp on Öland, which was reoccupied on a permanent basis during the late Viking Age.

We do not yet know as much as we would like about ordinary farms in the Viking homelands – no doubt because many of them lie beneath their modern counterparts, given the restricted areas available for farming settlements in much of Scandinavia. At Ytre Moa, in western Norway, one such farm complex has been excavated and has been found to consist of a small scatter of houses and farm buildings (although not all were in use together) amid the burial mounds of its former inhabitants. A similar close relationship between the living and the dead may be assumed at Lindholm Høje in Jutland, which came to an end c. 1100, to be smothered with sand. This mantle has been stripped away, to reveal a dense concentration of pre-Viking and Viking Age graves. Elsewhere in Jutland new finds of villages and farms – such as that at Vorbasse – are currently under excavation. Some of these appear to substantiate the suggestions that cattle- and horse-ranching were of particular importance to the Viking Age economy of Denmark.

Excavations outside Scandinavia are also continuously increasing our knowledge of the Viking world. For instance, work in recent years in Dublin has transformed our understanding of the Viking presence in Ireland, while that in progress in York will enable us to assess the true impact of the Danes on this Anglo-Saxon town, which they turned into the capital of a Viking kingdom. Details of Viking farmhouses and their associated buildings are still best appreciated from sites that have been uncovered in the western settlements – in Scotland, the Faeroes and Iceland – yet here too a great deal remains to be done. As will become apparent, much information of the greatest importance is the result of recent excavation, as well as work in the many related fields that together constitute Viking Age studies. One archaeological find, such as that of the Skuldelev ships, may bring entirely new light to bear on the Vikings and their activities, but so does the patient excavation of towns, farms and middens. And we can be sure that far more remains to be revealed wherever in the Viking world the resources are made available for such research to be carried out.

At Lindholm Høje in northern Jutland, beside the Limfjord, an extensive Viking Age cemetery has been excavated, together with part of its associated settlement and even a ploughed field. Most of the burials were cremations placed within stone settings, often in the outline of a ship.

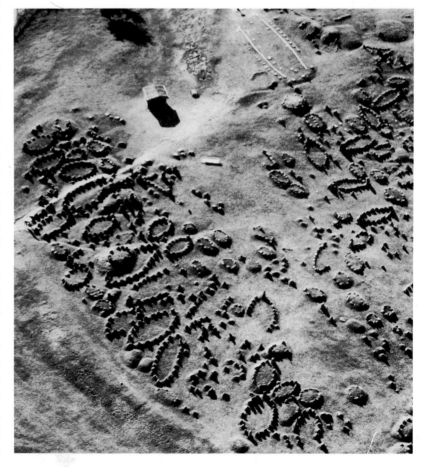

Viking
Warriors

Lindisfarne, or Holy Island, is a small tidal island off the coast of
Northumbria where a monastery had been established in 634.
Its shelving beaches provided a perfect landing for the shallow-
draft ships of the Viking raiders who fell upon its unsuspecting
and unprotected monks in the summer of 793. This bloody
assault on 'a place more venerable than all in Britain' was one of
the first positively recorded Viking raids on the West.

Salt-water bandits

'Salt-water bandits with brutal vices' or 'stout-hearted gentlemen of the north'? From the time of their first raids onwards, the Vikings have always aroused strong passions in their commentators. In twelfth-century England they were recalled as 'stinging hornets' and 'fearful wolves', while in Ireland at the same period they were remembered as 'ruthless, wrathful, foreign, purely pagan people'. Their initial impact on Western Europe fell heavily on the Church, for monasteries were prime targets; and monastic scholars have left us contemporary chronicles with bitter accounts of their misfortunes.

That monasteries were frequently raided in the ninth and tenth centuries was not because the Vikings were actively anti-Christian, but because these sites were centres of wealth, and ill protected. They had ecclesiastical treasures and accumulated gifts; they were well supplied with provisions and Mass wine. Above all, they were centres of population, whose abbots, monks and nuns might be captured for ransom; or, if funds were not immediately forthcoming for their release, sold into slavery. Repeated raids on monasteries in Ireland and western France suggest that their inmates were being culled to feed the demands of the slave trade on which much of Viking Dublin's prosperity was based.

The Vikings were not the only people to attack monasteries, which were liable to fall victim also to local political disturbances, or even to native bandits, as the Irish annals show. Nor was the Church always hostile to Viking forces: accommodation was sometimes felt to be a better course than valour. Archbishop Wulfhere of York, for instance, collaborated with the Danish conquerors when they took the city. But it is important to remember that our principal historical sources, being written by churchmen, are naturally biased. All the same, running through their accounts there is a very real sense of fear, even of panic.

For a couple of centuries the Vikings as *víkingr*, in the true sense of raiders, brought terror and destruction to much of Western Europe. They fell on the monasteries and towns around the North and Irish Seas, down Europe's Atlantic coast and even around the western Mediterranean. Any settlement, however small, could serve to revictual a ship, or have sons and daughters who would fetch a price in the slave market. It was not just the coasts that suffered. Viking longships, with their shallow drafts and good manoeuvrability under both sail and oar, allowed their crews to strike deep inland up Europe's major rivers; from the Shannon to the Seine and from the Rhine to the Rhône there was hardly a watercourse, with its ports and markets that escaped the attentions of the Vikings in their quest for booty. Throughout the West the relics of saints had to be moved to safety: those of St Columba were transferred from Iona in the Hebrides to Kells in Ireland; those of St Cuthbert, removed from Lindisfarne off the Northumbrian coast, finally came to rest in Durham; those of St Philibert from the isle of Noirmoutier, at the mouth of the Loire, ended up at Tournus.

By no means all of those who sailed west and south from Scandinavia were after loot; there were merchants among them, and people seeking new livelihoods as settlers or as mercenaries in the service of whoever had need of them. But raids were the hallmark of the Viking Age; and it is as raiders that the Vikings have been remembered.

Right One of a pair of silver miniatures (enlarged) from Birka in Sweden. Adam of Bremen wrote in the 11th century that the Swedes were 'very great warriors both on horses and on ships'.

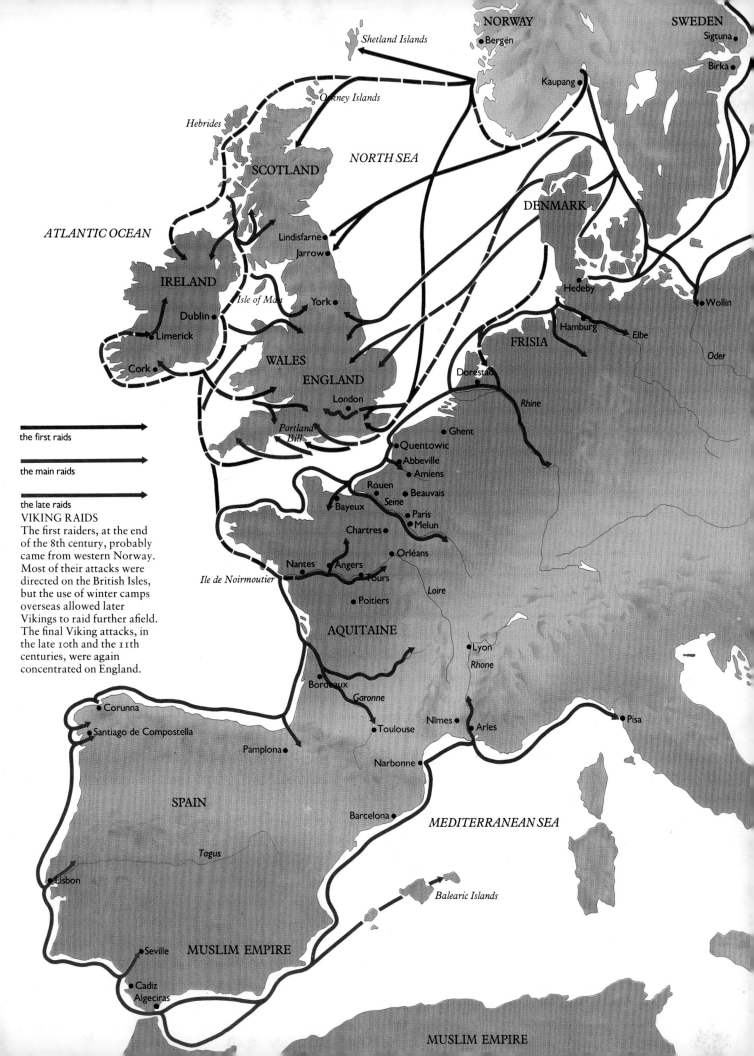

NORWAY
Bergen

SWEDEN
Sigtuna
Birka
Kaupang

Shetland Islands

Orkney Islands

Hebrides

SCOTLAND

NORTH SEA

DENMARK

ATLANTIC OCEAN

Lindisfarne
Jarrow

Hedeby
Wollin

York

FRISIA
Hamburg
Elbe

IRELAND
Dublin
Isle of Man

Oder

Limerick

WALES

ENGLAND
London

Dorestad

Rhine

Cork

*Portland
Bill*

Ghent

Quentowic
Abbeville
Amiens

the first raids

Rouen
Seine
Beauvais

the main raids

Bayeux
Paris
Melun

the late raids

Chartres

VIKING RAIDS
The first raiders, at the end
of the 8th century, probably
came from western Norway.
Most of their attacks were
directed on the British Isles,
but the use of winter camps
overseas allowed later
Vikings to raid further afield.
The final Viking attacks, in
the late 10th and the 11th
centuries, were again
concentrated on England.

Nantes
Angers
Tours

Orléans

Loire

Poitiers

AQUITAINE

Lyon

Ile de Noirmoutier

Rhone

Bordeaux
Garonne

Corunna

Nîmes
Arles

Pisa

Santiago de Compostella

Toulouse

Pamplona

Narbonne

SPAIN

Barcelona

MEDITERRANEAN SEA

Tagus

Lisbon

Balearic Islands

Seville

MUSLIM EMPIRE

Cadiz
Algeciras

MUSLIM EMPIRE

The equipment of the warriors

The 10th-century Viking warrior crudely carved on one side of the Middleton cross, in Yorkshire, is shown surrounded by his weapons. On his head he wears a conical helmet and by his left side are placed his shield, sword and axe; to his right is his spear. A large knife in a sheath hangs from his belt.

The success of the Vikings' raids depended in the first place on the special qualities of their ships. But in addition they were well provided with weapons of exceptional efficiency, among which swords were the most important. These were carefully balanced for maximum effect as slashing implements, and were designed to be used single-handed. Their blades were double-edged and the finest seem to have been imported from the Rhineland. Great care was naturally taken of such weapons and this often found expression in the elaborate ornamentation of their hilts. Apart from the sword, the commonest weapon found in the pagan Viking Age graves is the spear. Both javelins for throwing and lances for thrusting were in use; again the finest of these were richly ornamented.

The weapon with which the Vikings are most often associated in the popular imagination is the axe. Axes were certainly much used in battle throughout the Viking Age – they can be seen being wielded on the Lindisfarne stone (page 26), and on the Bayeux Tapestry they are among the weapons being loaded to equip William the Conqueror's invasion fleet. The principal means of defence was the shield, which consisted of a circular wooden board with a central iron boss to protect the hand.

It is, one fears, too late to scotch the myth that the Vikings wore horned helmets. You may search among the contemporary illustrations of Viking warriors from Iceland to Sweden and almost all will be found to show men with pointed heads. A simple conical cap, most probably of leather (for helmets of any description dating from the Viking Age are very rarely found), seems to have been the normal protection for the head of a Viking warrior. The most complete find of an iron helmet is from the grave of a tenth-century Norwegian Viking and consists of a simple rounded cap, made in several pieces, with a spectacle-like guard for the eyes and nose.

Rare exceptions among the representations, such as a small figure from Uppland (page 179), have horned helmets. But the explanation for such figures is to be found in the period before the Viking Age. Even then such helmets were not worn in battle, but were cult objects with birds' head terminals worn by dancing warriors at festivities probably connected with the worship of Odin.

Body protection in the form of chain mail seems to have been a rarity for most of the Viking Age, although the Norwegian chieftain who was buried with his helmet also possessed a mail shirt. By the end of the Viking Age such shirts were clearly becoming more common; not only are they depicted frequently on the Bayeux Tapestry, they are mentioned in the Anglo-Saxon poem known as *The Battle of Maldon*, after the encounter between an English and a Viking army that took place in 991 – a Viking was 'wounded through his mail in the breast', by the thrust of an Anglo-Saxon spear.

This poem tells also how 'They let the spears, hard as files, fly from their hands, well-made javelins. Bows were busy. Point pierced shield. The rush of battle was fierce, warriors fell on both sides, men lay dead.' The Anglo-Saxons had, at the beginning of the fight, formed a wall with their shields in order to hold their line against the Vikings; this was also a Viking practice. But, on the whole, a battle seems to have consisted of a general *mêlée* with the principal concern being to knock hell out of the opposition in whatever manner was most effective.

The use of horses in fighting seems to have become increasingly widespread as the Viking Age developed. In the tenth century we find Vikings buried not only with their weapons, but with their riding equipment and horses as well. The successes of the Vikings in England in the late Viking Age seem to have been due in great part to their mobility, resulting from their use of horses. They would normally have seized horses on landing, but the Viking ships could carry horses when necessary.

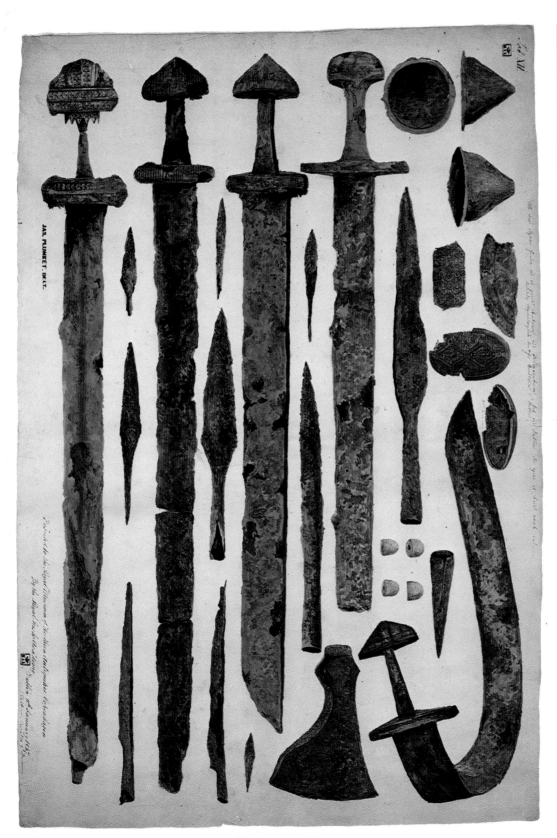

Above Spear-heads richly encrusted with silver and copper wires, from 10th-century graves at Valsgärde in Sweden, demonstrate the wealth and care that could be lavished on Viking Age weapons.

Left A 19th-century watercolour records the weapons of 9th-century Viking warriors, found in the pagan cemetery at Kilmainham-Islandbridge outside Dublin. Swords with ornamented hilts, spear-heads, arrow-heads, shield-bosses, and an axe, are all illustrated, together with women's bronze brooches and four playing pieces.

Viking raids on Britain

This Anglo-Saxon stone grave-marker was raised on Lindisfarne in the 9th century. It seems probable that the scene depicted is that of a Viking raiding party brandishing their axes and swords – perhaps recalling the attack on the monastery of 793.

ut of the north an evil shall break forth upon all the inhabitants of the land' (Jeremiah 1:14). This prophecy came true for the Anglo-Saxons on 8 June 793, when 'ravages of heathen men miserably destroyed God's church on Lindisfarne, with plunder and slaughter.' The *Anglo-Saxon Chronicle* prefaces this entry with an account of the 'dire portents' that had appeared over Northumbria earlier in the year, to be followed by famine. To the Anglo-Saxons the first Viking raids seemed to be a divine judgment on their sins.

The long sandy beach of Lindisfarne, or Holy Island, where monks from Iona in Scotland had established themselves in 634 to bring Christianity to the Northumbrians, provided a perfect landing for Viking longships. The raid was a hit-and-run affair, typical of those that were to follow. The English scholar Alcuin wrote of it to the King of Northumbria:

> . . . never before has such terror
> appeared in Britain as we have now
> suffered from a pagan race, nor was it
> thought that such an inroad from the
> sea could be made. Behold, the church
> of St Cuthbert spattered with the blood
> of the priests of God, despoiled of all its
> ornaments; a place more venerable
> than all in Britain is given as prey to
> pagan peoples.

The success of this raid was such that a party of Vikings, no doubt the same ones, returned to the coast of Northumbria the following year and raided a monastery, probably Jarrow. However, their leader was killed, others were drowned in a severe storm and those who clambered ashore were killed. Following this disaster for the Vikings, Northumbria seems to have escaped their further attentions for a generation. The focus of Norwegian piracy, for it is a reasonable assumption that these raiders of 793/4 were from Norway, shifted westwards.

The Northumbrian raids are the first of which we have certain knowledge, but disturbances in the English Channel may have started even earlier. Offa was arranging for the defence of Kent against pagan seamen in 792, although we are not told who they were. That the south coast of England was in danger is confirmed by the *Anglo-Saxon Chronicle*'s entry under the year 789 of an event that occurred during the reign of King Beorhtric of Wessex (786–802). From the various versions of what took place, it appears that men from three ships put ashore at Portland and the King's official, who rode out from Dorchester to investigate, was killed by them. It is probable that these were Vikings from Hordaland in western Norway, although the *Chronicle* passes the comment that 'Those were the first ships of Danish men which came to the land of the English.'

The Anglo-Saxons were frequently confused as to the distinction between Norwegians and Danes. They were 'heathen men' alike and both races spoke the 'Danish tongue'. As a further complication, certainly at a later period if not at the very beginning, Viking armies and even groups of raiders included men of more than one nationality.

In 795 Iona was plundered for the first time, as was an island off Ireland, probably Lambay, to the north of Dublin. There are no chronicles to tell us of the raids that must have preceded these, on the monasteries of the Northern Isles. In the north and west of Scotland, raiding and settlement seem to have gone hand in hand. The new settlements provided a network of fellow Norsemen along much of the sea route from Norway to Ireland and bases where additional crewmen or ships might be recruited, or storm damage repaired, before heading southwards.

Ireland

Raiding on Ireland was at first sporadic and confined to the coastline. But in the 830s the frequency of the raids increased and Viking ships began to penetrate Ireland's rivers and

BRITISH ISLES AND NORMANDY
Viking settlement in these areas can be plotted from the occurrence of Scandinavian place-names. In 886 Alfred's treaty with the Danes in England confined them to the area known as the Danelaw. Normandy was granted to the Viking chieftain Rollo and his followers in 911, but by the end of the century their descendants were speaking French and had lost their Scandinavian heritage.

Danish

Norwegian

‒ ‒ ‒ ‒ ‒ ‒ ‒ ‒
Danelaw frontier established by treaty 886

·········
Normandy ceded to Rollo by treaty 911

Shetland Islands

Jarlshof

Westness
Birsay
Orkney Islands

Hebrides

The Udal

SCOTLAND

Iona

Lindisfarne

Jarrow

Wearmouth

Ouse
Whitby
Ribblehead
York

Cuerdale
Stamford Bridge 1066

ENGLAND

Humber

Larne

IRELAND

Armagh

Isle of Man

Kells
Annagassan

Tara 980
Clonmacnoise
Clontarf 1014
Dublin

Clonfert
Shannon

Wicklow
Arklow

Limerick

Anglesey

Chester

Dee

Lincoln

Nottingham

Derby
Repton
Stamford

Leicester

Norwich

WALES

Waterford

Wexford

Cork

Thames

Maldon 991
Mersea Island
Northey Island
Shoeburyness
Benfleet
London
Thanet
Canterbury

Bristol

Ethandun 878

Winchester
Southampton

Appledore

Hastings 1066

Quentowic

Portland Bill

✿ The Five Boroughs

⚔ battle

◉ Viking capital

▣ Anglo-Saxon capital

♟ monastery

○ temporary Viking camp

● other Viking settlement

▥ hoard

■ Anglo-Saxon town

Rouen

Bayeux

Seine

NORMANDY

Paris

operate on her inland waters. One by one her great monasteries were plundered for their treasures and their occupants, some of them many times. Partly in response to these continuing attacks the Irish invented the tall conical 'round tower'. The remains of some eighty of these, built between the tenth and twelfth centuries, survive on the sites of early monasteries; although they were used primarily as bell towers, their doors were always raised well above ground level to make them a safe place for both monks and valuables. One anonymous monk expressed his anxiety in some lines penned in the margins of his manuscript – one of the few poems written in praise of bad weather. In translation, it reads: 'The wind is rough tonight, tossing the white hair of the ocean; I do not fear the fierce Vikings, coursing the Irish sea.'

In the 840s events took a sinister turn when groups of raiders began to establish *long-phorts*, fortified sea bases in which they could over-winter. Whereas the raiders had previously appeared annually, as the raiding season had come round again, now they became a permanent part of the Irish scene. At about the same time the Norsemen who had mounted the earlier raids were joined by Danes. Some of the fortified bases came to nothing, as at Annagassan in County Louth, where a rampart-enclosed area awaits excavation. But at the first base, established in 841 by the *Dubh-Linn* (Black Pool) at the ford of the river Liffey, there developed a settlement that in time became (with one brief interlude) the capital of a Norse kingdom and one of the premier trading centres of Western Europe. Up-river from medieval Dublin, at Kilmainham-Islandbridge, numerous graves of well-equipped Viking warriors – and their women – were discovered and destroyed when the Great Southern Railway was built in the mid-nineteenth century. Enough was salvaged to suggest that from the mid-ninth century onwards there was a permanent settlement here that numbered craftsmen and merchants among its inhabitants. Its site

also suggests that the first settlement of Dublin may have been slightly different from the one, dating from the tenth century, that has been excavated from beneath the heart of the medieval and modern city.

This putative change in location might be attributable to the fact that in 902 the Irish succeeded in expelling the Norse from Dublin; some went to Scotland, others to north-west England. However, about ten years later the pillaging of Ireland began again in earnest and in 917 Dublin was re-established as a Norse settlement, soon to expand and develop into a great port and manufacturing centre. To the tenth century belongs also the development of the other Norse towns in Ireland: Wicklow and Arklow, Wexford and Waterford, Cork and Limerick, a familiar list to which recent studies suggest that Larne should now be added. Yet it was only in the neighbourhood of Dublin that any extensive area of Irish countryside came directly under Norse rule. Land-taking on any significant scale had been successfully resisted by the scores of small Irish kingdoms. At the battle of Tara in 980 the Norse suffered a severe defeat at the hands of the Irish, to whom they henceforth paid tribute. The Irish were prepared by then to tolerate the Vikings in their midst, if kept under control, because of their skill as traders and the wealth that their towns generated. Many words in the Irish language connected with both ships and trade, such as *margadh* for a market, are borrowed from Norse, which illustrates well the permanence of their impact on the Irish economy. Struggles and battles continued, for they were a major feature of Irish politics to which the Vikings had only added a further dimension. The battle of Clontarf, fought near Dublin in 1014, is often regarded as the ultimate confrontation between the Vikings (who numbered among their army allies from the Orkneys and the Isle of Man, together with the Irish of Leinster) and Brian Boru, King of Munster and High King of Ireland. The Norse were defeated, although Brian Boru was killed. Of such victories are legends made, but in reality Clontarf was not the ultimate confrontation between the Irish and the Vikings, and final overthrow of the Vikings, that it was built up to be. It was Irish against Irish and Norse, and the vanquished King Sigtrygg Silkenbeard of Dublin ruled on for a further twenty years, until his own death.

The Norse remained distinct in their coastal communities, outward-looking with their concentration on trade. But under Irish influence they had long since become Christians, which had done much to ease cross-fertilization between their two cultures. In the late eleventh and twelfth centuries Irish art was strongly influenced by the late Viking styles, providing them with a final flourish of glory far from Scandinavia. Dublin was still Norse-speaking when it fell to the Anglo-Norman invaders in 1170.

Renewed Viking attacks on England

The 830s saw a major new impact by the Vikings on England. A Danish expedition that had fallen on Frisia in 834, sacking its prosperous trading centre of Dorestad on the Rhine, turned across the Channel in 835, when the 'heathen men ravaged Sheppey', a small island at the mouth of the Thames. During the next fifteen years there were more Viking raids on England, from Somerset and Dorset to Lindsey and Northumbria. Some would have been the work of the Norse from Ireland, most were by Danes, including those who had established bases in Frisia. In 850 they began to over-winter in England, at first on the island of Thanet, and in 865 the first payment of a Danegeld is recorded. For the promise of peace the people of Kent paid the Vikings money and were rewarded with treachery, for 'under cover of that peace and money the army stole away inland by night and ravaged all eastern Kent.'

The *Anglo-Saxon Chronicle* for 865 records an event that marked a turning point in the intervention of the Vikings in England. 'In this year a great heathen army came into England and took up winter quarters in East Anglia; there they were supplied with horses, and the East Angles made peace with them.' This 'great army' (*micel here*) had come after land for settlement, an aspiration that was to be fully realized, although their progress through England cannot be followed in detail. In 866 they captured York and placed a puppet Anglo-Saxon king on the throne of Northumbria. By the early 870s the Vikings controlled the greater part of eastern England from York to London. In 874 the 'great army' divided and subsequently in 876 those under the leadership of Halfdan 'shared out the land of the Northumbrians and they proceeded to plough and to support themselves.' Other groups from the 'great army' also took land, in Mercia in 877, and in East Anglia in 879 under the leadership of King Guthrum. Guthrum had previously attempted to settle in Wessex, but had been defeated by King Alfred at *Ethandun* (Edington). In victory, Alfred was able to force the invaders to accept his terms, which included the baptism of Guthrum and his chief followers.

Five years after settling in East Anglia Guthrum broke the terms of his agreement with Alfred, but after a successful campaign Alfred imposed a new treaty on Guthrum in 886. Its terms survive, with its first clause defining the frontier between the English and the Danes: 'up the Thames, and then up the Lea, and along the Lea to its source, then in a straight line to Bedford, then up the Ouse to Watling Street'.

During the last twenty years of his reign Alfred was troubled by a new group of Vikings, who were raiding on both sides of the Channel. Meeting with a severe defeat by the Franks in 891, they crossed to England and attempted to seize land for settlement. They were successfully resisted and so finally split up in 896, some settling in areas already under Viking control – in East Anglia and in Northumbria – others returning across the Channel to continue their raiding.

A large amount of metalwork from the British Isles has been found in 9th-century Scandinavian graves. This stylized human figure, his body inlaid with enamel and chequered glass, is from an Irish bronze bowl found in a man's grave at Micklebostad in western Norway.

Above A gilt-bronze mount, made for the cover of an 8th-century Northumbrian book, was plundered by a Viking and converted into a woman's pendant.

Right 'Ranvaig owns this casket', states the runic inscription on the base of this small Scottish or Irish reliquary now in Copenhagen. Was it looted to make a jewel box or acquired by an early convert as a shrine?

By the turn of the century there had been Vikings resident in England, in greater or lesser numbers, for a period of fifty years. A great deal of disruption and destruction had taken place. The Danelaw – the area of accepted Danish settlement and rule in eastern England – now included the kingdoms of York and East Anglia, and the area around the fortified towns of Derby, Leicester, Lincoln, Nottingham and Stamford (the Five Boroughs) in between. Within it the Church had survived, but numerous monasteries had been abandoned and their estates shared out following Viking attacks. Lindisfarne, Wearmouth and Jarrow all came to an end in the ninth century, as did Whitby in Yorkshire, which was raided in 867. A stone mould for casting ingots found at Whitby Abbey may well have been used by Vikings for the melting down and sharing out of the looted treasures. Alfred, in his writings, recalled the time 'before everything was ravaged and burnt', and in his will remarked that 'we were all harassed by the heathen army.' Alfred, however, was the leader who had beaten back the Vikings and whose policies for the defence of his kingdom, initiated during his own lifetime, enabled his successors to turn the tide and establish a united English kingdom by the middle of the tenth century. The last Viking king of York was Eirik Bloodaxe, who was expelled by the Anglo-Saxons in 954 during the reign of Alfred's grandson, Eadred.

Loot from the British Isles

A large amount of metalwork from the British Isles has been found in ninth-century graves in Scandinavia, especially in Norway. There is obviously a problem, however, in trying to determine what is loot and what may have been obtained by other, non-violent, means. It is now realized that much of what was once accepted as ecclesiastical metalwork, and therefore necessarily loot, may well have been secular in origin and use.

The Frankish Empire & Europe

he earliest contacts between Scandinavia and the Continent seem not to have taken the form of Viking raids, but to have been based on trading relations. The Frisians were the traditional North Sea traders and would have been involved in commercial contacts with Denmark before the Danish King Godfred invaded Frisia (the low-lying southern coast of the North Sea) in 810. Although this first raid was successful, Frisia was by then part of the Carolingian Empire and its defence was well organized. A subsequent attack was beaten off during 820, the year when Viking ships (perhaps the same ones) also appeared for the first time on the Seine, and again were driven away. It was in 834, with the sack of Dorestad, that Viking attacks on the Frankish Empire began in earnest; thereafter it was pillaged regularly for a generation. In 841 it was the turn of Rouen on the Seine to be sacked, and in 842 of Quentowic, opposite the Straits of Dover. In 844 Viking ships sailed up the Garonne, and in 845 Paris was plundered and the Vikings bought off by Charles the Bald for 7,000lb (3,000kg) of silver, the first of thirteen Danegelds known to have been paid in France up to 926. This one achieved a respite of six years. In 845 Hamburg was sacked. In the years 862–3 the Vikings were operating up the Rhine to Cologne, and in 882 Trier received their attentions. These are but a few dates from the catalogue of misfortunes that fell upon the northern coasts of the Frankish Empire in the ninth century.

The loot and the Danegelds received, totalling 685lb (310kg) of gold and 43,042lb (19,500kg) of silver according to contemporary Frankish sources, have left their mark in Scandinavia, but not to the degree that might be expected. Very few ninth-century Frankish (or Anglo-Saxon) coins have been found in Scandinavia and the reason must be that for the most part they were melted down and turned into ornaments. The great Hon hoard, hidden in the ninth century in Buskerud, Norway, consists of 5½lb (2.5kg) of gold objects, with some glass beads. The Frankish coins among these have been mounted with loops to convert them into pendants. The prize of the collection is without doubt a massive trefoil-shaped mount, with acanthus-leaf ornament of Carolingian workmanship – an object of exceptional splendour by any standards. To complete the picture of Viking depredations on the West, the hoard also contains the only Anglo-Saxon gold object to have been found in Scandinavia, a finger-ring. Again, it is difficult to decide whether Frankish objects that found their way to Scandinavia did so by fair means or foul. In 864, in desperation, Charles the Bald had prohibited any further sale of weapons and horses to the Vikings.

Meanwhile the Vikings who had been active down the western coasts of the British Isles had penetrated south to the Atlantic coasts of France. There were raiders active off Aquitaine as early as 799. In 835 the monastery on the island of Noirmoutier, at the mouth of the Loire, was plundered; this was a centre for the trade in salt and wine. In 843 the Vikings penetrated the Loire to attack Nantes, before retiring to establish a winter base at Noirmoutier, by then abandoned by the monks because of earlier attacks. A monk from Noirmoutier, writing in the 860s, sums up the events of these years:

> The number of ships grows: the endless stream of Vikings never ceases to increase. Everywhere the Christians are victims of massacres, burnings, plunderings: the Vikings conquer all in their path, and no one resists them: they seize Bordeaux, Périgueux, Limoges, Angoulême and Toulouse. Angers, Tours and Orléans are annihilated and an innumerable fleet sails up the Seine and the evil grows in the whole region. Rouen is laid waste, plundered and burned: Paris, Beauvais and Meaux taken, Melun's strong fortress levelled to the ground, Chartres

occupied, Evreux and Bayeux
plundered, and every town besieged.
It was not just the towns and monasteries
that suffered. In western France there was
disruption of cultivated land and dispersal of
the peasantry. When the land around the
towns was devastated, to remain within the
walls would have meant starvation. The
result was the depopulation of both town and
countryside. Bordeaux, which had become
increasingly prosperous up to the ninth
century, then experienced disaster without
parallel in its history and reached its nadir in
the middle of that century. As Bordeaux
suffered, so too did Aquitaine. The population of the Périgord was driven to take
refuge in the Haut-Limousin. From the north
refugees fled to Burgundy, and there were
others who sought safety in the Ardennes and
the Auvergne.

In the mid-ninth century, Lothar, son of
Charles the Bald, had granted the island of
Walcheren in Frisia to the Danish brothers
Harald and Rorik. He was buying their protection and assistance against other Vikings
and against his own brothers. It was a first
step in the direction that led to the Viking
chieftain Rollo receiving Normandy by treaty
in 911. Rollo, probably a Norwegian himself
although leading a force of Danes, had evidently been plundering in France for a
number of years before Charles the Simple
settled Normandy on him in return for his
promise to defend it. Rollo did homage to the
King and in 912 he was baptized; Normandy
was shared out among his men. During the
tenth century the Normans drifted away from
their Scandinavian origins and became assim-
ilated into French ways. After a couple of
generations their language had been lost,
although their presence lives on in Normandy
(as in the English Danelaw) in the place-
names of the region.

The Vikings in Frisia and in France have
left few archaeological traces of their presence. There is a man's grave at Antum,
near Groningen in the Netherlands, and a
woman's grave at Pîtres on the Seine, between
Rouen and Paris. There is otherwise only a
pair of gold arm-rings from Dorestad and a
scatter of swords and spear-heads across the
Continent, until one reaches a little island off
the south coast of Brittany, the Ile de Groix.
Here, beneath a mound, were found the
cremated remains of two bodies buried in a
ship during the second half of the tenth century. At its centre was a large iron cauldron,
surrounded by weapons and smith's tools;
there was gold and silver wire from richly
ornamented cloth, and a gold finger-ring. The
grave-goods form a mixture of Scandinavian
and West European objects, so this Viking sea
captain, buried with a slave or follower, can
scarcely have just arrived from home before
meeting his death by the Atlantic. He must
have been operating in the West for some
time, active perhaps in Normandy, Ireland
and around the Loire. The island of his burial
might well have served as his 'pirate's nest' for
part of his life; it would have been well suited
for the purpose.

Spain and the Mediterranean

Other Atlantic Vikings followed the coast of
France yet farther south to one of the richest
and most splendid of Europe's kingdoms in
the Viking Age – that of the Moors in Spain.
While it is possible that some Vikings had
reached Spain as early as the end of the eighth
century, the first raid of which we have
definite evidence took place in 844 when
Seville was taken and held for a week. The
raiders subsequently received short shrift at
the hands of the Moors and suffered severe
losses; only by ransoming their prisoners
were those still surviving able to re-equip and
make good their escape.

The next year the Moorish kingdom of
Spain sent an embassy under Al-Ghazal to the
King of the Majus – *majus*, meaning fire-
worshippers or heathens, was the Muslim
name for the Vikings. The embassy may have
gone either to Ireland or to Denmark,
unfortunately we cannot be sure which, or

The magnificent hoard buried at Hon in south-east Norway in the 860s consists of 5½ pounds (2.5 kilos) of gold with a little silver and some beads. The large trefoil-shaped mount (top left) is one of the finest surviving pieces of Carolingian goldwork; some of the coins mounted as pendants were also obtained from the Franks, the others are Roman, Byzantine, Arabic and Anglo-Saxon.

what was the outcome, although the object may well have been to encourage trade in slaves and furs.

The most famous expedition to Spain and beyond was that led by Bjorn and Hastein, which set out from the Loire with sixty-two ships in 859 and which did not return until 862. They passed through the Straits of Gibraltar, plundered Algeciras, and then headed for North Africa. After considerable success they turned back and harried the southern coast of Spain, before moving on to the Balearics. They found winter quarters for themselves in a traditional type of location, on an island in the Camargue in the Rhône delta; this had the incidental benefit of providing them with a base from which they were able to raid up-river as far north as Nîmes, Arles and Valence. Finally, beaten off by the Franks, they moved on to Italy. Pisa was sacked and so was Luna, in mistake (it is said) for Rome; their subsequent movements are largely unknown, but there is a suggestion that they continued on into the eastern Mediterranean. Their attempt to pass back through the Straits of Gibraltar in 861 was contested by the Moorish fleet. Those that escaped made one last bid for yet more booty. On reaching Navarre they went inland and captured its prince, for whom they obtained a ransom of 90,000 *denarii*. Although only a third of the ships that had set out four years previously reached the Loire again in 862, the survivors must have been immensely richer for their expedition.

Arabic sources for events in Spain are far from complete, but there does seem to have been a gap of almost a century before the next concerted raid in 966, which was unsuccessful. The Iberian peninsula had not, however, gone unvisited in the intervening period; some trade may well have been involved. Around 966 eighteen of the cities of the Christian kingdom of Asturias in northern Spain fell to Viking attacks; among them was Santiago de Compostella. But all in all it is hard to assess the extent and significance of the western Vikings' contacts with Spain, although it is clear that the western Mediterranean, at any rate, lay outside the sphere of regular Viking activity.

Viking mercenaries

From early in the Viking Age there seem to have been plenty of men prepared to hire themselves out as fighters wherever the demand existed. In Ireland, bands of Vikings became involved as mercenaries in the eternal disputes between the numerous kingdoms into which the country was divided. In Frisia Lothar engaged the services of Harald and Rorik in return for Walcheren. We are told that in England on several occasions the Vikings aided the Britons of the south-west in their struggles to hold off the Anglo-Saxons of Wessex. In the late Viking Age, as we shall see, there was a permanent force of Scandinavians maintained for the defence of England against other Scandinavians. But the most famous of such mercenary undertakings must be the so-called Varangian Guard of the Emperor at Byzantium.

Scandinavians may have served in the Imperial Bodyguard from soon after the establishment of contact with the capital in the ninth century. An agreement of 911, between the Rus, those of Scandinavian origin settled or active in Russia, and the Byzantines, contains a clause concerning those of the Rus who wished to enter military service under the Emperor. The Byzantines applied the term Varangians to Scandinavians in general and there does not seem to have been a separate band of them in the Imperial Guard until the late tenth century. In the eleventh century the Guard appears to have become a mainly Scandinavian company and the most famous among its number was Harald Sigurdson, later to be nicknamed 'the Hard-ruler', who was King of all Norway from 1047 to 1066. In the later eleventh century, however, the complexion of the Guard changed when it was augmented by Anglo-Saxons leaving England after the Norman Conquest.

Helmeted Viking warriors with their dogs ornament the splendid Ledberg rune-stone in Östergötland. They carry circular shields and the man at the top is armed with a sword and spear.

Return to England

A second Viking Age began for England in 980, when the *Anglo-Saxon Chronicle* recorded attacks on Southampton, Thanet and Cheshire; the following year the coasts of Devon and Cornwall were ravaged. Then in 982 Dorset was attacked and London burned. These were the first in a new wave of Viking expeditions carried out by men who had no interest in land-taking; they were after treasure. They found England once again vulnerable as well as wealthy, and therefore concentrated their attentions upon it. These renewed raids reached their peak at the turn of the tenth century and the first of a new series of Danegelds was paid in 991.

The attacks of 991 were led by Olaf Tryggvason (later to be King of Norway) at the head of a fleet of ninety-three ships. It was during his campaign that the Battle of Maldon was fought, against the English in Essex. The Anglo-Saxon poem renders thus the words of the Vikings' messenger.

> Bold seamen have sent me to you, and
> told me to say that you must send
> treasure quickly in return for peace,
> and it will be better for you all to buy
> off an attack with treasure, rather than
> face men as fierce as us in battle. We
> need not destroy each other, if you are
> rich enough. In return for the gold we
> are ready to make truce with you.

Rich enough England proved to be, for the Vikings victorious that year received £10,000 as the first of the Danegelds. The sums needed to make truce rose rapidly: £16,000 (994), £24,000 (1002), £36,000 (1007), £48,000 (1012). The silver hoards of Scandinavia contain dramatic evidence of this continued drain on the pockets of the English.

The Danegeld of 994 was again paid to Olaf, who had returned allied with King Svein Forkbeard of Denmark. Although Olaf thereafter engaged himself in Norwegian affairs, Svein followed this venture with many campaigns of his own. There were those, however, who, not sharing in the raiders' booty, were prepared to sell their services to the English. Thorkel the Tall, with forty-five ships, became a mercenary in the pay of King Æthelred in 1012, helping to save London from Svein in 1013. His troops were richly rewarded for their services.

In 1013 Svein had arrived by way of the Humber and had been accepted by the Danelaw as king; he died the following year ('a happy event', said the chronicler). But his son Cnut remained, and was chosen as king of England when Æthelred died in 1016. He ruled until his death in 1035 (see page 196); his court reintroduced Scandinavian tastes to the English. The splendid tombstone from St Paul's churchyard in London must have been raised in memory of one of his followers; it is ornamented in the mainstream fashion of Viking art of that period. Even after the restoration of the English monarchy in the person of Edward the Confessor, Scandinavian mercenaries were still employed by the English. When in 1051 this force was disbanded, the stream of English silver to Scandinavia dried up, although kings of both Norway and Denmark continued to regard England and her wealth with longing eyes.

It was from a victory over Norwegian invaders, at Stamford Bridge, when their king, Harald the Hard-ruler, was killed, that King Harold of England had to speed southwards to meet a second invasion – that of Duke William of Normandy – and his own defeat at the battle of Hastings. These events of 1066 did not bring England's Viking Age quite to its close. In 1069 a Danish royal fleet entered the Humber and supported an English revolt against their Norman invaders. The following year the Danish king, Svein Estridsson, came himself, but was bought off by William. Finally, in 1085, Cnut, Svein's son and successor, planned a mighty invasion of England, but the attempt came to nothing and the fleet never set sail. This was the last serious effort by the Scandinavians against England; the Viking Age was over.

Several Swedish rune-stones from the 11th century mention England and men who died in the West. The Yttergärde stone in Uppland was raised in memory of a man called Ulf who 'took three payments of geld in England. The first was the one that Tosti paid, then Thorkel, then Cnut.'

Ships, Shipwrights & Seamen

For 300 years the Vikings were the most accomplished shipbuilders and seamen of the northern seas, operating from the Arctic to the Caspian and across the Atlantic to the New World.

Sources of evidence

he Viking longship has become
a symbol of Scandinavian
achievement, encapsulating
the essence of the Viking Age
and excellence in ancient shipbuilding. But how did the Viking shipwrights
build ships of such speed and elegance? How

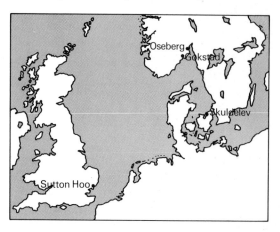

were these ships navigated? Why were they so
successful and why finally were they super-
seded by the bulky, slow-moving ships of the
Middle Ages? Unfortunately there are no
Viking shipbuilding manuals to provide
immediate answers to such questions, but
there are many other sources of evidence,
which when painstakingly pieced together
offer a surprisingly complete picture of the
ships and the men who built them.

Two 1,000-year-old ships, excavated eighty
to a hundred years ago from Norwegian
burial mounds, at Oseberg and Gokstad on
the west side of Oslofjord, and now reconstructed and displayed in a building of
cathedral-like proportions at Bygdøy near
Oslo, are everyman's idea of a Viking ship.
But these two ninth- to tenth-century ships
were rather special ones – possibly the Norse
equivalent of royal yachts; although we can

Thousand-year-old
Norwegian vessels from
burial mounds at Oseberg
and Gokstad are
everyman's idea of Viking
ships and are among the
chief sources of evidence
for Viking Age
shipbuilding techniques.
Right The burial chamber
of a royal lady was found
in the centre of the 9th-
century Oseberg ship,
excavated in 1904. This is
the richest ship grave yet
discovered.

The 10th-century Gokstad ship, seen here during its excavation in 1880 and reconstructed in the Viking Ship Museum at Bygdøy, near Oslo, is less ornate than the earlier Oseberg ship, but was found in a better state of preservation.

The superb carvings on the bow and stern of the reconstructed Oseberg ship can also be seen at the Viking Ship Museum at Bygdøy.

learn much from them about certain aspects of Viking Age shipbuilding, we have to look elsewhere for evidence of how earlier and later ships were built, for the distinctive features of Viking merchant ships, and for details of sails and rigging.

Ships and impressions of ships in other burial mounds in Scandinavia and Britain have provided some of this additional information. Sagas, sea laws, poetry and travellers' tales (such as those recounted to King Alfred) have also helped to fill out the picture, as has the evidence from woodcarvings, stone en-

gravings and the eleventh-century Bayeux Tapestry. There are problems in interpreting all these forms of evidence: for example, the sagas were not written down until the twelfth century and thus many contain post-Viking material. Nevertheless, careful investigation can reveal valid information about Viking ships. More recently, our knowledge has been greatly increased by the excavation of wrecked or abandoned vessels. Research by Ole Crumlin-Pedersen, Director of the Viking Ship Museum in Roskilde, Denmark, on the five Skuldelev ships excavated from Roskilde

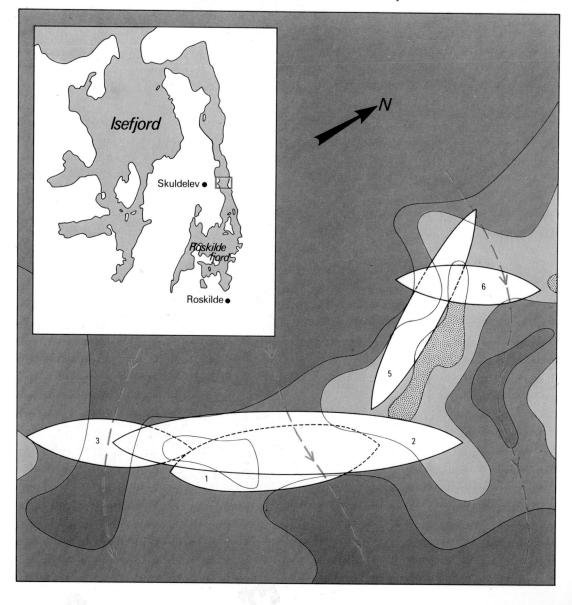

Unlike the burial ships at Oseberg and Gokstad, the 11th-century ships excavated at Skuldelev in Denmark were working vessels, deliberately sunk to blockade the shallow Roskilde fjord – thus protecting the Danish royal town of Roskilde from an attack from the sea. The diagram, *right*, shows how the five wrecks were laid across the navigable channel.

Museum, Greenwich, recently built and tested a replica of one of the small boats – a *færing* or four-oared boat – found inside the Gokstad ship. During the process much was learned about how the ninth-century craftsmen probably tackled the job of building such a boat; and the replica's characteristics under oars and under sail were assessed.

Similar evaluations can be made by calculation using data from reconstruction drawings, or by testing a small-scale model in a special tank fitted with instruments that record the boat's speed and resistance to motion, or possibly in a wind tunnel. The advantage of such evaluations is that several different versions of the ancient vessel can be tested, under variable conditions. However, the results from both theoretical and practical experiments can only be as sound as the data used; this, and the authenticity of the experiment, will determine their value in estimating the performance of ancient ships.

All these forms of evidence have been used in this chapter to describe what is known and conjectured about Viking Age boats and ships.

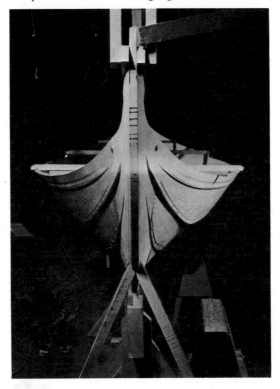

fjord in 1962, and on other Danish finds, and by Arne Emil Christensen of the Viking Ship Museum in Oslo, on recent Norwegian finds, means that we can now begin to recognize both functional and regional variations in Viking Age boats and ships. The ability to identify and date ship finds by the stage of technological development they had reached is but a short step away.

Study of modern wooden boatbuilding methods in such places as western Norway, where there has been a great degree of continuity over the past 1,000 years, has also proved fruitful, and evidence of a different sort is now coming from the building and trials of replicas of ancient boats. The aims of this experimental archaeology are to learn how ancient boats and ships were rowed, sailed and steered; what sorts of loads they could safely carry; and what their performance might have been in various states of wind and sea. The National Maritime

Building modern replicas of Viking Age boats provides considerable information, both on the use of timber and tools and on performance under oars and sail. A replica of a *færing* (a four-oared boat) was built and tested at the National Maritime Museum, Greenwich; *above left*, one of the boat's oak stems is hollowed out with an adze; *left*, the boat on the stocks nearing completion.

The ships & boats

Of the 7th-century royal burial ship excavated at Sutton Hoo, England, in 1939, only an impression in the sand, with iron nails, remained. But this distinctively clinker-built, equal-ended vessel may be considered as a fore-runner of the Viking ship.

hether the Viking urge to expand stimulated shipbuilding, or whether improved boatbuilding techniques paved the way for Viking exploration and expansion, is still being discussed by scholars. What is certain, however, is that the Viking ship was not invented at the start of the Viking Age, but was developed from boats used in earlier times. North European finds dating from about AD 400 onwards, including the Nydam and Kvalsund boats, in Schleswig-Holstein and Norway, show early forms that were subsequently perfected by Viking Age shipbuilders. Although not in Scandinavia, the ship found at Sutton Hoo, Suffolk, England, may be considered as one forerunner of the Viking ships. Here a large open boat some 75ft (23m) in length had been used for a royal burial dated to c. AD 625. During its 1,300 years of interment the timber

of the ship had decomposed, leaving in its place an impression in the sand that revealed details of the ship's construction: a clinker-built, equal-ended vessel of distinctive form and structure.

Ships and boats dating from the ninth to the eleventh centuries, of a similar though more advanced construction, are now known, the main bulk of the evidence coming from two groups: the ninth- to tenth-century Oseberg, Gokstad and Tune burial ships; and the tenth- to eleventh-century Skuldelev ships, which were working ships that were deliberately sunk to blockade Roskilde fjord.

Ole Crumlin-Pedersen, joint excavator of the Skuldelev ships, has concluded from studying these and other ship remains of Nordic origin, that although each ship was unique in some way, they have many characteristics in common. This basic shape and structure, which in its developed form we can now recognize as the Viking ship, is illustrated and described in the visual glossary on pages 44–5. There were of course variations in the ships over time, recognizable regional differences and also functional modifications. For example, the method of supporting the mast changed between the ninth and eleventh centuries; and the way planks were fastened together in the eastern Baltic, where treenails (or wooden pegs) were used and the overlaps made watertight with moss, differed from the method of the western Baltic, where iron nails and animal hair were usually employed. Within the Skuldelev group of ships itself there are differences, Skuldelev ships 1 and 3 being much broader in relation to their length than ships 2 and 5. This reflects the different functions of the ships, 1 and 3 being cargo carriers and 2 and 5 being warships. Possibly other variants remain to be identified or to be discovered by excavation.

This distinctive style of boat- and ship-building greatly influenced the shipwrights of those lands where Vikings settled. Unfortunately, except for finds of re-used boat timbers from Viking Age Dublin and some poorly documented boat graves in Scotland, the archaeological evidence is scarce. However, the many Norse shipbuilding and seafaring words borrowed by the Irish, French, and, to a lesser degree, the English, indicate this influence. And by post-Viking times, illustrations on the Bayeux Tapestry, on Irish monuments, and on English, Irish and French town seals, show a form of ship that has unmistakable Norse characteristics, as do the fragmented remains of ships built from Irish timber recently excavated from the thirteenth-century Wood Quay site in Dublin. It seems safe to say, therefore, that during the Viking Age and for some time afterwards the dominant vessel in north-west Europe was this Nordic type: the Viking ship in its several forms.

Nevertheless, some requirements for water transport were more efficiently satisfied by other types of boat. For instance, on inland waterways, lakes and fjords the Vikings used log rafts and log boats (dugout canoes), as did their contemporaries in other European countries. Boats of skin and bark were used on the northern and eastern fringes of the Viking homelands, and skin boats were almost certainly used in the Celtic west of the British Isles during the period of the Viking raids and settlement. Furthermore, the flat-bottomed boat found in 1966 at Egernsund on the Flensburg fjord in southern Denmark, and dated to about 1090, shows that not all Viking Age planked boats were what we think of as 'Viking boats'. This boat is believed to have been a ferry and therefore probably built locally. It has none of the Nordic boat's characteristics of form and probably few (if any) of the structural features, its role as a ferry on inland waterways determining both form and structure. Similar ferries were used elsewhere in Europe, especially on the Rhine. In regions uninfluenced by Viking building methods other types of planked boat were constructed, such as the forerunners of the medieval cogs and hulks, which were ships of great cargo capacity.

Above Skuldelev ship 1 was an ocean-going merchant ship and represents the peak of Viking Age shipbuilding. Its remains are on display at Roskilde, Denmark, the missing parts being outlined by metal strips.

A late form of the Nordic type of ship depicted on this 13th-century town seal of Winchelsea, England, reveals the continuing influence of Viking shipwrights on the lands they settled.

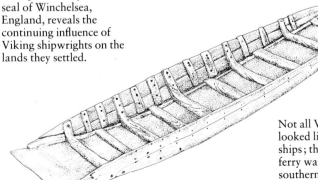

Not all Viking Age boats looked like the Skuldelev ships; this flat-bottomed ferry was built in southern Denmark at the end of the 11th century.

The Viking ship: a visual glossary

This visual glossary illustrates the parts of a Viking ship and explains the terms used in the chapter. The cutaway ship is a composite drawing including details taken from more than one vessel. In order to show the main structural features, many of the internal timbers have been omitted.

The shape and size of Viking ships varied with their function, as cargo vessel, warship or royal yacht, and there were also variations during the 300 years of the Viking Age, but they all had certain distinctive characteristics in common. The hull was symmetrical at the ends, with a slightly curved keel blending into a curved fore-stem and after-stem at the bow and stern. The top line of planking (the sheerline) had a distinctive curve, being higher at the ends than amidships. The hull was built with clinker-laid

This body plan shows the characteristic shape of the Viking ship, with round bottom and flared sides. The light draft – resulting from the thin planking – allowed the ship to go close in to the shore before grounding and to be taken far inland up shallow rivers, while the deep keel and steeply angled lowest planks reduced sideways drift (leeway) caused by the wind.

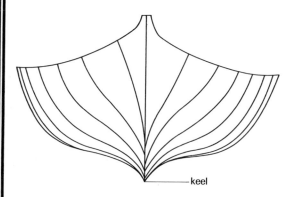

keel

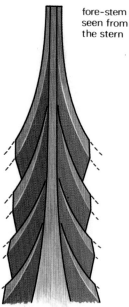

fore-stem seen from the stern

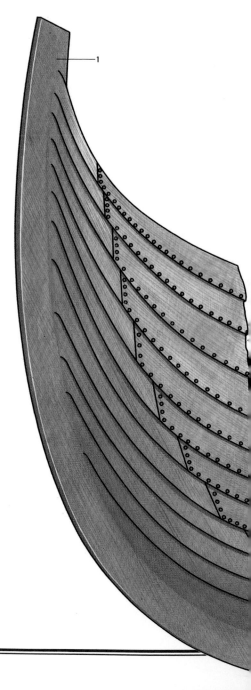

1

A cross-section (looking towards the bow) shows the internal supporting system of floor-timbers and crossbeams. The slender floor-timbers were individually chosen to match the curve of the hull, as were the beam knees used to attach the crossbeams to the planking beneath. In a warship the upper crossbeams could be used as rowing benches, with the rowers' feet resting on bottom boards at lower crossbeam level. In a cargo ship decks might be laid on the upper beams at either end of the vessel with an additional layer of crossbeams used as rowing benches.

The curved fore- and after-stems were each carved from a single piece of wood and might be marked as here to simulate an effect of overlapping planks – the real planking being fastened to the stems some way back from the bow and stern. Other Viking Age stems were of simpler design. The base of each stem was nailed to the keel at the keel scarf.

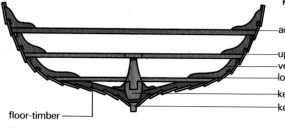

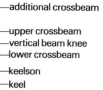

additional crossbeam

upper crossbeam
vertical beam knee
lower crossbeam

keelson
keel

floor-timber

strakes (overlapping planks), which were fastened to the 'back-bone' of keel and stems. Internal supporting timbers were added only after the bottom planking had been completed. The evenly spaced floor-timbers were attached to the planking but not to the keel, producing a flexible structure, and the system of crossbeams above each floor-timber could be used to support decking or rowing benches.

1 fore-stem
2 top strake
3 horizontal beam knee
4 stringer or beam shelf
5 additional crossbeam
6 upper crossbeam or mast!beam
7 vertical beam knee
8 side-timber
9 lower crossbeam
10 floor-timber
11 keel scarf
12 keel
13 keelson
14 keelson knee
15 mast step
16 first strake or garboard
17 snelle
18 stanchion
19 bulkhead
20 rudder with tiller
21 after-stem
22 oarport

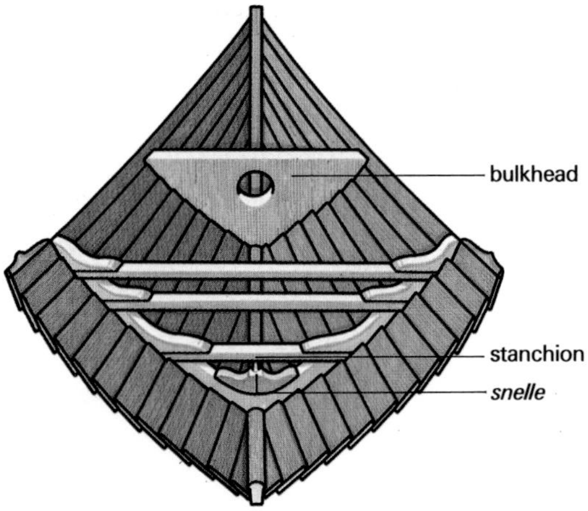

The lower edge of each strake of planking overlapped outside the one below it. Individual planks in a strake were joined at plank scarfs, which (except the ones at the forward stem) had their opening facing aft to minimise the ingress of water when underway.

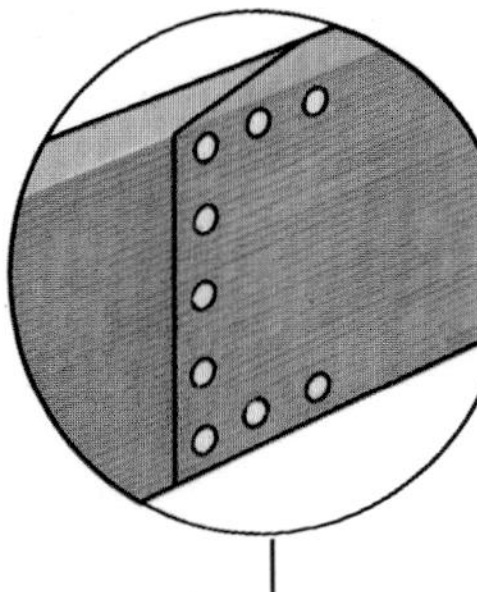

The overlapping strakes were fastened with iron nails (a), the ends hammered flat over a rove (washer) to hold them. A caulking of tarred animal hair between the planks kept the hull watertight. Floor-timbers were either lashed on to cleats left standing proud of the strakes (b) or fastened by treenails, wooden pegs driven through strake and floor-timber (c) and jammed in position by a wedge hammered into the inboard end of each peg.

a

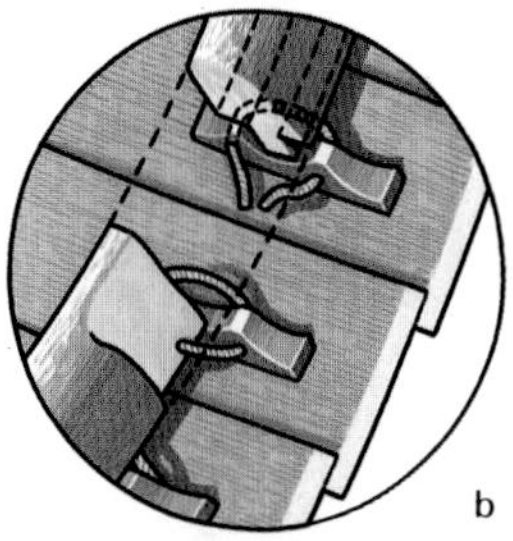

bulkhead
stanchion
snelle

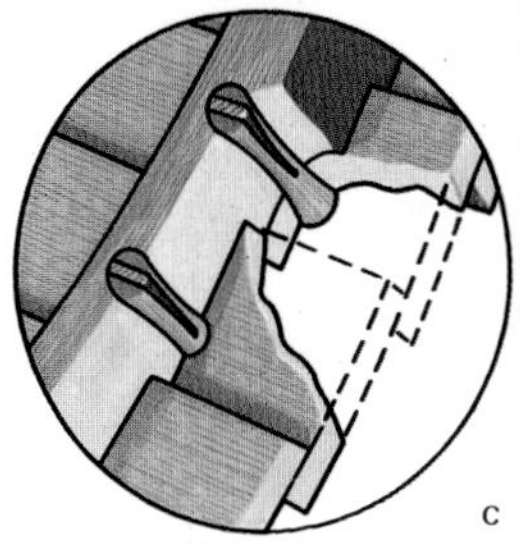

b

c

Oarports were cut at either end of a merchant ship or along the full length of a warship. Small boats had tholes — vertical projections from the top strake — as oar pivots.

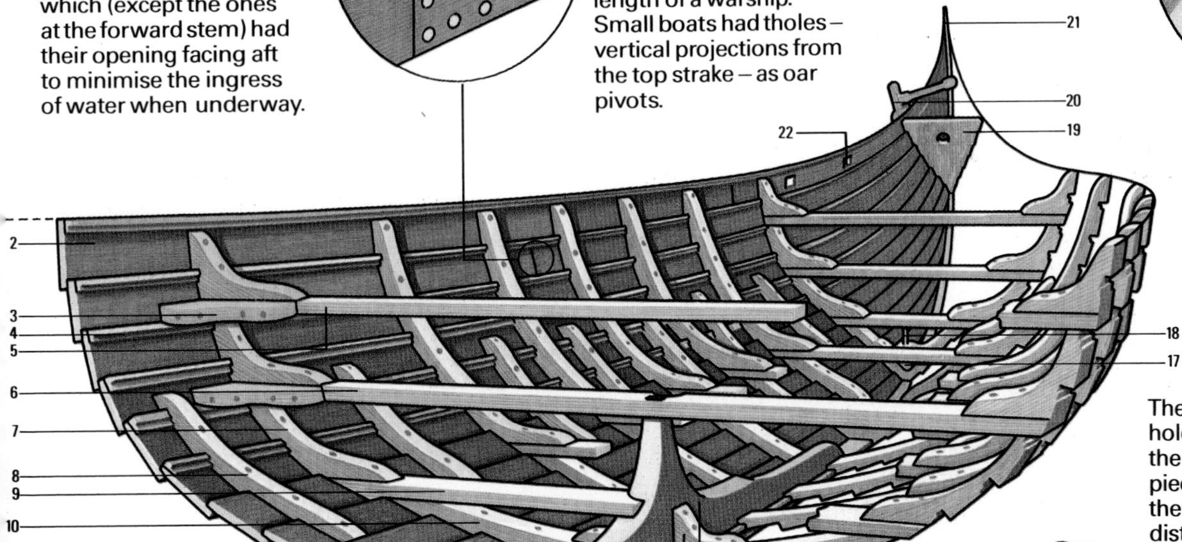

The mast slotted into a hole or mast step cut in the keelson, a heavy piece of wood resting on the keel, which distributed the weight of the mast and had a vertical projection to support it.

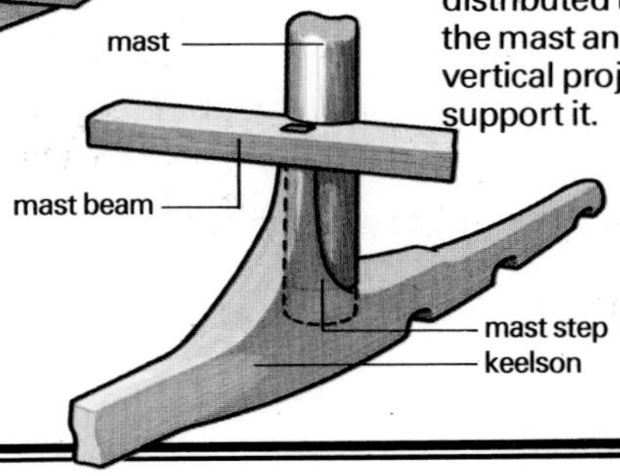

mast
mast beam
mast step
keelson

Ship sizes & shapes

The Viking boats and ships could be classified by size. Smaller boats, sufficiently narrow for each man to pull a pair of oars, were known as ... *æring* according to the number of oars: thus a four-oared boat is a *færing*, a six-oared vessel a *sexæring*, and so on. Bigger vessels in which each man pulled only one oar were described by the number of thwarts or rowing benches they had. In addition to these two groups, documentary sources mention various types of ship by name, but it is generally impossible to equate archaeological remains with them.

For the present it seems best to recognize only functional types: the merchant ship, the warship, and possibly the fishing boat, each with distinctive characteristics. Ships such as

Plans and profiles of eight Viking Age vessels: from the Skuldelev longship to the Gokstad *færing*, each has the same equal-ended shape and distinctive curve of the upper line of planking (sheerline). The merchant ships Skuldelev 1 and 3 are clearly deeper and broader than the others in relation to their length.

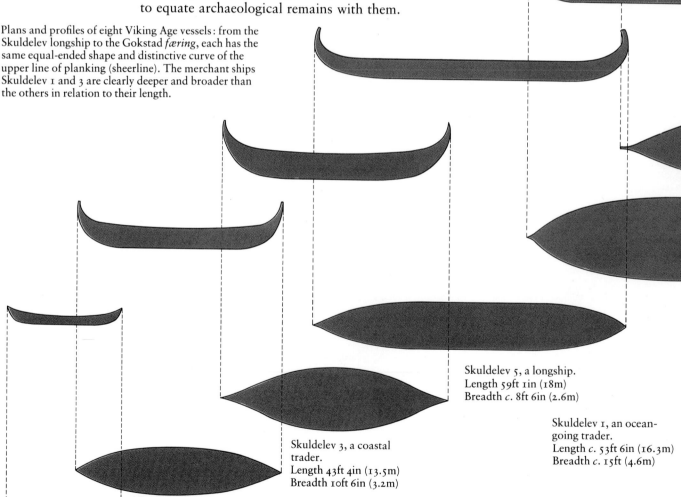

Skuldelev 5, a longship.
Length 59ft 1in (18m)
Breadth *c.* 8ft 6in (2.6m)

Skuldelev 1, an ocean-going trader.
Length *c.* 53ft 6in (16.3m)
Breadth *c.* 15ft (4.6m)

Skuldelev 3, a coastal trader.
Length 43ft 4in (13.5m)
Breadth 10ft 6in (3.2m)

Skuldelev 6, a ferry or fishing boat.
Length *c.* 39ft 5in (12m)
Breadth 8ft 2in (2.5m)

Færing, a small four-oared boat from the Gokstad ship.
Length 21ft 4in (6.5m)
Breadth 4ft 7in (1.4m)

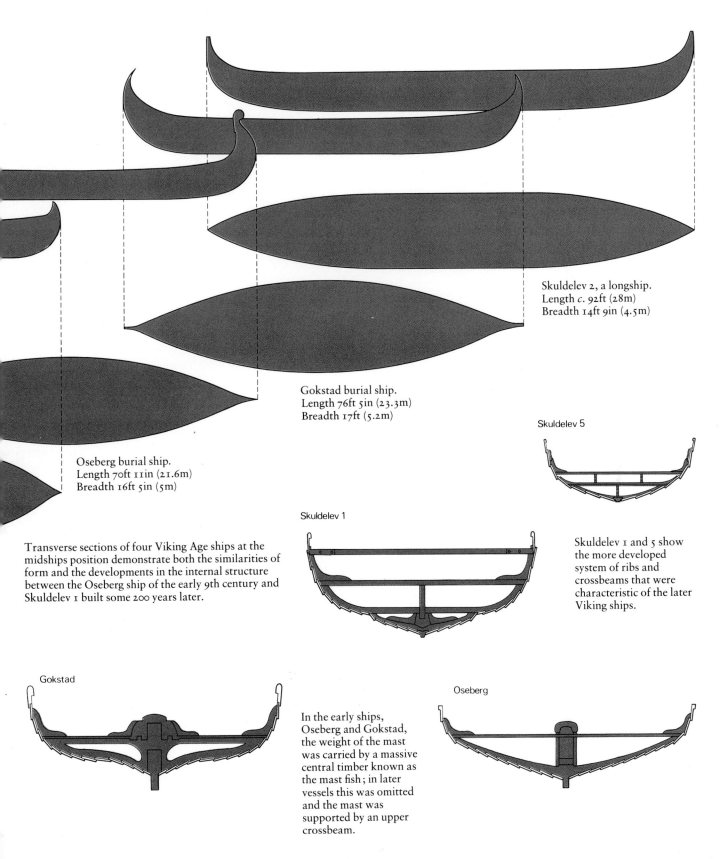

Skuldelev 2, a longship.
Length *c.* 92ft (28m)
Breadth 14ft 9in (4.5m)

Gokstad burial ship.
Length 76ft 5in (23.3m)
Breadth 17ft (5.2m)

Skuldelev 5

Oseberg burial ship.
Length 70ft 11in (21.6m)
Breadth 16ft 5in (5m)

Skuldelev 1

Transverse sections of four Viking Age ships at the midships position demonstrate both the similarities of form and the developments in the internal structure between the Oseberg ship of the early 9th century and Skuldelev 1 built some 200 years later.

Skuldelev 1 and 5 show the more developed system of ribs and crossbeams that were characteristic of the later Viking ships.

Gokstad

Oseberg

In the early ships, Oseberg and Gokstad, the weight of the mast was carried by a massive central timber known as the mast fish; in later vessels this was omitted and the mast was supported by an upper crossbeam.

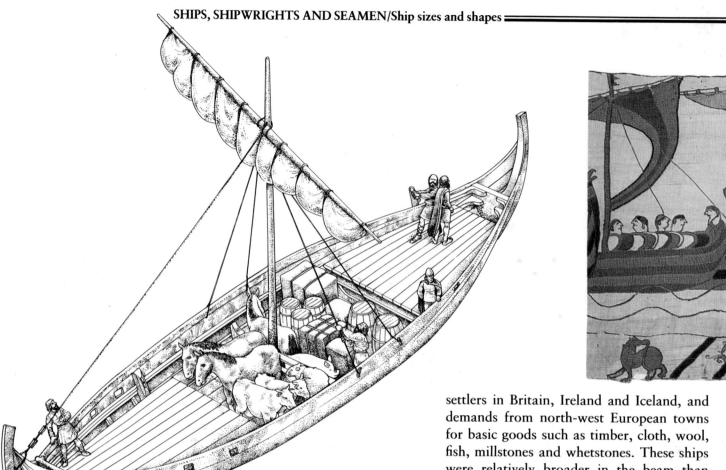

The Viking Age merchant ships were built for cargo capacity and seaworthiness and did not have the speed and manoeuvrability of the longships. They were relatively deeper and broader in the beam and, as can be seen from this conjectural reconstruction, had an open cargo hold amidships with decking and oarports only at either end. Although this was an ocean-going vessel designed for long voyages, there was little protection for either cargo or crew. (In this illustration the rowing benches have been omitted.)

those from Gokstad and Oseberg are difficult to classify by this scheme. They may be either special ships built as royal yachts or general-purpose ships built before specialization of function had developed.

Raiders and traders

The warship or longship may be recognized by its relative slenderness, its continuous full-length decking, a full outfit of oars, and an easily unstepped mast. These ships were built for speed, for operating semi-independently of the wind, and for the carriage of men and of goods of high density and high unit value, such as coins and other booty from raids. The development of the Viking Age merchant ships, built for cargo capacity and sea-worthiness rather than speed, was probably stimulated by the requirements of early

settlers in Britain, Ireland and Iceland, and demands from north-west European towns for basic goods such as timber, cloth, wool, fish, millstones and whetstones. These ships were relatively broader in the beam than longships, had a cargo hold amidships, with decking and oarports only in the fore and after parts, and a more firmly seated mast designed to be unstepped only rarely. Despite their sea-going capacity they were still basically open boats with the cargo covered by skins, and the crew and any passengers exposed to the elements. On coastal voyages it may have been possible to beach, or to go ashore at night using the ship's boat, which was towed astern, to cook and to sleep in tents, but on the voyages to Iceland and Greenland and even crossing the North Sea this would not have been possible. Seamen, merchants and passengers slept where best they could on the deck, between the thwarts, covered with hides or possibly in two-man skin sleeping bags for extra warmth. Food was mainly dried, pickled, salted or possibly smoked fish and meat, with unleavened bread. For drink there would be water in skin bags, and beer or sour milk in tubs. Some of these stores (and indeed other cargo) could

HIC EXEVNT:CABALLI   DENAVIBVS · ET HIC:MILITES: FES

have been carried under the half-decks.

Merchant ships relied mostly on their single square sail for propulsion, using their few oars only when temporarily becalmed or when manoeuvring near landing places. At times they would need to await a favourable wind to round a headland or to take them on a long passage across the ocean. These ships could be crewed by relatively few men: a helmsman, a lookout, someone bailing, and others sufficient to handle the sail: the ocean-going Skuldelev 1 probably carried a twelve-man crew, the 43ft (13m) coastal trader Skuldelev 3 required only five or six.

Although only 10ft (3m) longer than the coastal trader, Skuldelev 1 had space for something like 1,060–1,235 cubic feet (30–35 cubic metres) of cargo in the hold, plus more under the half-decks, compared with an estimated 355 cubic feet (10 cubic metres) space in Skuldelev 3. What precisely could be carried would be determined by density, for a bulky load, with a high centre of gravity, might impair stability, while a high-density load might reduce freeboard dangerously. The reconstruction drawing of a cargo ship shows horses, cattle and sheep in the hold. On the Bayeux Tapestry horses are shown being

offloaded from what is probably a cargo ship, as it is without the continuous line of oarports shown on the other vessels. It is also possible that longships carried horses. *Imme Gram*, a replica of the Danish warship from Ladby, carried horses during sea trials in 1970. With a low freeboard the horses were able to step on board in shallow water.

Longships, being fighting ships, were operated to make good use of favourable winds but also to be as independent as possible of contrary winds and the weather in general. Their main source of power was therefore the oar, with the mast unstepped to reduce wind resistance and to improve stability. There were no supernumaries in the crew, all being seamen at sea and soldiers on land. Where there was room, two or more men could man each oar; and for long passages it would have been necessary to change crews at intervals. Thus extra crew would have to be available or the full complement of oars could not be continuously manned. Estimates of crew are therefore difficult: the 92ft (28m) Skuldelev 2 is thought to have had a crew of fifty to sixty men; Skuldelev 5, which had twelve oars each side, may have had twenty-six to thirty men.

The Bayeux Tapestry shows the Norman invaders disembarking horses from their Nordic-style ships, at Pevensey, Sussex, on 28 September 1066. This is probably a cargo vessel, but horses may also have been transported in the longships (already drawn up on the beach).

Preparing the timber

Timber for shipbuilding was selected to suit the job in hand: planking was cut from straight-grained trees, while ribs and other curved members followed the grain of crooked trunks and limbs.

Oak was most commonly used, the logs being split radially to produce thin wedge-shaped planking ideal for clinker construction. Pine planks (used in Norway and possibly Sweden) were fashioned from near the widest part of the log.

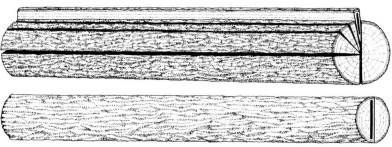

Smaller curved structures were also cut from naturally angled pieces of wood to ensure maximum strength. This modern replica of a thole or oar pivot was made from a log with a projecting branch and follows the curved grain of the 'crook'.

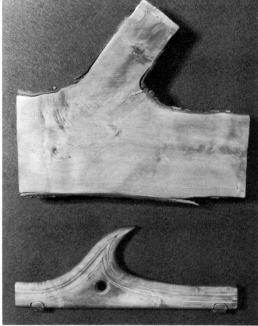

Wherever it was available, oak seems to have been the timber preferred for building Viking ships and boats, although ash, beech, alder, birch, lime and willow were also used, probably for their specific qualities; pine was used in Norway and possibly in Sweden. Forest oaks that had grown tall with straight grain and no low branches were selected for keels and planking. Such oaks are a rare commodity today, and the single oak timber required for the 60ft (18m) keel of the Gokstad ship would be hard to find. Isolated oaks, free to grow outwards, produced the crooked timber for ribs and other curved components. After felling by axe the timber was cut, without seasoning, into planks and other structural parts. Green timber was used, probably because it was easier to work than when seasoned, and to avoid the shrinkage and splitting that occurs on drying. The danger of dry rot – the main reason for the modern insistence on seasoned timber – would be minimal in these Viking vessels, which were mainly open and well ventilated.

The oak logs were split radially, using beech or hafted metal wedges, each log being cut in half and half again until wedge-

shaped planks of uniform breadth and triangular cross-section were produced, somewhat in the manner of slicing a cake. Experiment has shown that an average of twenty sound planks, some 12in (30cm) broad, can be produced from a log of 39in (1m) diameter. These radially split planks, or clove boards, worked from sound, straight logs without a spiral grain, have several advantages over modern sawn boards: they are stronger, shrink less, and are not so liable to warp or split. They are also very suitable for clinker construction, as their wedge shape allows more wood along one edge for the cutting of the bevel where the planks overlap. Nevertheless, this planking is generally remarkably thin, the bottom planks of the Gokstad ship being only 1in (25mm) thick, while those of the *færing* are ½in (15mm).

Keels, keelsons, masts, yards and cross-beams were fashioned from suitable straight-grained logs, and stems (and possibly some keels) were worked from timber with an appropriate slight natural curve. More curvaceous timbers were used for ribs and knees. Tholes and those keelsons with a mast-supporting projection required forked timbers.

More wood was required for treenails and wedges, oars, rudders, rigging blocks, gang-planks and bailers; for clamps, battens, stakes, shores and the stocks on which the boat was built; and for skids and launching ways. All this necessitated a good supply of choice timber. Ole Crumlin-Pedersen calculated that 1,765–2,050 cubic feet (50–58 cubic metres) of oak was probably required to build a 65–80ft (20–25m) longship. This would be equivalent to about eleven trees each 39in (1m) in diameter and 16ft (5m) in length of trunk, together with another tree 50–60ft (15–18m) long for the keel.

Naturally curved timbers (crooks) not immediately required were stored underwater to keep the timber green and workable. In Scotland and Norway partly fashioned stems have been found which had probably been laid by in this way.

Other raw materials

Other essential raw materials included iron for anchors and for nails and the roves or washers over which they were flattened (clenched) to fasten the planking; wool for sails and as a caulking (luting) between the planks; leather (walrus or sealskin), hemp, lime bast and willow for rigging; and pine tar for waterproofing the seams and as a protection against rot.

Scenes from the Bayeux Tapestry depicting the Normans preparing their invasion fleet give a good impression of the way Viking shipwrights must have worked. Here William's men use different types of axe to fell trees, lop branches and trim planking from the logs.

Shipbuilding tools

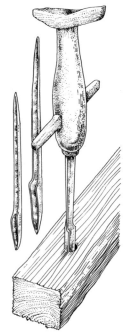

Woodworking tools found in several Viking Age graves show the wide range of tools available. Most of these would have been used by the boat- and shipbuilder, who would also have used certain metalworking tools to produce the thousands of nails and roves. Examination of these tools, of boatbuilding scenes depicted by early medieval artists, as for example on the Bayeux Tapestry, and of the toolmarks left on boat finds leads to the conclusion that the axe was by far the most important of the Viking Age shipwright's tools: incredibly, even the final finish of oak planking was done with axes, although pine planking in the Skuldelev finds was finished with a draw-knife, and adzes must have been used to shape certain curved surfaces. Four different types of axe can be seen in the Bayeux boatbuilding scenes, being used for felling trees and lopping off branches, fashioning planks from logs and for the final trimming of the plank after fitting. Holes were bored with a spoon-shaped bit inserted in a T-shaped handle, and knives, chisels, gouges, hammers and mallets were all in frequent use.

Excavations have produced a wide range of Viking Age wood- and metalworking tools, most of which would have been used by the shipwrights. A selection is illustrated here.

Above T-shaped wooden breast auger with metal bits (as seen on the Bayeux Tapestry, *right*), for boring holes in timber.

Below Adze (the main woodworking tool after the axe) for shaping curved structures.

The axe was the most important tool to the shipwright, for fine work as well as for cutting timber. Here axes are used for the final trimming of the planking, while in the background holes are bored with a T-shaped auger. The man standing on the left, who is apparently assessing the run of the planking, may well have been the master shipbuilder.

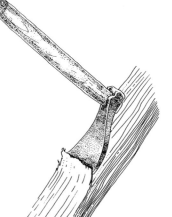

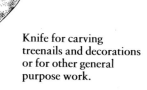

Axe (also seen on the Bayeux Tapestry) for trimming planks or the flat sides of curved timbers.

Knife for carving treenails and decorations or for other general purpose work.

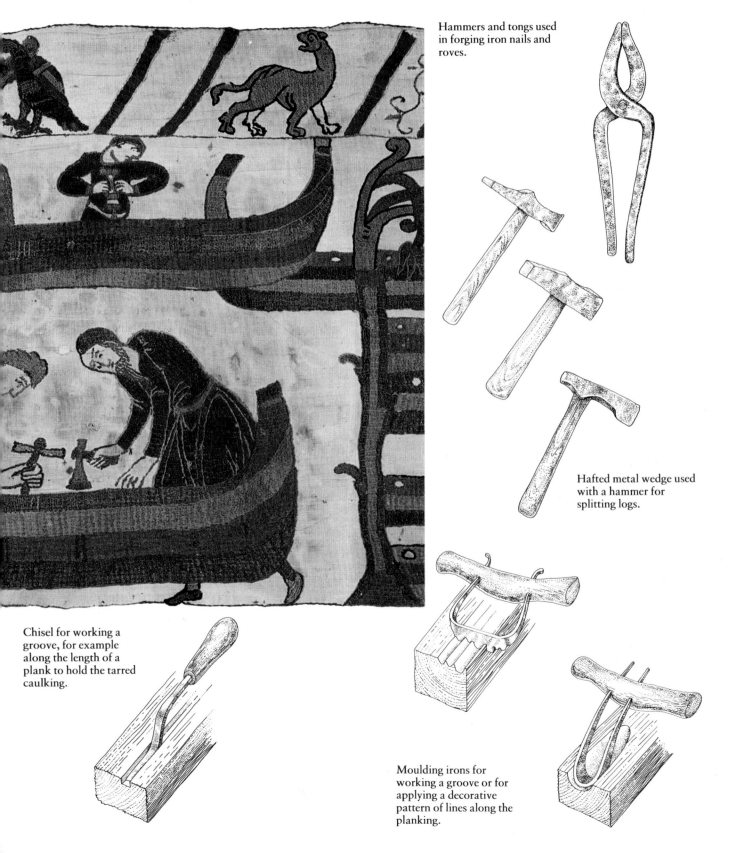

Hammers and tongs used in forging iron nails and roves.

Hafted metal wedge used with a hammer for splitting logs.

Chisel for working a groove, for example along the length of a plank to hold the tarred caulking.

Moulding irons for working a groove or for applying a decorative pattern of lines along the planking.

Building methods

The sagas and other documentary sources can tell us something of the various grades of skill required in building a medieval Scandinavian ship. Doubtless small boats would be built by one man, possibly with an assistant, as they are today. But for ships greater specialization was required and under the master boatbuilder worked a range of craftsmen including woodsmen, specialist stem-smiths and craftsmen plank-cutters, as well as labourers.

Today we instinctively think of boats and ships being built from designs or plans. But the Viking Age master builder had no such aids: he built by eye and rule of thumb, as was the case until recently in Norway and in Shetland. The optimum ratios of length to breadth and depth required for boats to perform different functions were learned

from experience. It has been established, for example, that Viking merchant ships had a length/breadth ratio of approximately 4:1, whereas for warships this was 7:1. Such rules were handed on by oral tradition, but Arne Emil Christensen has suggested that design details may also have been transmitted in code on a boat ell, a form of measuring stick, or on a boat level, which recorded the angle between the runs of planking.

Within such traditions there was scope for individual variation to cater for specific requirements or differences in available raw material, and vessels were built with the same general characteristics but differing in detail. The eye of the individual master boatbuilder determined the final result.

Stages of construction
Viking ships and boats were not built in yards

The first stage in the construction of a Viking ship or boat was to place the prepared keel on a base of securely laid stocks and to join the fore- and after-stems to it (at the keel scarfs) with iron nails and one or two wooden treenails. Once the backbone of the ship had been thus set up and firmly supported at either end it was ready to receive the garboards (first strakes).

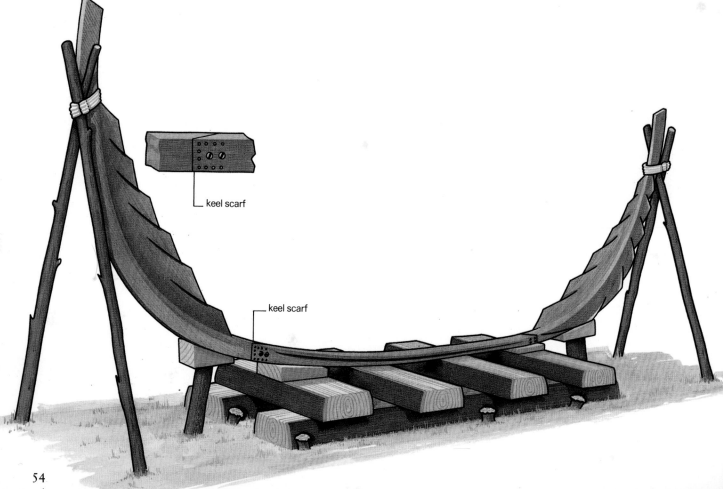

keel scarf

keel scarf

or in sheds, but in the open, perhaps under a simple shelter, as close to the water as possible. Work began with the fashioning of the keel and the forward and after stems, and the preparation of the firm, level base upon which the ship was to be built. Meanwhile other men would be splitting logs and fashioning planking from them.

The backbone of the ship was set up, by fastening the stems to the keel. The garboards or first strakes (each layer of planking is called a strake) were then fastened to the keel and stems, using iron nails driven through the two pieces of wood then beaten flat against a metal washer (rove) on the inside of the ship (the western Baltic method), except at the ends, where iron spikes were used. The second pair of strakes was then fastened overlapping the lower strakes, a caulking (luting) of tarred animal hair having first been placed in the overlap to fill any irregularities and thus keep the hull watertight. Ships built in the eastern Baltic, however, had moss caulking in between planks fastened by treenails or wooden pegs. As planking-up continued the varying breadths of the planks and the angles at which succeeding strakes were fastened to the lower ones determined the form of the boat. Thus, as the master builder saw the shape emerging he could achieve the required hull shape by altering the breadth of the next pair of strakes or by altering the angle at which they were fastened. The top strake of the ship's bottom – the layer of planks at or near the waterline – was often stouter than other strakes, in order to give longitudinal strength at that point.

Internal supporting timbers were added only after the bottom planking had been completed: for the Oseberg and Gokstad

The first strakes (each made of two or more planks) were fastened to the keel and stems with iron nails, iron spikes being used at either end where the wood was thick. Subsequent strakes were then added in clinker fashion, again using iron nails clenched over roves (see page 45), and with tarred animal hair in the overlaps. Clamps held the planking temporarily in place; the angle and position of each strake may have been checked by a device similar to the level shown here, or possibly by a boat ell, measuring the distance from a central line as illustrated.

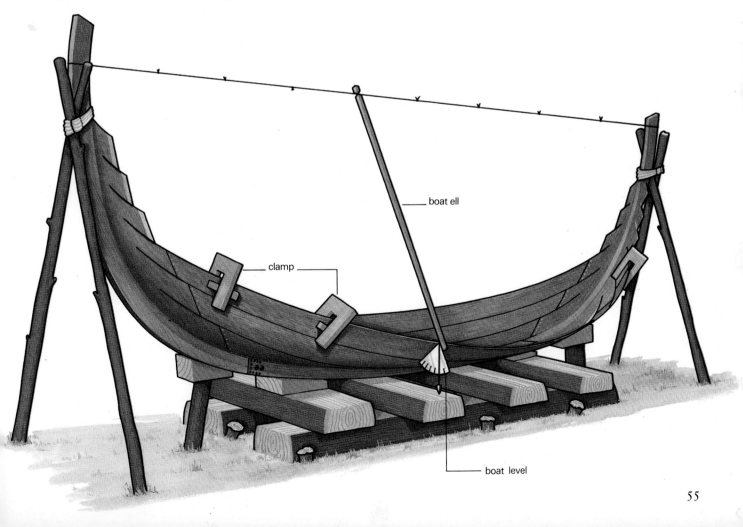

boat ell

clamp

boat level

ships this was after ten or eleven strakes had been fastened each side; for the Skuldelev ships it varied from three to seven strakes. Thus Viking ships were built shell first, rather than by the method recently used in Britain in which the planking is fastened to a preformed skeleton of ribs, keel, stem and stern that determines the shape of the hull.

In the Oseberg and Gokstad ships the regularly spaced floor-timbers were lashed to cleats left standing proud of the planking. But in almost all other Viking Age finds these floor-timbers were fastened by wooden pegs or treenails. The treenail method has the advantage of saving in material, labour and skill, but the drawback is that many holes, each a potential source of leakage, have to be made in the planking. The characteristically slender floor-timbers were fashioned from timbers chosen to match the transverse curves

of the hull. Notches were cut in their lower surfaces so that they fitted close to the clinker planking, and limber holes were also cut to allow free passage of bilge-water.

A keelson was fitted on top of the keel in those ships destined to have a mast. In the eastern Baltic this was a transverse timber, but in the normal Viking design it was a heavy longitudinal timber, with notches at appropriate places in its undersurface to accommodate the floor-timbers, to which it was fastened by knees (timbers that had naturally grown with two arms approximately at right angles). There was a vertical supporting projection (again a natural branch) from the upper surface of the keelson immediately forward of the hole in which the mast would be stepped. Keelsons distributed the weight of the mast and yard over the keel, and thus the larger they were the more efficient they

Internal supporting timbers were added only after the bottom planking had been completed, and were attached to the strakes, not to the keel. The slender floor-timbers were chosen to match the curve of the hull and notched in their lower surfaces to fit close against the overlapping planks. They were either lashed to cleats left standing proud of the planking or fastened by wooden pegs or treenails as shown on page 45.

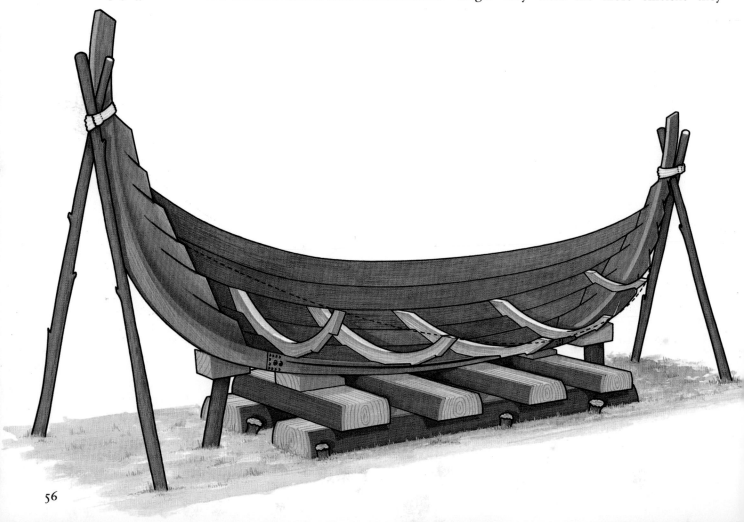

became. The Skuldelev keelsons were about half as long as the keel, and some were of sufficient size significantly to reinforce the longitudinal strength of the ship.

Slender crossbeams (known as *bite*) were next fastened across the ends of the floor-timbers, often supported by a wooden pillar (a stanchion or *snelle*) between floor-timber and beam. Vertical knees were fastened to the ends of the beams and to these the lower side planking was secured. When possible, a beam and a knee were worked out of one suitably curved timber, thus increasing the strength of the structure.

At crossbeam level in the earlier ships the mast was supported by a massive timber known as a mast fish or mast partner; in later ships this was omitted and the mast was supported by an upper crossbeam.

In the Skuldelev ships more side planking was added and reinforced by longitudinal timbers known as stringers, and the internal structure was further developed to include upper crossbeams with their ends resting on the stringers, and vertical and horizontal knees to reinforce the upper side planking. Where there was to be a cargo hold amidships upper crossbeams were omitted, except for a central mast-bracing beam of stouter dimensions supported by the vertical projection from the keelson. The upper crossbeams could be used as thwarts or rowing benches, with the rowers' feet resting on bottom boards at lower crossbeam level. In the large cargo vessel Skuldelev 1 a half-deck was laid on these crossbeams both forward and aft, and there was a third tier of crossbeams at the ends that could be used as thwarts. Knees attached to these crossbeams supported further strakes, with side timbers providing

A keelson (to support the mast) was fitted on top of the keel and over the floor-timbers, to which it was fastened by angled knees. Crossbeams were then laid across the ends of the floor-timbers, braced centrally by a wooden pillar or stanchion and attached by knees to the strakes at either end. Planking-up could now continue, further beams, knees and stringers (horizontal supporting timbers) being added as necessary.

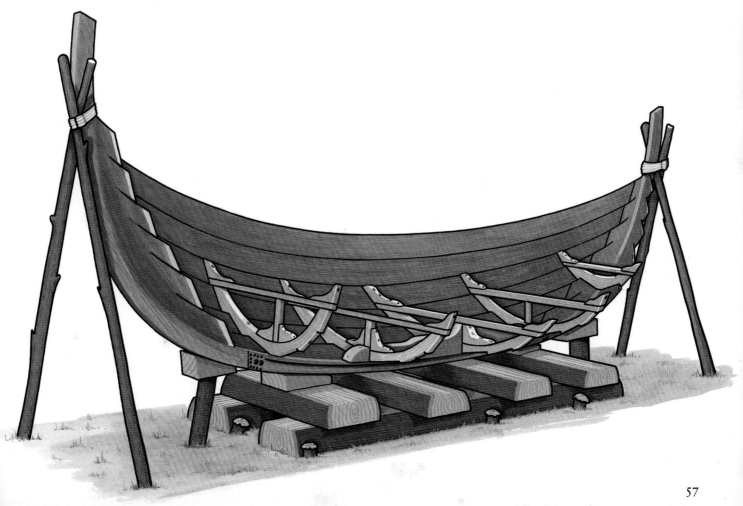

The stern of the Oseberg ship shows the distinctive Viking Age side rudder, fastened by a rope or thong through the upper planking and pivoted on a boss lower down.

Sails and ropes do not survive the passage of time, but coins and graffiti give some idea of Viking Age rigging. The ship depicted on a silver coin minted at Hedeby has a wide sail and carries a row of shields along the gunwale.

additional support between the crossbeam stations. This distinctive combination of crossbeams and knees above each floor-timber, with longitudinal stringers providing a housing for the beams, transversely reinforced the shell of thin planking at each station along the boat's length, thus giving Viking craft maximum strength and resilience despite their lightness and flexibility.

With the hull completed, and probably after tarring and launching, the ship was fitted out. The mast was stepped and the yard fitted, held to the mast by a parrel, a yoke of rope and wooden beads. Mast steps on cargo vessels tended to be deeper than those on war-ships: the former's mast could withstand greater forces and thus could be used in worse weather. Excavated evidence for mast, rigging, yard and sail is minimal: stumps of masts and yard fragments from Oseberg and Gokstad; cleats and twisted osier rings (grommets) in Skuldelev 3; iron rings in the Ladby ship; and fittings to receive the heel of a tacking boom in Gokstad and Skuldelev 1. Representations of sailing ships, ranging from those on the Gotland stones of the seventh century and later, to those of graffiti, coins and seals of the thirteenth century, provide useful information, however, and documentary evidence also helps. From this evidence it seems that the standing rigging was very simple, with a forestay to the bow, shrouds fastened to the top strakes or to thwarts, crossbeams or knees either side of the mast, and a backstay that perhaps doubled as a halyard to hoist the yard and sail.

The running rigging to hoist and lower the yard and to control the head and foot of the sail was also simple, leaving little specific evidence to be found on excavation, as these ropes could be made fast to structural elements of the ship and thus would not need special fittings. There were probably braces to each yardarm, sheets and tacks to the foot of the sail, and a bowline to the leading edge, supplemented by the *beitiáss* spar (tacking boom) when tacking. Sails have not survived,

but it is thought that the Gokstad ship's loose-footed sail was rectangular, about 23ft (7m) high and 36ft (11m) across, while the sail of Skuldelev 1 was probably twice as wide as high: the representations on the Gotland picture-stones appear to agree with these proportions.

Oars were made of varying lengths to match their station in the ship. For oar pivots, tholes (forked pieces of wood) were fastened to the top strakes of planking – or, in ships with greater freeboard, rounded or rectangular oarports were cut through one of the upper strakes. Oarports were required the full length of warships, whereas they were fitted only near the ends of merchant ships.

The side rudder was made to a distinctive shape, somewhat like a broad oar, and fastened on the starboard quarter by a thong or rope lashing through the upper planking and by a withy thong through an external projection or boss on the lower planking. The skilled craftsmanship of the Viking Age ship-wright is apparent in the way side rudders were given a cross-section similar to that of an aircraft wing: thus the 'lift' or sideways thrust generated on the rudder by the flowing water compensated for the drag or water resistance, which would otherwise have caused the ship to turn to starboard.

In warships bottom boards were fitted at lower crossbeam level, thus providing deck-ing the full length of the ship, with possibly a raised section at the stern for the steersman and in the bow for the lookout. In cargo ships, there could be similar bottom boards in the central area where the cargo was stored, with half-decks forward and aft at upper cross-beam level.

Anchors, gangplanks, bailers and other essential equipment completed the fitting out of the ship. The more important ships were decorated with carvings and some had detachable figureheads, but even small boats had moulding patterns of lines cut along the planking, a sign of the craftsman's pride in a well-built vessel.

We get some idea of the performance of these ships at sea from the fact that the Vikings could maintain fairly regular contact with Iceland and Greenland, and undertake countless voyages in the Arctic, the Baltic, the North Sea, the eastern Atlantic and the Mediterranean, though prudently limiting their sailing season to between April and early October. For further information we must

Viking's voyage also demonstrated the reliability of the thin planking. Thin planking results in light draft and thus Viking vessels could be taken far inland up shallow rivers; some could even be manhandled overland between rivers or across a peninsula.

Steering

Magnus Andersen was also favourably impressed by the side rudder, which, because it was balanced, he found easy to use even in

turn to recent experimental work with replicas of Viking ships and boats.

Seaworthiness

In 1893, *Viking*, a Norwegian replica of the Gokstad ship, under the command of Captain Magnus Andersen, sailed from Bergen to Newfoundland in twenty-eight days. This voyage demonstrated the seaworthiness and the seakeeping qualities of this form of hull. Andersen noted the flexibility of her distinctive method of construction, yet the vessel successfully endured several stormy days and proved reasonably watertight. Viking ships were designed to be supple and to 'ride the punch' of the sea, rather than be rigid and battle against it. In this they were probably more successful than any rigid structure could have been, for, with the materials and technology of those days, a rigid structure would inevitably have had to be more massive. Leakage at the seams and through fastenings must always have been a problem, however, and bailing out a constant task.

heavy seas. Viking Age side rudders projected well below the keel but in shallow water they could be raised quickly by unlashing the upper fastening and pivoting the rudder about the external boss.

Speed

Theory indicates that long, light-displacement craft should have high speed potential, and this was in fact demonstrated during trials of the Greenwich *færing* of longship proportions; the *færing* achieved an unexpectedly high speed of 7 knots under oars, probably because she rode up out of the water and skimmed along in a semi-planing posture, almost like a power boat. Experiment and theory thus show that in favourable conditions the Viking longship could have achieved high speed under oar or sail, provided that she had a competent crew.

Under sail

The simple standing rigging evidently used in Viking ships gave freedom to trim the yard

A late 11th- or early 12th-century ship graffito on a wooden plank found in the Winetavern Street excavation, Dublin, provides further evidence of shrouds and stays. The arrow at the mast head is possibly a wind vane.

Various types of rigging are tested on *Imme Gram*, a replica of a Danish warship from Ladby.

into the optimum position, especially if the shrouds were readily adjustable. The relatively short mast would mean better stability and less need for support, while the long yard made a large sail area possible. Calculations indicate that the Gokstad ship did in fact have good sailing potential. Precisely how fast and how close to the wind a Viking ship could sail is at present difficult to quantify, for these qualities also depend on the material and the cut of the sail, the match of the sail and rigging to the hull, and the abilities of the crew. The deep keels and the characteristic steepness of the lower strakes imply that Viking hulls had relatively good windward capability and the use of the *beitiáss* or tacking boom to hold the leading edge of the sail taut shows that Viking seamen were striving to get as close to the wind as they possibly could.

Recent experiments in Denmark have shown that the Viking hull and rig can be sailed across the wind and even against it, though precise figures are not yet available.

Pilotage and navigation

With generations of experience and constant practice Viking seamen became familiar with landmarks that indicated their whereabouts in coastal waters, even when operating at extreme visual range, as would be prudent with an onshore wind when they might easily be wrecked. Crossing a channel such as the English Channel or the North Channel would also be relatively simple; wider stretches of water could be similarly navigated in conditions of refraction, when bending of the light rays means that peaks and headlands can be visible at sea level up to 60 miles away.

Voyaging out of sight of land was a different matter, for the Vikings had no compass and no accurate timepiece. Nevertheless, in the later Viking period they repeatedly achieved long, two-way ocean voyages to Iceland and Greenland during which they were out of sight of land for several consecutive days. They were thus proven ocean navigators, but we can only make a reasoned guess at the precise methods

HAROLD: HIC: APPREHENDIT: V

they used: possibly these were similar to those used by contemporary Arabs, for which there is some documentary evidence. If the course was known and the distance of the run estimated, a form of dead reckoning could have been used. On a clear night a course may be steered relative to the Pole Star, and we know that the significance of this was appreciated by early medieval seamen. The angle to a steady swell from a known direction can also be used, as can the relative direction of a prevailing wind: warm wet winds are from the south-west, cold wet winds from the north-east; thus the feel of the wind can be roughly equated with direction. Checks on these estimates could be made at certain times of day, providing the sun was visible. At noon, with the sun at its highest, or in northern latitudes at midnight, with the sun at its lowest, the direction of north and south can be established; sunrise and sunset, except in high latitudes, give the approximate directions of east and west.

Over generations, a body of knowledge would have been built up on the time usually taken to sail between two places. There are accounts of traditional routes and their associated number of sailing days in the sagas and we may deduce that there were similar oral accounts in the earlier, Viking times. Such records would have to be based on a standard speed, possibly allowing for currents. Deviations from this theoretical speed could be estimated on a particular voyage from a knowledge of the past performance of one's own ship, and the existing weather and sea conditions. Alternatively, speed could be estimated from the position of the bow wave, or by counting the number of standard oarstrokes used to propel the ship past a floating object thrown overboard from the bow, or by a sandglass. Use of a simple traverse board (similar to the gaming boards found in Viking contexts) would enable these estimated courses and speeds to be plotted to give the ship's approximate position, although there is no direct evidence of such use. For a more accurate position estimates would have to be

Their light draft enabled the Viking ships to be run close in shore before grounding – hence the success of the fast and unexpected beach landings of the Viking raiders.

made of the leeway experienced (the amount the ship had been blown sideways) and the effects of any currents.

The length of daylight and the angular altitude of Polaris and of the noon sun change as one moves north or south of a known place. If such variations could be detected on board ship it would be established that the ship was north or south of a known 'latitude'. It may have been possible to estimate altitudes against the ship's rigging, although with questionable accuracy. Another method could be to compare the apparent height of sun or star above the horizon with the outstretched hand (a finger's breadth is *c.* 2°; wrist span, *c.* 8°; clenched fist, *c.* 10°; extended fingers, *c.* 19°), or against a calibrated stick. The ship's movement would cause inaccuracies, but the mean of several readings could be used to reduce error. The ability to appreciate significant deviations from the known 'latitude' of the home port, or of destination, could lead to a form of latitude sailing, striving to maintain a constant 'latitude' as indicated by the altitude of the Pole Star or the sun, and there are indications in the sagas that the Vikings may have used this method.

Navigation based on celestial observation requires relatively clear skies; a succession of overcast days would almost inevitably lead to loss of bearings, unless, as some authorities believe, Viking seamen had discovered the sun-seeking property of double refracting cordierite or Icelandic feldspar crystals. Whatever methods were employed, it seems clear that the Vikings had developed ocean navigation to a fine art, possibly with the aid of skills that we no longer realize we possess.

Approaching land, navigational problems would be eased, although risk of shipwreck increased. Cloud sitting over an island is visible before land is sighted, and ice may be detected many miles away in good weather by its reflection in the sky. Nearer land the line of flight of seabirds, the boom of the surf, the shallowing of the water revealed by lead and

line, even the smell of sheep indicate its proximity. Landmarks and beacons were built as aids for navigators in certain places. Using these aids the master or pilot would identify his landfall and decide which way to turn along the coast in order to make the intended destination.

Landing places

Viking ships, at least until the eleventh century, did not need the formal facilities of quays and jetties to load and unload. Raiders would naturally prefer to run aground unobserved on a remote strand where their attack would be mounted. But the marked wear on the keel and the extensive repairs to the bottom planking of Skuldelev ship 3 show that some merchant ships were also run ashore on beaches with suitable gradients, on river banks, estuary shores or coastal sites protected from the prevailing wind. On muddy beaches simple hardstandings of parallel timbers might be used; otherwise ships were run direct on to the sand or shingle, their relatively light draft allowing them to go in close before grounding. For a long stay or in

NAVIGAVIT ETVE LIS VE NIT WIC CON

tidal conditions they might subsequently be dragged clear of the water. As we see on the Bayeux Tapestry, ships could also be anchored off a landing place or moored to posts in shallow water. They were then unloaded and loaded by men wading through the water or by carts driven into the water. For ships moored further away from land, small boats could be used to ferry the cargo to and fro.

That it was foreign to their nature to bring Viking ships alongside a waterfront or another ship is illustrated by the presence of cleats on the outboard side of Skuldelev 3's top strake, where they would be vulnerable to damage; similar considerations apply to the external shield rails on Skuldelev 5 and on the Oseberg ship. The tholes (oar pivots) protruding from the top strakes of the Greenwich *færing* replica also proved to be a hazard when alongside a jetty, where they were likely to be broken or to catch under a projection.

Only with the development in the post-Viking period of ships of significantly greater draft, and structurally unsuited for beaching, did vessels of this type need to use quays with relatively deep water. Even then boats and the smaller ships continued to use beach or river-bank landing places.

The Viking achievement

Many of the achievements described in other chapters would have been impossible without the Vikings' mastery of shipbuilding, seamanship and navigation. For a period of 300 years or so, they were the most accomplished seamen of the northern seas. Their ships operated from the Arctic to the Caspian Sea and across the Atlantic to the New World: some were on raiding missions but many were trading ships or on voyages of exploration and settlement.

The Viking ship type appears to have been replaced as the dominant northern ship in the twelfth century by the larger and more unwieldy cog. This was mainly because the cog could carry more cargo and not because it was a more seaworthy ship. Although ships with Viking characteristics may have virtually disappeared by the fourteenth century, the style of building lived on in the small boats of many countries, in some places even up to the present day.

Land-seekers

Viking explorers and settlers sailed out across the Atlantic to discover and colonize new lands in the West. Eirik the Red who explored Greenland, *left*, in the 980s gave it this name in order to attract prospective settlers. Although much of its coastline is grim and forbidding, pastureland exists at the head of certain fjords. The early settlers flourished, but the Norse colonies were eventually abandoned in the 14th and 15th centuries.

The first explorers

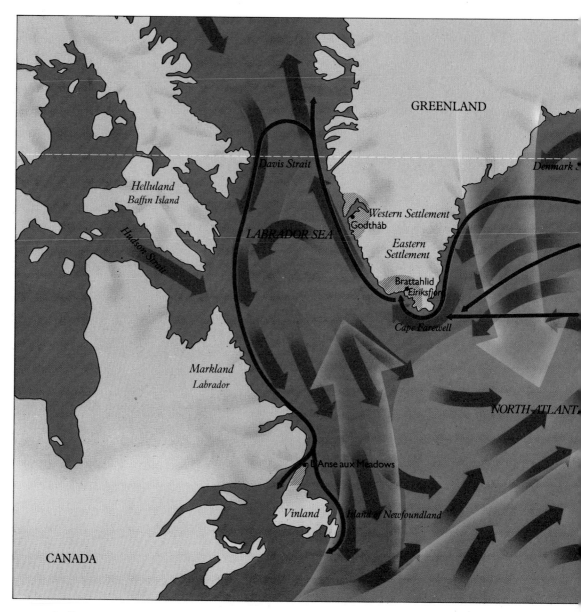

mong the Viking raiders who swept across the sea to attack the British Isles during the closing years of the eighth century, there must have been men who would return in later seasons as settlers, bringing with them their families and friends. These first land-seekers came to the Northern and Western Isles of Scotland, where they found familiar landscapes that would support them in their accustomed manner, by mixed farming, hunting and the resources of the sea. Others followed, travelling farther south to the lands around the Irish Sea. In Ireland there were few opportunities for land-taking, although Viking towns would flourish. But the Isle of Man and northwest England were to offer considerable scope for rural settlement.

In previous decades Irish monks had discovered, and sought solitude in, the north Atlantic islands. Now the most venturesome Viking explorers set out from their new settlements in the British Isles in the wake of

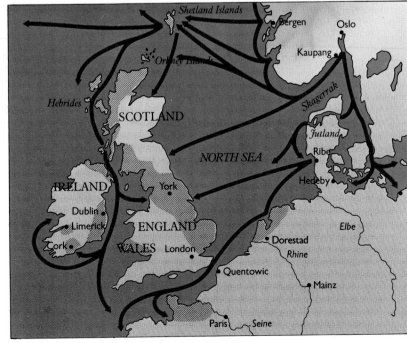

WESTERN ROUTES AND SETTLEMENTS Pushing ever further west in their search for fertile lands in which to settle, the Vikings first sighted America in about 985.

- tundra
- mountains
- pastureland
- modern limits of pack-ice in spring
- modern limits of drift ice
- ➡ currents
- ➡ prevailing winds
- ➡ Viking Routes
- areas of Viking settlement

It is impossible to plot Viking Age limits of drift and pack-ice, but the Atlantic Ocean was warmer at that period and drift ice probably rare south of North Cape. The northern voyages of the Vikings would have been difficult under present ice conditions.

the monks' leather curraghs to the Faeroes and to Iceland. From there, an intrepid few sailed on to countries as yet unseen by Europeans, to Greenland and thence to America.

Medieval sagas and histories

The early settlers are anonymous men and women, for there was none among them able to chronicle their voyages and their struggles to establish new farms. It was not until much later that the events of these centuries of exploration and settlement came to be written down in the medieval Icelandic sagas and histories. *Orkneyinga Saga* (*The Saga of the Orkneymen*), *Færeyinga Saga* (*The Saga of the Faeroemen*), *Eiríks Saga Rauða* (*Eirik the Red's Saga*), and *Grœnlendinga Saga* (*The Saga of the Greenlanders*) all have much to offer the historian as well as the student of medieval literature. But such saga-history must be treated with caution, for the information recorded about the events that took place several centuries before is in the form of stories that had been preserved by constant retelling, and thus were always liable to distortion by personal, political and religious interests, before finally being committed to parchment. For Iceland, however, in addition to the various *Íslendinga Sǫgur* (*Sagas of Icelanders*), there are two historical works compiled in the twelfth century that deliberately set out to record the country's early history: the *Íslendingabók* (*Book of the Icelanders*), and the *Landnámabók* (*Book of the Settlements*). But even these depend ultimately on unwritten traditions for the earliest events that they describe.

We cannot tell exactly when the first Vikings settled in Shetland and the Orkneys – certainly in the ninth century, but not necessarily any earlier, as is often claimed. Place-name scholars in particular have suggested that there was extensive settlement already in the eighth century in the Northern Isles, but archaeology has not confirmed this version of events. The evidence from excavated Viking graves and farmsteads in Scotland indicates that settlement was taking place during the ninth century with expansion in the tenth. More recently controversy has centred on the manner in which these settlements came to be established in the territories of the Picts and Scots, who lived respectively in the northern and western areas of Scotland. Was it by violent conquest, or peaceful assimilation? If the latter was the case then why are nearly all place-names in the Northern Isles Norse in origin? The two most obvious explanations for this state of affairs would be either that the Vikings found the islands empty or that they

On Unst in the Shetland Isles, ponies graze today in front of the excavated remains of a Viking farm at Underhoull. The bay behind served as the harbour. The boat would normally have been pulled up on the beach, although there was also a boathouse for its protection during the winter months.

exterminated the native population of Picts. But neither of these somewhat simplistic suggestions can be accepted today.

Recent excavations have now demonstrated that some established Pictish settlements were indeed taken over by the Norsemen, such as that at Buckquoy on the main island of Orkney. Buckquoy faces the tidal islet of the Brough of Birsay, where there stood a Pictish monastery and community, including metalworkers capable of producing fine ornaments. This monastery was deserted by its monks and replaced by a major Norse settlement that in time was to be the seat of Orkney's greatest earl, Thorfinn the Mighty, who died in 1065.

Fine examples of pre-Norse metalwork of the type made at Birsay were found in 1958 as part of a silver hoard buried under the floor of the small church on St Ninian's Isle, off the south-west coast of Shetland. Its excavator lifted a cross-marked slab to reveal the remains of a larchwood box filled with twenty-eight pieces of silver and (rather surprisingly) part of the jawbone of a porpoise. This Pictish treasure, consisting largely of bowls and distinctive penannular brooches, had been hidden about AD 800, presumably to keep it safe from Viking raiders; the fate of its owner is unknown. The St Ninian's Isle hoard is an eloquent witness both to the wealth available to the Pictish population of these islands and to their obvious fear of attack by Vikings.

On the other hand, Buckquoy is considered by some to have produced evidence for the peaceful assimilation of the native culture by the Norsemen, because its ninth- and tenth-century houses contained pottery, bone pins and combs in the Pictish tradition. But how could there have been a mingling of Norse and native on a peaceful basis when we see the Picts obliged to bury their treasures, and their monks put to flight? Why then should all their own names for places have been replaced? The Norse takeover must have been complete; the Pictish population can only have been subjugated by force. They would have

been put to work as slaves, farming the land, building the houses, making pins and pots for their Norse masters. They made them, of course, in the manner to which they were accustomed. This then would explain the presence of such Pictish material in Norse houses on sites like Buckquoy.

A further argument in the case for friendly Viking settlers is the fact that weapons are not found on such settlement sites. But then weapons are valuable objects that are not discarded on middens, lost about the house, or left lying around in abandoned buildings. They are treated with care, as excavations at Westness, on the Orkney island of Rousay, have shown. Here, for the first time in Scotland, a ninth-century farmstead has been discovered *together* with its family cemetery. The grave-goods buried with the dead show that the men were warriors as well as farmers, for their weapons were placed beside them in their graves.

The tidal island of the Brough of Birsay, off the north-west of Orkney mainland, was the site of a monastery when the Vikings arrived. Here they established a settlement that was to become the seat of Orkney's earls and ultimately the site of a Norse church, built over the ruins of its Pictish predecessor.

The settlement at Jarlshof

The clearest picture that we have to date of the type of farmstead built by the first Viking settlers in Scotland is provided by the multi-period site of Jarlshof, on the southern tip of Shetland. The settlement is located in a sheltered bay, behind the cliffs of Sumburgh head. It had been occupied for centuries, and still was on a small scale, when the Vikings arrived and recognized its potential for their own purposes. The name, though, meaning 'Earl's Mansion', is romantic nonsense, dreamed up by Sir Walter Scott

Above Jarlshof on Shetland was continuously occupied from the late Bronze Age. The complex of early settlements is dominated by a 17th-century ruin, behind which may be seen the long, rectangular outlines of several Norse houses. The earliest Viking farmstead, outlined *right*, was a simple two-room dwelling with a number of outbuildings.

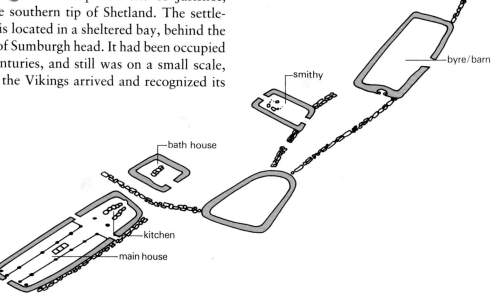

byre/barn

smithy

bath house

kitchen

main house

in his novel *The Pirate* for the later ruins that still dominate the site. The first Norse dwelling house was a bow-sided building about 75ft (23m) long and built of drystone

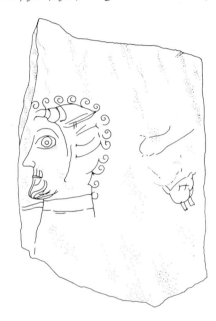

An old man's head scratched on slate by an inhabitant of Jarlshof, perhaps even a portrait drawn from life, is an unusual example of naturalism in Viking art.

and turves, except for its east gable, which was of timber. It was divided into two rooms, the hall or living room, and a much smaller kitchen or pantry. The hall was provided with a characteristic long-hearth down its centre, with raised platforms on either side for both sitting and sleeping. The outbuildings consisted of a byre for wintering the animals, a barn for their fodder, stables, a small smithy and another building of similar size that is thought to have been a bath house where water would have been thrown on hot stones to make a steamy sauna.

The settlers at Jarlshof were principally farmers, although as time passed fishing appears to have become of increasing importance to their economy, perhaps because of the need to feed the growing population. The little community grew and prospered over the next 400 years, with new buildings and extensions being added when necessary to the original farm complex.

urials of Viking warriors and their wealthy ladies have also been discovered in the Hebrides, but to date only two settlements have been excavated and both of these are in the Outer Isles. The most important is the Udal, on a sandy peninsula projecting from the Atlantic coast of North Uist. Here again the story is one of a ninth-century takeover of what had been a flourishing native settlement, the characteristic rectangular buildings with their central long-hearths being built among the pre-Norse ruins. At this moment in the history of the site a small but strongly defended enclosure was constructed on its highest point. It cannot now be established whether it was built by the natives against the Norsemen, or by the Norse settlers against native reprisals (or even against other Vikings). Whichever it may have been, it certainly does not speak of peaceful penetration of the Hebrides.

The pattern of Norse settlement in the Hebrides is still far from fully understood, but it appears to have been more concentrated in some areas than in others, so that different degrees of co-existence must have been practised. On Skye, for instance, only the northern half of the island has any significant number of Norse settlement names. The same was true for the Scottish mainland, where there was scattered settlement, particularly in the north and down the east coast as far as the Dornoch Firth.

Christianity in the Scottish isles

The conversion of these pagan settlers in a Christian land was a gradual process, dependent on personal inclination. But pagan burial practices were gradually abandoned during the tenth century. The Orkneys were forcibly converted in 995, when Olaf Tryggvason, about to seize the throne of Norway, forced Earl Sigurd the Stout to be baptized and to see that the islands followed his example. On the other hand there was nothing at all militant about Scandinavian

The Isle of Man

The Hebrides were settled by Norse Vikings in the 9th century, but not as intensively as the Northern Isles. *Above* The fertile, sandy plain of North Uist's Atlantic coast proved attractive to Viking land-takers. Here, at the Udal, later buildings overlie the Norse settlement, itself established among the ruins of native houses.

paganism and many Vikings seem to have respected the holy places of others. Even raiding monastries was not done with their destruction in mind. The settlers at Birsay did not build over the Pictish church and its cemetery, so that when they erected their own church there in the eleventh century they were able to superimpose the new building on the ruins of the old. This church, of which the remains still stand, is likely to have been the minster of Christchurch, built by Earl Thorfinn the Mighty. It was the predecessor of St Magnus cathedral in Kirkwall, begun in 1137 while Orkney was still a powerful Norse earldom (but using masons from Durham, so that it is hardly a Norse building).

The decline of Norse power

Norse power in Scotland gradually declined from the twelfth century. After the defeat of the Norwegians at Largs in 1263, the Hebrides were ceded to the Scottish Crown. In 1468-9 the Orkneys and then Shetland were pledged as part of the dowry of the Danish princess Margaret on her marriage to King James III of Scotland (Norway and Denmark being then united). But no such transfer could obliterate the Viking heritage of the Northern Isles, where Norse dialects continued to be spoken into the nineteenth century.

The Hebridean chain of island settlements led south to the Isle of Man, a connection recalled in the title of the Bishop of Sodor and Man (Sodor, from *Suðreyjar*, meaning the Southern Isles, as the Hebrides were known to the Norsemen). Viking graves, among them that of a warrior buried in his boat in the Christian cemetery at Balladoole, suggest that the first settlements on Man were made during the second half of the ninth century – at the same time as those in Ireland, after fifty or more years of raiding in these waters and beyond. One curious fact is that, except for the slave girl apparently sacrificed with her master at Ballateare, there is not a single burial of a woman among the forty or so Viking graves known from the Isle of Man. Given this number of burials, it seems probable that few Scandinavian women can have been involved in the settlement of Man. Indeed it is unlikely that the island was settled in the same way as Scotland; more probably it was seized by Viking warriors who then intermarried with the Manx women. Evidence for this supposition comes not only from their rapid adoption of Christianity, presumably by example, but also from the fact that native Celtic names are among those carved in runes on the tenth-century stone slabs and crosses that are so finely decorated with Scandinavian ornament and mythological scenes.

Viking-period settlements on Man include small defended homesteads on coastal promontories, a type of fortification that appears at that time to have been peculiar to this island, perhaps because of its position exposed to all the traffic through and across the Irish Sea. More familiar in type is the massive bow-sided hall at the Braaid, replacing the circular houses of the earlier native settlement.

On Man, the legacy of its Viking past is alive above all in the fact that it retains independent status under the British Crown, administered by its own parliament – the Tynwald. The name is derived from the Norse *Þingvǫllr*,

Above One of the first Viking warriors to settle in the Isle of Man was buried in his boat, marked by a stone cairn, in a corner of the early Christian churchyard at Balladoole.

Left At the Braaid in the centre of the island, a pre-Viking round house was replaced by rectangular and bow-sided Norse buildings (foreground). Unfortunately, few finds were made when the site was excavated.

meaning Parliament Plain (as in the modern place-name Thingvellir, in Iceland). This assembly, originally known as the Thing, still meets annually in the open air on Old Midsummer Day (5 July), seated on an artificial mound called Tynwald Hill, in the south-west of the island, to promulgate the laws passed during the previous year. In 1979 the Isle of Man celebrated the millennium of the Tynwald, although no one knows for certain when the first Viking assembly was held. Man remained a Scandinavian possession until 1266, when the last of its own kings accepted the overlordship of King Alexander III of Scotland. Today it is Queen Elizabeth II who holds the position of Lord of Man over this independent country, unique in its relationship to the British Crown.

Ireland, Wales & England

This unique early 10th-century cross at Gosforth in Cumbria is the largest surviving piece of sculpture in England from before the Norman conquest. It is ornamented with interlace patterns (including the Borre-style ring-chain), scenes from the life of Christ and from pagan Norse mythology. Irish monastic sculpture influenced its design.

I n the nineteenth century a small Viking cemetery was discovered on Rathlin Island, off the north-east coast of Ireland, suggesting that a Norse settlement awaits discovery there. Other such sites may well be scattered along Ireland's northern, eastern and southern coasts, but they must be few and far between, for the only concentrations of Scandinavian settlements were around the new Viking towns of Dublin and Waterford. They were anyway of little importance in comparison with the wealth and influence of the Scandinavian towns in Ireland, above all of Dublin (see page 100).

When the Irish drove the Norse out of Dublin in 902, some Vikings sought land unsuccessfully in North Wales and were forced to move on to England. Silver hoards from Anglesey and Bangor tell of Viking activity in these parts and the development of the trade route between Dublin and Chester. In the latter part of the Viking Age, Bristol replaced Chester as the principal focus for Hiberno-Norse trade with Anglo-Saxon England. Many Scandinavian place-names along the coast of South Wales testify to the importance of this sea route. The establishment of small markets and settlements must be the explanation for the adoption of these names into common usage, although there is no archaeological evidence for this. It could be that those involved were second- or third-generation settlers, from say Ireland, without distinctive Scandinavian objects or tastes. If so, it would be hard to recognize the archaeological remains of the Haralds, Hakons and others who left their names for places around Milford Haven. It is possible, however, that they also left their mark in other ways. A study of blood-group frequencies showed the frequency of A genes among the indigenous population of Pembrokeshire to be at levels of up to 33.6 per cent, which is far higher than in adjacent parts of Wales and only matched in parts of Scandinavia.

The settlement of north-west England, by Vikings from Ireland, also got under way at the beginning of the tenth century. Historical references to this are supported by a handful of Viking burials from Cumbria and Lancashire. The most dramatic testimony to the events of these years is that provided by the great Cuerdale silver hoard, concealed in a lead chest in a bank of the river Ribble. Its contents of some 90lb (40kg) of silver objects and coins make it by far the largest Viking hoard known in the West, exceeded only by some coin hoards found in Russia on the routes along which the Arabic silver travelled to the Baltic. The 4,000 or so coins in the Cuerdale hoard include some that are Arabic and others from the Continent, but the majority are Anglo-Saxon and from the Viking kingdom of York. Among the many fragments of silver objects, or so-called 'hack silver', are arm-rings and brooches of distinctive Hiberno-Viking types.

The great cross standing at Gosforth also speaks of the Irish origins and connections of the settlers of Cumbria. The form of the cross itself and its Christian scenes are inspired by the High Crosses of the Irish monasteries, although combined with Scandinavian ornament and mythological figures. It is its Irish elements that make it quite unlike the Anglo-Scandinavian sculpture of Yorkshire, which still remains among the most important archaeological evidence for the Danish descendants and followers of the 'great army', who established the Viking kingdom of York.

Most Scandinavian farms in England will lie beneath their modern counterparts, but of those placed on marginal land, and subsequently deserted, we may hope to learn something. There is, however, a real problem of identification, as is illustrated by the excavations at Ribblehead in the far west of Yorkshire. Here a bow-sided hall with outbuildings, one of which was a kitchen, was uncovered around a yard from which radiated the drystone walls of fields, running off across the high limestone plateau. No

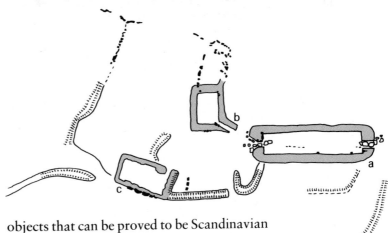

objects that can be proved to be Scandinavian were found, but there were three small bronze coins struck in York to point to its occupation in the latter part of the ninth century. The buildings could have been built by Scandinavians, but equally well by the Anglo-Saxons. We do not know the answer at present and will not be able to tell until a number of Viking Age farms, both Scandinavian and Anglo-Saxon, have been located and excavated across northern England. Meanwhile it remains possible that Ribblehead is a settlement of some of the first Vikings to penetrate England from the west, or represents a western outpost of the Danish settlers who spread from the east after their leader Halfdan had shared out the land of Northumbria among his army in 876.

Excavations at Ribblehead, *top*, on the weathered limestone of Gauber High Pasture in Yorkshire, have revealed a farm that may have been built either by some of the first Viking settlers in the north of England or by native Anglo-Saxons. The buildings, grouped around a farmyard, *above*, consist of a bow-sided dwelling (a), a kitchen (b), and a workshop or smithy (c).

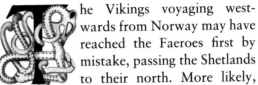

The Vikings voyaging westwards from Norway may have reached the Faeroes first by mistake, passing the Shetlands to their north. More likely, they will have learned of their existence in Britain or Ireland. For this cluster of islands, rising steeply from the Atlantic almost half-way between Shetland and Iceland, was already inhabited by Irish hermits before the ninth century. The Irish monk Dicuil, living in France, wrote a treatise in 825 in which he described some islands (generally agreed to be the Faeroes) that lay 'two days' and nights' direct sailing' from 'the northernmost British Isles'. He states that Irish hermits had been living there 'for roughly a hundred years', but 'now, because of Norse pirates, they are empty of anchorites, but full of innumerable sheep and a great many different kinds of sea-fowl.' To the Norse they were the *Færeyjar*, or Sheep Islands, and provided unoccupied land and pasture for settlers.

The settlers were forced to build in turf and stone on these treeless islands, as they had done previously on Orkney and Shetland. An early Norse farmstead has been excavated at Kvívík, where the hall was placed beside a combined barn and byre. This had stalls, on either side of a central drain, for perhaps a dozen cattle. One end of each bow-sided building is now missing, eroded by the sea. Apart from their dependence on sheep and a few cattle, the Faeroese have always lived by fishing, fowling and whaling – that is by driving inshore and killing the herds of pilot whales that arrive in their fjords each August.

The Faeroe Islands rise so steeply from the sea that settlements, such as that at Kvívík, *opposite*, have always been strung out along the only level ground available, at the foot of the hills. The Norse farmstead found at Kvívík, *left*, was built so close to the shore that part of it has been eroded away by the sea. It consists of two turf buildings: a bow-sided building, with a central long-hearth, and a combined barn/byre.

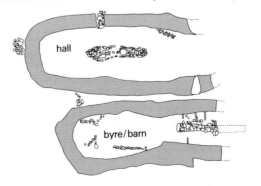

hall

byre/barn

Iceland

The Norse settlers in the Faeroes were true colonists in an empty landscape, but for others these islands merely provided a stepping stone on their route to Iceland. Dicuil knew also of Iceland's existence, noting the perpetual daylight at midsummer and that 'the frozen sea' lay one day's sailing to the north. The early Icelandic historians mention that there were Irish hermits living there when the first Norsemen arrived, but *Íslendingabók* states that 'They went away because they were not prepared to live here in company with heathen men.' Three men are separately accredited with the discovery and naming of Iceland, but it is the name *Ísland* (simply Ice Land), given by a man called Floki, that it has borne ever since. Floki chose this name because of the harshness of the first winter he spent there and the drift ice he saw to the north. It seems from the various stories that there were a number of exploratory voyages, both accidental and otherwise, around 860, preceding the main sixty-year period of land-taking that took place between about 870 and 930.

Landnámabók records the names of roughly 400 men who are said to be the initial settlers, of whom perhaps one-seventh can be shown to have had connections with Britain and Ireland – some arrived with Celtic wives, others with Celtic slaves. Again blood-group frequencies have been studied and the results confirm the presence of Celtic blood among Iceland's Scandinavian population.

Birth of a nation

Iceland's medieval historians believed that there was one reason above all why Norse Vikings had come to settle in Iceland – to escape the tyranny of King Harald. This is certainly a later exaggeration, but the Icelanders were particularly proud to have established an independent republic, even if it was ultimately to submit to King Hakon of Norway between 1262 and 1264. Iceland can still boast the oldest (but revived) national

assembly in Europe. This general assembly, the Althing, met in the open air for two weeks each summer at Thingvellir – a spectacular plain, bounded by cliffs of lava, thirty miles to the east of Reykjavík. The traditional date for its first meeting, and thus the birth of a nation, is 930. It was here in 1000 that it was decreed that Iceland was to become a Christian country. There had been Christians among the very early settlers (including one Ketil the Foolish, who had been given his nickname for just that reason!), but there was still a very strong pagan faction at this critical meeting of the Althing. A compromise was reached whereby everybody in the country should be baptized, but pagans were permitted to practise their religion in private, although their rights were withdrawn in subsequent years.

Iceland's landscape has been formed by fire and ice. Lava shaped the great plain in south-west Iceland, which was chosen for the annual open-air meeting of the national assembly, or Althing. Known as Thingvellir (Parliament Plain), it was accessible to all the settlers, although some would have journeyed on horseback for a fortnight or more to reach it.

This T-shaped bronze crozier-head, ornamented with a pair of Urnes-style animals, was found at Thingvellir, where Iceland was declared a Christian country in 1000. The crozier dates from a few generations later.

Icelandic farmsteads

One of the earliest settlers was a man named Ingolf Arnarson, who established himself at Reykjavík, the Smoky Bay, so named from the steam of its hot-water springs, which today provide the heating for the nation's capital. Such men constructed farmsteads with buildings similar to those at Jarlshof and Kvívík – having the long-hall design with at most one or two ancillary rooms on the end. An example has been excavated at Hofstadir, in the north of Iceland, which is of exceptional length (some 130ft, 40m). It consisted simply of a hall with a single small room on one end. It may perhaps have been a chieftain's farm used for feasting on pagan festivals, since *hof* means 'a building used for cult purposes'; and these might well have required extra space.

This basic type of hall-house was developed and modified during the Viking Age in Iceland, becoming divided into specific rooms and also growing additional rooms at the back. Such changes appear to have been in response to local conditions, both to the weather and to the lack of suitable building timber and stone on this volcanic island. The result was a more compact building, in which a variety of tasks might be comfortably undertaken. This developed type of farmhouse is well represented by those found in a series of excavations in the southern Icelandic valley of Thjórsárdalur, which was smothered in ash when Mount Hekla erupted *c.* 1104. What was once a fertile valley, supporting up to twenty farms during the Viking Age, still presents today a desert-like landscape.

The Stöng farmhouse

The farm at Stöng was one of several that were smothered by volcanic ash during an eruption of Mount Hekla, *c.* 1104, destroying not only the buildings but also the fertility of the valley. Today its excavated remains are protected under cover. *Below right* A full-scale reconstruction has recently been built in the original manner, with turf walls on stone footings.

he particularly well-preserved remains of one of these farms, cleared of its mantle of volcanic ash in 1939 and now roofed over for protection, stands at the heart of the valley on a small rise above a stream. Few objects were found here at Stöng, for its inhabitants appear to have had time to evacuate their farmstead in the face of the eruption, but its plan and many of its structural details are complete. These have recently been used as the basis for a full-scale reconstructed farmstead, built in the original manner, with massive turf walls placed on stone foundations; the living rooms were panelled on the inside, but with the wood panels standing free of the walls to protect them from damp.

The main hall at Stöng – just over 40ft (12m) long – opens off a vestibule entered through the single exterior door. In one corner of this vestibule was a rectangular structure that might have been the bed-closet of the owner and his wife, or was perhaps simply for storage. On either side of the hall's stone-lined long-hearth were the wide sleep-

ing benches; leading directly off this hall, on the same axis, was a smaller living room (25ft, 8m, long) with a central fireplace and narrow benches, suitable only for sitting; spinning was certainly one task carried out in this room. One of the two rooms that open off the back of the building was a stone-lined dairy, with impressions in the ground for three large vats; opposite its entrance from the hall stood the quern for grinding grain. The other back room was entered from the vestibule and has a drain down either side; it was most probably a lavatory.

To the east of this house is situated the byre, with its cattle stalls formed from vertical slabs of stone on either side of a paved alley to facilitate the mucking out. Nearby was a building that presumably served as the barn. Set apart from all these structures was the smithy, which contained a sunken fire-box, an anvil stone, a basin for quenching the hot iron, and a small quern that might have been used for grinding volcanic ash to make red dye. The remains of the bog iron ore used by Icelandic smiths also abounded. There is every reason to suppose that farm complexes like this at Stöng were typical in Iceland during the later Viking period.

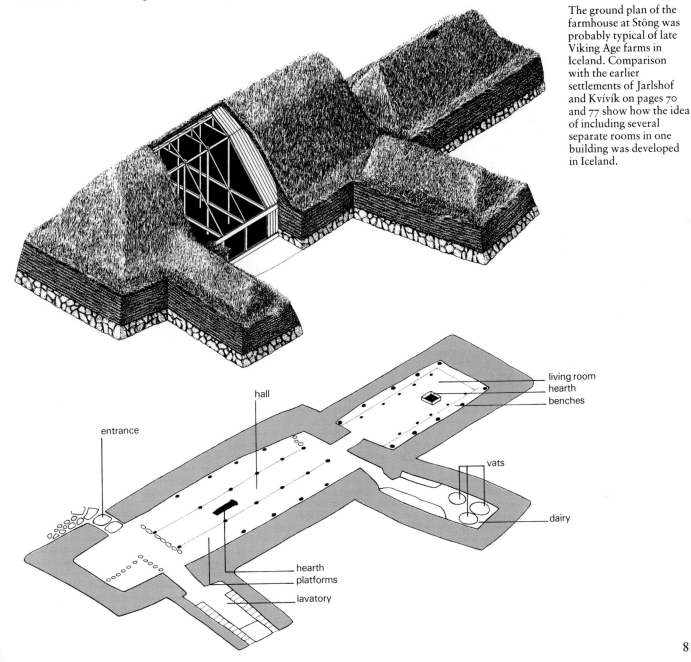

The ground plan of the farmhouse at Stöng was probably typical of late Viking Age farms in Iceland. Comparison with the earlier settlements of Jarlshof and Kvívík on pages 70 and 77 show how the idea of including several separate rooms in one building was developed in Iceland.

entrance

hall

living room
hearth
benches

vats

dairy

hearth
platforms

lavatory

Greenland & Vinland _____

lood-feuds and storms were
the first links in the chain of
chance events that led to the
Norse settlement of Greenland
and so to the Viking discovery
of North America. The chief character in this
stirring adventure story was reputedly one
Eirik the Red – 'Red' from hair and beard, but
also apparently of a quarrelsome nature –
who was born in Jæren, the fertile district of
south-western Norway. 'Some killings', or so
it is stated in the medieval saga that recounts
his exploits, were behind the hurried depar-
ture of the adolescent Eirik and his father for
the Norse colony in Iceland in about 980.
However, Iceland was to prove no more
peaceful for him than Norway, and further
killings led to his banishment from the island.
With his followers Eirik escaped once more
by ship, this time to look for a land in the
western ocean that had been discovered some
sixty years earlier by a man named Gunn-
bjorn, who had been blown far off course
while endeavouring to sail from Norway to
Iceland – a land that had since remained
unvisited and without a name.

For three years Eirik remained in exile, then
returned to Iceland with tales of *Grœnland*.
the Green Land. He had chosen the name
deliberately as being far more alluring to
prospective settlers than that of Ice Land, for
he sensibly maintained that 'Men would be
much more eager to go there if the land had
an attractive name.' But it is not entirely in-
accurate if one thinks of the inner reaches of
the great fjords and their inland valleys,
forgetting at the same time the wet and windy
coasts and the high, ice-clad interior.

There were many in Iceland prepared to
listen to Eirik's propaganda and to follow him
in a venture of colonization. We are told that
twenty-five ships set sail that summer (about
985) for Greenland, but the hazards of their
journey into the unknown were extreme and
only fourteen of the twenty-five are said to
have arrived – some being forced back, while
others disappeared without a trace.

The Eastern and Western Settlements

Eirik himself survived and returned to the
fjord where he had first built himself a house.
He 'took Eiriksfjord by right of settlement
and lived at Brattahlid.' Farmers could exist
in only two main areas situated some 400
miles apart, around Julianehåb bay and
Godthåb fjord, which became respectively the
Eastern and Western Settlements – although
to modern eyes conditioned by other orienta-
tions, they would more naturally be described
as the 'Southern and Northern Settlements'.
Only by these fjords lay the grazing land
required by the Norse stock-raisers, who had
brought with them their cattle, horses, sheep,
goats and a few pigs. Today Eiriksfjord is
frozen from October to May, but although
the climate was milder then, it was a hard life.

The landscape of Greenland is also treeless,
but the settlers knew how to build their farms
of turf and stones, lined and roofed with
driftwood, since these were what they had left
behind them in Iceland. They were inevitably
scattered to make the most of the grazing for
the animals on which their livelihoods
depended, and to enable sufficient hay to be
gathered to see the stock through the winter.
Today their houses, byres and barns are
grassy mounds, amid green pastures at the
foot of barren mountains. Further to the
north, up the western coast, were rich hunting
and fishing grounds (and beaches where
driftwood could be gathered). Hunting and
fishing were important, for reindeer, hares
and game-birds supplemented the Vikings'
diet, and above all they ate seals and fish.

Julianehåb bay and Godthåb fjord were
marginal settlements for men who had been
brought up in the traditional Scandinavian
economy, for they were dependent on trade to
supply many of their accustomed needs –
unlike the self-sufficient Eskimos, whom they
later encountered and who were ultimately
to replace them. Timber, iron and corn were
always required, quite apart from luxuries.
These imported goods were exchanged for
furs, sealskins, ropes of hides, walrus and

The site of Eirik the Red's farm at Brattahlid, which lay at the heart of Greenland's Eastern Settlement, overlooks Eiriksfjord. The stone ruins are those of later medieval buildings. It was Eirik's son, Leif, who set sail from Brattahlid to become the first Norseman to set foot in North America.

narwhal ivory, woollens, and in time ferocious Greenland falcons, and even polar bears. From the tenth to the twelfth centuries the settlements flourished (so that nearly 300 ruined farmsteads are now known). All was well as long as nothing changed. But then commercial neglect, climatic deterioration and disease began to take their toll, while the Eskimos were drawn southwards in pursuit of the seals that spelled survival for them. The Western Settlement was deserted by the middle of the fourteenth century; the Eastern Settlement was able to struggle on for around another 150 years.

The route to the New World

As accident and chance had led to the discovery of Greenland, so the story continues. When Bjarni Herjolfsson sighted a western land that was flat and covered with woods, it was clear that this was not the Greenland for which he had set sail from Iceland. He was attempting to follow his parents, who had sailed that year with Eirik the Red to settle there, when he got lost in foggy seas, blown off course by north winds. Thus, in about 985, Bjarni was probably the first Norseman to sight America – maybe indeed the first European to do so, unless one

The bronze ringed-pin, excavated at L'Anse aux Meadows, in northern Newfoundland, is of a type well known on Norse sites around the Atlantic.

An American Indian arrow-head of Labrador quartzite, found on the Norse site of Sandnes in Greenland's Western Settlement.

believes that St Brendan or some other Irish monk achieved this in a leather boat (and returned to tell the tale). But Bjarni never stepped ashore for he was no explorer, rather a man with a cargo to deliver in Greenland, where he eventually landed.

The privilege of first setting foot in the New World fell to Leif the Lucky, Eirik's son and an experienced sailor. Inspired by Bjarni's account of his sightings, he retraced his journey in reverse, sailing first to Helluland, Flatstone Land – a barren mountainous land with glaciers – identified today as the southern part of Baffin Island, then on south to Markland, Wood or Forest Land – which was no doubt the coast of Labrador. After two further days sailing to the south-west, Leif came to what he termed Vinland – most probably Berry or Vine Land – an area with an island lying to the north of what appeared to be mainland, with a projecting cape.

Here Leif Eiriksson built winter accommodation and waited with his crew before returning to Greenland the following spring. Excited by his stories, his brother Thorwald decided to follow in his footsteps. Thorwald's expedition also explored a beautiful and well-wooded coast but, while returning home, encountered the first inhabitants of America yet to be sighted. In a bloody skirmish, Thorwald was killed by an arrow – perhaps with the same kind of Indian arrow-head as that of Labrador quartzite found in 1930 during excavations at Sandnes, in the Western Settlement of Greenland. There were other expeditions, most notably that of Thorfinn Karlsefni, who attempted to establish a permanent colony in Vinland. But after three winters, harassed by the native Indians, his party returned to Greenland.

Vinland

Vinland – with its frost-free winters, wild grapes and self-sown wheat – has been sought by many a scholar, both in armchair and in boat. And it will continue to be so. For although Vinland must begin at New-

foundland, how far south the Norse explorers travelled is another matter and as yet quite unknown. But what evidence must we look for? Certainly more than that provided by the later Icelandic sagas, or the controversial Vinland Map, or even by the isolated discovery of a Norse penny recently reported from Blue Hill Bay, Maine.

During the 1950s the Norwegian Helge Ingstad was drawn on voyages of exploration in the wake of his Norse forebears to the meadowlands of northern Newfoundland. Here, at Epaves Bay, into which meanders the Black Duck Brook, he and his wife have excavated the site of L'Anse aux Meadows, where the first undoubted ruins left by Norsemen from Greenland were discovered. Over several seasons, three groups of turf-built structures were excavated, each with its own house; a separate smithy and boathouses were also found. Radio-carbon dates have supported the suggestion that they were built and occupied during the Viking Age, but the indisputable evidence that they were used by Norsemen derives from a combination of factors. The chief among these is a bronze ringed-pin of a type well known from Norse graves in the British Isles, the Faeroes and Iceland, while a spindle-whorl of a type common in the settlements of Greenland also reinforces this interpretation. However, whether this was a permanent settlement is open to doubt, for there is no definite evidence that the occupants had livestock with them, nor has pollen analysis revealed evidence for farming there at this period. It is possible that each group of buildings was used by successive expeditions.

The Vinland Map

The significance of the Ingstads' discoveries was first overshadowed by the excitement that surrounded the publication of the Vinland Map in October 1965. This is a pen and ink drawing of the world, on a sheet of thin parchment, that includes the depiction of land in the north-west Atlantic, west of

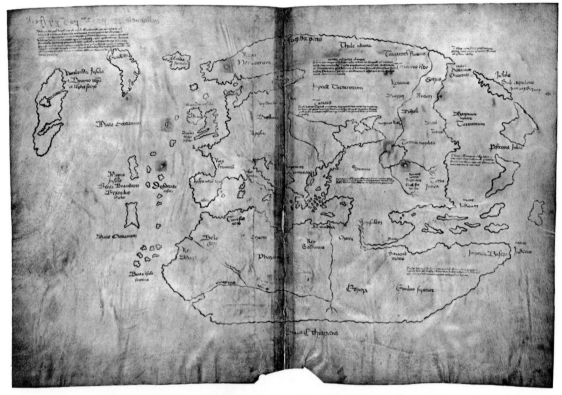

The pen and ink drawing of the world known as the Vinland Map purports to have been made in the 15th century. It records, among other information, the discovery of Vinland by Bjarni and Leif. However, various of its features, including the nature of the ink, suggest that the Map is in fact a 20th-century forgery.

Greenland, labelled 'Island of Vinland, discovered by Bjarni and Leif in company'. The Map was then given a date of *c.* 1440, but doubts were rapidly cast on its authenticity for various reasons, including the fact that it has several features that do not fit the known framework of medieval European cartography. One such problem is the accuracy of the delineation of Greenland as an island; this alone suggests a date for the Map of no earlier than the 1890s. Subsequently tests were made on its ink, which have demonstrated that it contains a pigment not known to have been available before 1917 at the earliest. Thus the Map appears to be a twentieth-century forgery, although there are those who still believe that evidence will be forthcoming to demonstrate its authenticity. Be that as it may, there is no question that the Map's importance in relation to the Norse discovery of America has been greatly exaggerated in the popular press, for it contains no information about the Viking Age that was not already available from the literary sources.

The end of the settlements

The Norsemen managed to keep a permanent toehold on a minute part of the great island of Greenland for about 500 years from the time of the first settlement. But to make this possible, the first arduous voyages of exploration and colonization had to be repeated time and again as voyages of commerce in order to sustain the colonies. Ultimately this western outpost proved too remote, and trade dwindled and finally ceased. The settlements in North America were remoter still, for there no regular chain of communications had ever become established to support any colony. Those who chose to settle would have been dependent on local resources, or on their own return journeys to Greenland – and even then, like the Greenlanders, they would still have had to look farther afield to Iceland and Norway for supplies. It is hardly surprising therefore that we have little evidence of permanent Viking settlements in America, for they can only ever have been extremely few in number.

Merchantmen

Silver was the prize most coveted by the Vikings. Scandinavian merchants travelled the great Russian rivers with furs and slaves to bring back Arabic silver coins, while others traded or raided in Western Europe for coins or objects of silver and gold. For safekeeping the Vikings buried their wealth in hoards, many of which they never returned to retrieve.

Trade & towns

The image of a Viking as a trader rather than a raider may be unfamiliar, but the achievements of the Vikings in this sphere are among their most dramatic and enduring. Piracy was all very well, but could scarcely ensure a regular income of the kind that might be had, for instance, by supplying the Arabs with slaves in exchange for their excess wealth of silver.

The first small trading centres in Scandinavia had been established before the ninth century, but with the great growth in trade during the Viking Age larger towns came into being. Many were royal foundations such as Hedeby in Denmark and Bergen in Norway, for the Scandinavian kings were naturally anxious to control trade, since taxation of merchants produced a substantial revenue.

Trade around the Baltic had been stimulated by the establishment of Swedish settle-

VIKING TRADERS
Viking merchants travelling along the great Russian rivers penetrated far to the east. Here they joined the international caravan routes and met foreign traders with goods from such distant countries as China and Persia. In the West other Vikings traded with England and the Frankish Empire.

——————
Viking sea and river routes

– – – –
land routes used by the Vikings

——————
international trade routes

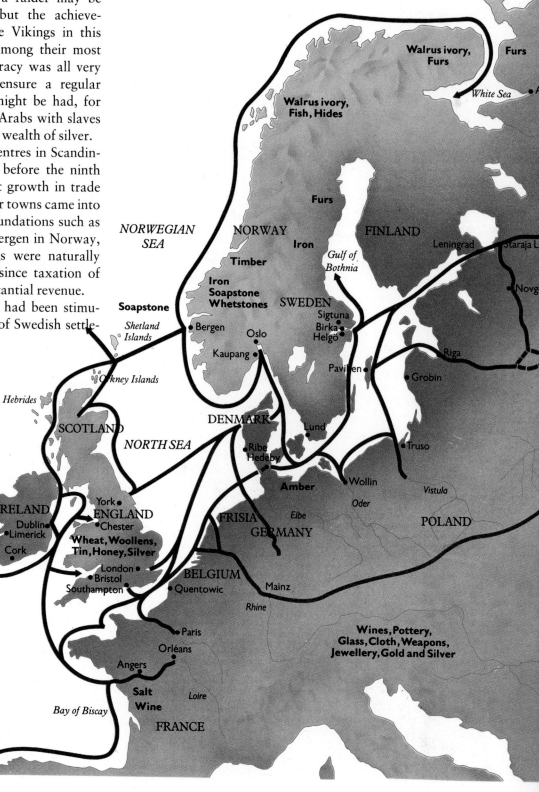

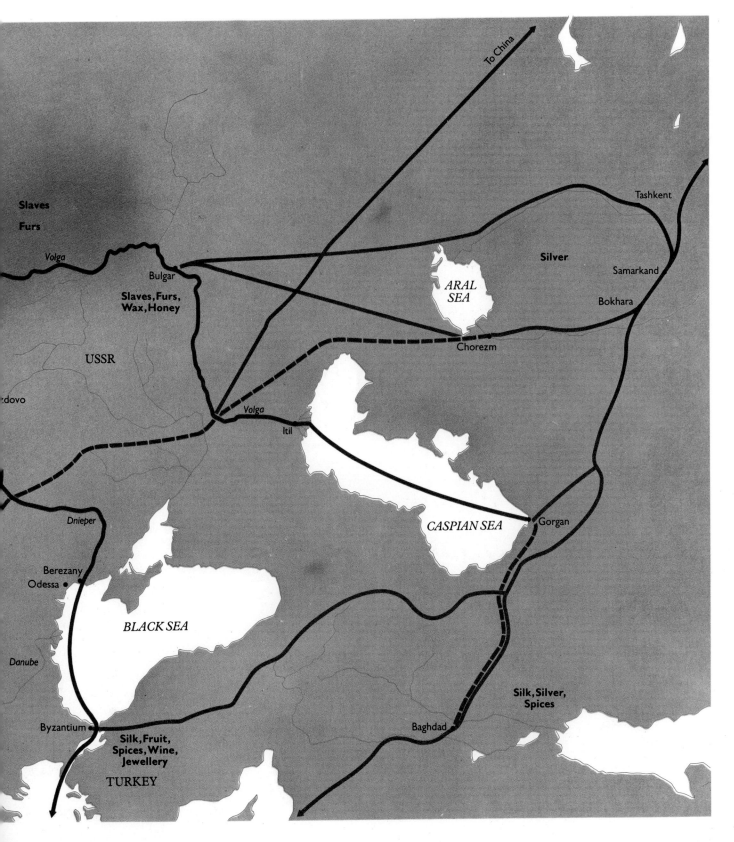

Slaves

Furs

Volga

Bulgar

**Slaves, Furs,
Wax, Honey**

USSR

.dovo

Volga

Itil

Dnieper

Berezany

Odessa

BLACK SEA

Danube

Byzantium

**Silk, Fruit,
Spices, Wine,
Jewellery**

TURKEY

To China

Tashkent

Silver

*ARAL
SEA*

Samarkand

Bokhara

Chorezm

CASPIAN SEA

Gorgan

Baghdad

**Silk, Silver,
Spices**

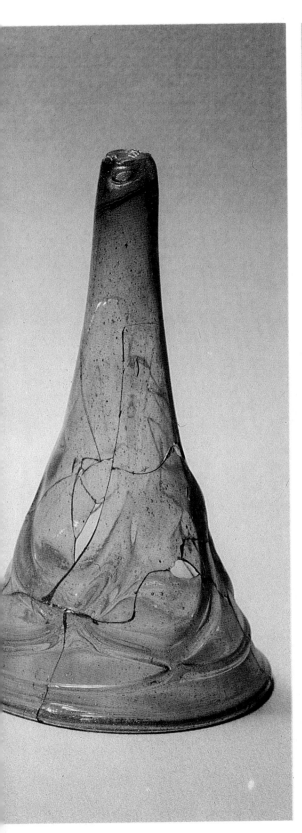

ments on its eastern shores, as at Grobin in western Latvia, well placed to control eastern trade along the Vistula, or Wollin at the mouth of the Oder – described by Adam of Bremen in 1070 as the largest town in Europe (although by then under Slav rule). Commercial traffic was intensive, both within Scandinavia and in the Baltic, but it was the development of regular long-distance trade that distinguished the Viking Age, for by the end of the tenth century Viking merchants had established a network of trade routes that stretched from Iceland to the Caspian Sea.

Silver from the East was chiefly what the merchants sought, for which they traded furs, honey, wax, weapons and slaves. Of the other surviving imports into Scandinavia, the most exotic may simply have been the souvenirs and curios of travellers in distant places: a buddha, a painted Arabic glass, a glazed cup from Iran and a bronze brazier in the form of a mosque are all examples found in Sweden. Silks, on the other hand, were traded and are found in rich graves throughout Scandinavia. Most will have been brought back from Byzantium, but a few pieces are more likely to be Chinese. Trade goods from Western Europe tended to be of a more domestic nature – cloth from Frisia, black basalt from the Eifel region for querns – but there were also luxuries such as barrels of wine from the Rhineland, and pottery jugs and drinking glasses from which it might be consumed.

Exotic objects reached Scandinavia by both fair means and foul. *Opposite* Glasses found at Birka were luxuries imported for the rich from the Rhineland. *Above* An Arabic glass and a Persian glazed cup are travellers' curios, brought back to Sweden. *Below* An enamelled bronze mount found at Helgö was made in Ireland; it may be a looted crozier-head.

Hedeby

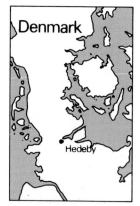

Denmark

Hedeby

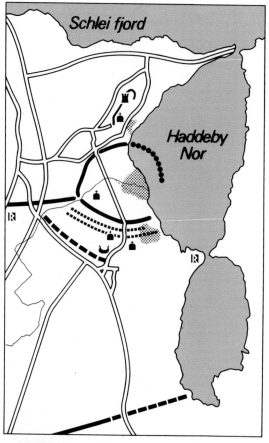

Schlei fjord

Haddeby Nor

○ settlement areas
— remaining rampart
-- demolished rampart
R rune stone
♔ hill-fort
♜ cemetery
♨ ship burial
●●● palisade
···· ditch
— Hedeby stream

Hedeby owed its success to its key position at the base of Jutland. This site plan shows the rampart, settlement areas and modern course of the Hedeby stream; a broken line indicates its course during the Viking Age.

lesvig is a large town at the very end of the world ocean.' Thus related Al-Tartushi, an Arab merchant from the Caliphate of Cordoba, after visiting Hedeby about the year 950; for the town that the Danes called 'Hedeby' was 'Slesvig' to their southern neighbours, the Saxons. If the well-travelled Al-Tartushi thought Hedeby 'large', then large it was.

When Al-Tartushi passed that way he would not, however, have seen the feature that makes Hedeby an impressive site even today – the immense semicircular rampart. Thought to have been built in the late tenth century – and repaired and rebuilt on subsequent occasions before the town was abandoned in the mid-eleventh century – this runs down to the water's edge, continuing as a curving palisade into the Haddeby Nor, the inlet that provided both a sheltered harbour

and access to the Schlei fjord and so to the Baltic Sea. The rampart was linked to the Danevirke, the system of great earthworks that protected the Danish border.

Hedeby owed its success as a market town, manufacturing centre and port to its frontier position at the base of the Jutland peninsula, which gave it control over the most important trade routes from Western Europe to the Baltic. The *Hærvej*, the northern extension of the long trans-European land routes, passed through the Danevirke near Hedeby. More important, however, was the flow of traffic from the North Sea to the Baltic, which avoided the dangerous coastal journey round Jutland by travelling the short distance overland behind the protection of the Danevirke and thus through Hedeby. Hollingsted, only eleven miles west of Hedeby on the banks of the Treene, was the primary port of disembarkation for goods arriving from Western Europe and further afield.

From the Frankish annals of 804, we learn that Godfred of Denmark, having destroyed the Slav town of *Reric* (?Rostock), established its merchants by the site of an early settlement at Hedeby. This was a shrewd political act, for Hedeby grew and prospered, to become a rich prize held by the Danes, the Swedes and the Germans in turn.

The earliest occupation, the South Settlement, was largely Frisian. It lay beside the brook to the south of the later rampart, with a cemetery to its west. Traces of amber- and metalworking and of such imports as Eifel stone and Frisian coins have been found in its late-eighth-century levels. From the start of the ninth century there was also a small North Settlement. Both these Settlements, however, were abandoned in the late ninth century, by which time the Central Settlement had been in existence for some one hundred years.

The Central Settlement was established about 800 beside the Hedeby stream, with its own cemetery to the west. In the following years, the course of the stream was diverted and its sides planked as the settlement ex-

Above The great trading centre of Hedeby is today a patchwork of small fields. All that remains above ground is the massive semicircular rampart, seen *right*. Still standing in part to a height of 30ft (9m), it encloses an area of 60 acres, about twice the size of Birka.

panded around it. The fact that the streets were laid out at right angles and parallel to the stream, and that the building plots seem to have been regulated in size, indicates a strong urban control, presumably under Godfred's authority, from the beginning of Hedeby's existence. The Central Settlement was later surrounded by the rampart, although we do not yet know how intensively the walled area came to be inhabited.

Overshadowing the North Settlement is a small hill, now overgrown with trees. On the top is an oblong fortification of two periods, but of unknown date. As it was never lived in, it must presumably have been used as a refuge in times of danger – perhaps before Hedeby was walled, for its position is similar to that of the fort beside Birka.

Unlike the rich grave-fields of Birka, Hedeby's five cemeteries have produced only one exceptional burial, that of a warrior placed in a chamber beneath a boat. In this respect, it is clear that Hedeby was influenced early on by the Christian religion, for many of the several thousand bodies in the large western and southern cemeteries were buried in a more or less Christian manner. The skeletons excavated show that life expectancy was about forty years.

Hedeby must always have been low-lying and a gradually rising water level meant that most of the Central Settlement occupation levels became waterlogged. Under such conditions of rapid deposition, where all air is excluded by waterlogging, timber and other organic remains may survive to a remarkable extent. The uppermost level of the Central Settlement was excavated in the 1930s by Professor Jankuhn, and the exacavations were renewed and extended in the 1960s by Dr Schietzel, who was able to drain off the water from his trenches and reach the natural sand on which Hedeby was founded.

By counting and studying the tree-rings of the preserved house-timbers at Hedeby, a dated sequence for the construction of the buildings has been established. It seems that the average life of a house was only about thirty years. Houses that had to be replaced were simply levelled and built over.

From the start of the Central Settlement, the merchants' and craftsmen's plots were fenced round, often with wattle hurdles, and contained both a dwelling and a storehouse or workshop. Only one such outhouse had stalls for animals, though there may have been others near the outskirts. Many plots had a timber-lined well.

The houses were generally thatched with

reeds, with a hole left either above the central hearth, or at the top of the gable end, to allow smoke to escape. Apart from their central hearths, little is known about the internal arrangements, although some at least were divided into separate rooms. One well-preserved house had three: a central living room with a hearth, and a smaller room at either end, one containing a large bread oven.

After its peak in the tenth century, Hedeby seems to have declined. Certainly it never recovered from being burnt by Harald the Hard-ruler from Norway just before 1050, and raided by the Slavs in 1066. Its inhabitants moved to the site of modern Schleswig, north of the Schlei, and by the late eleventh century Hedeby had been abandoned.

Houses in Hedeby's Central Settlement were built a
little back from, but facing, the streets. They were
rectangular, measuring on average about 20ft by 50ft
(6m by 15m). Some were constructed of horizontal
planking; others were 'stave-built', with vertical
planking generally consisting of wedge-shaped sections
of treetrunks; others were timber framed, with panels
of wattle daubed with clay or dung to make them
waterproof. Smaller houses for the poorer inhabitants
have been found elsewhere in the Settlement. These
were simple wattle huts, 10ft by 10ft (3m by 3m), with
a sunken floor and a hearth in one corner.

Birka

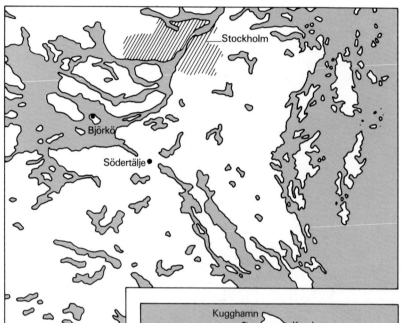

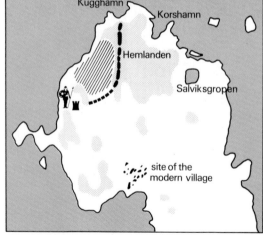

'garrison'

hill-fort

black earth

An area of Black Earth lies at the centre of the 30-acre settlement of the Swedish town of Birka, situated at the northern end of an island in Lake Mälar. Birka is surrounded by some 3,000 graves from the 9th and 10th centuries, and is overlooked by a hill-fort, to which it was linked in the 10th century by a rampart that enclosed the town. There were three harbours to the north and east of the settlement.

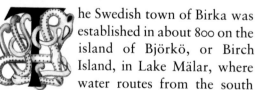

he Swedish town of Birka was established in about 800 on the island of Björkö, or Birch Island, in Lake Mälar, where water routes from the south and east converge. The choice of Birka as a trading centre may well have been influenced by the fact that there was a royal estate on the adjacent island of Adelsö. We know that Birka was governed by a representative of the king and had its own Thing. Although in the tenth century Birka is estimated to have had a population of about 1,000, the town had completely disappeared by the time Adam of Bremen was writing in about 1070.

The coastline of Björkö has changed since the Viking Age because the land level has risen, so altering the appearance of Birka's harbours. But the site remains dominated by a small hill-top fort on its southern edge. This probably served as a refuge for the inhabitants before the town was walled in the tenth century. The rampart ran in an arc down to the water's edge, as at Hedeby, but only part of it remains. There are six gaps in it facing the burial mounds of the great cemetery of Hemlanden: these can scarcely all have been for gates and it is probable that they contained timber watch towers, linked together by a palisade that would have run along the top of the 6ft (1.8m) high, but 20–40ft (6–12m) wide earthen rampart.

This rampart encloses an area of about thirty acres within which lies the so-called 'Black Earth' – soil darkened by its content of charcoal and organic remains from one and a half centuries of intensive occupation. Little of it has been excavated, so we know nothing of the internal layout of the town itself, though both wattle-and-daub and stave-built houses have been found. The debris from manufacturing industries included iron-working, bronze-casting, leather-working and the carving of bone and antler into all manner of objects – in fact a range of crafts similar to those practised at Hedeby. A considerable number of scale-weights serves to remind us of the merchants with their portable balances for weighing out silver, for above all Birka was an *entrepôt* to which traders brought all manner of goods for distribution and dispatch.

There were probably markets in both winter and summer. In winter the trappers and middlemen would bring their furs over the ice on skates and sledges; in summer the merchant-skippers came with their trading ships. The waterfront was protected by a palisade, as at Hedeby, and there were also jetties in front of the Black Earth area. The natural harbours of Kugghamn, the Cargo Boat Harbour, and Korshamn, the Cross

Harbour, provided more sheltered accommodation. But such was the demand for suitable safe anchorages that an artificial harbour, now known as Salviksgropen, was constructed on the east side of the island.

We know that Swedish iron was exported from Sweden to Hedeby, but the fur trade was probably the major source of Birka's wealth. The furs were shipped by professional traders either to Hedeby for onward transport to Western Europe, or across the Baltic and down the Russian rivers to the Eastern Caliphate of the Arab Empire in return for a small part of its wealth of silver. The silver hoard buried in the Black Earth during the last years, or maybe even the last days, of Birka's existence, in the 960s or 970s, included Arabic coins.

Our most important information about the range of luxury goods imported into Birka comes from the late-nineteenth-century excavations by Hjalmar Stolpe of nearly 1,200 graves, out of the estimated 3,000 that surround the Black Earth. As well as coins, imports included wine, pottery and glass, bronze vessels, weapons and silks, demonstrating Birka's contacts with both Western and Eastern Europe, and with western Asia, in addition to those with the Lapps to the north of the country, and with the other Scandinavian kingdoms.

The decline of Birka occurred as a result of two circumstances: the falling off in the long-range transit trade, and the rise in the land level. The southern channel from Birka to the Baltic had always required a short overland haul of the ships at Södertälje, but as the land rose the distance seems to have increased to something like half a mile. Birka was abandoned, although the island itself continued to be inhabited, and its important role as a manufacturing centre and internal market was taken over by Sigtuna to the north, while Baltic trade focused more on Gotland.

The Black Earth area of Birka is now preserved as an open field (seen here from the north), enclosed in part by the remains of the earthern rampart. Trees cover the burial mounds of the great Hemlanden cemetery in the foreground. In the background rises the bare rock of the hill-top fort, surmounted by a modern cross to St Ansgar.

Kaupang

he Norwegian settlement of Kaupang – the name means 'market-place' – is situated on the west side of the entrance to the Oslofjord in the wealthy region of Vestfold in south-east Norway. Its Black Earth is far smaller than that of Birka and has been intensively cultivated, but nevertheless Charlotte Blindheim has been able to carry out some highly successful excavations. On the west side of the small bay she uncovered a complex of houses and workshops, with wells attached, placed right by the waterside, which was provided with stone jetties. Wooden objects discovered included a remarkable heavy anchor. The main crafts were metalworking (particularly with iron, but silver and bronze were being cast into ingots and ornaments), and the production of soapstone vessels; the latter were a major export to Jutland and Hedeby.

Coins and sherds of imported pottery from the Rhineland, similar to those found at Hedeby and Birka, demonstrate that Kaupang existed from the late eighth century throughout the greater part of the ninth. It must have been an important market centre for its region, and it was to Kaupang that northern merchant-skippers came with their cargoes of furs, skins, down, walrus ivory and much-prized walrus-hide ropes. The surrounding grave-fields contain the burials of wealthy merchant-farmers and their wives; their grave-goods include many trinkets from the British Isles, which (with the Rhenish imports) demonstrate that Kaupang's interests were concentrated in North Sea trade.

Kaupang probably remained a seasonal market and for some reason never grew as Hedeby and Birka did; and was never fortified. In fact for the whole of the middle period of the Viking Age, Norway seems to have been without a major market town of its own. Norse trade in the tenth century continued to look to the west, to Iceland and the British Isles, where it was focused on the Scandinavian towns of York and Dublin.

Opposite Excavations at Kaupang, beside a natural harbour on the west side of the Oslofjord in southern Norway, have revealed the remains of a small but apparently wealthy trading and manufacturing centre. This settlement flourished in the 9th century, but never developed in the same way as Hedeby or Birka, its role as a market-place for North Sea trade passing to the Viking towns of York and Dublin.

York & Dublin

York was seized from the Anglo-Saxons to become the capital of a Viking kingdom. Scandinavian merchants brought their ships up the Ouse (in the foreground) from the North Sea, as had the Romans before them. Behind York Minster can be seen the medieval city walls built on top of the Roman fortress ramparts, which were also used to defend the Viking town.

Among finds of Viking objects from York is a bronze chape for the end of a sword scabbard, decorated in the Jellinge style. Excavations in York are transforming our knowledge of the houses, workshops and crafts of its Anglo-Scandinavian inhabitants.

At York the Danes were able to settle themselves in an already thriving Anglo-Saxon town with an established trade, particularly with Frisia. New contacts were opened up with Scandinavia and, by about the year 1000, York is said to have been 'filled with the treasure of merchants, chiefly of the Danish race'.

The town had an area of intensive industrial and commercial activity to the south of the Roman fortress, in the angle made between the rivers Ouse and Foss (although the latter's course was a little different then from what it is today). The north-west and north-east walls of the Roman fortress were kept repaired and in use (they still stand, topped by the medieval defences), but on the other sides of the fortress the walls had decayed and the stones had been robbed away. On the north-east side the old wall was extended by a clay embankment running down to the Foss, and the rivers appear to have been considered adequate defences for the unwalled sides. The fortress area con-

tained the Anglo-Saxon minster, in the region of its great successor, and probably also the Viking royal palace. Excavation by the York Archaeological Trust of the waterlogged levels of Anglo-Scandinavian York have been revealing the details of the workshops of York's tenth-century inhabitants on Coppergate, with much debris from wood-turning, among other crafts. At High Ousegate tanning pits were discovered at the beginning of this century; hides were being stretched at Pavement, with cobblers active at Feasegate and Hungate. In the suburb across the Ouse tenth-century Viking burials were discovered around the church of St Mary Bishophill Junior, immediately above the remains of a fish-processing plant.

Dublin
At Dublin the Vikings did not take over an existing town but established their own trading centre, which rose to a position of great wealth in the tenth century. Dublin was ideally placed from the point of view of the Viking merchants who used it. To the north

their routes lay through the Hebrides to Orkney and Shetland, and then either to Iceland by way of the Faeroes, or straight on to Norway. Across the Irish Sea lay Chester, giving access to Anglo-Saxon merchants. Sailing southwards brought one to the Carolingian Empire and even to the Arabs in Spain. Dublin too has waterlogged levels from the Viking Age and years of patient excavation by Breandán Ó Ríórdáin, and most recently Pat Wallace, have revealed successive layers of small and crowded wattle houses, and even one that is stave-built in familiar Scandinavian manner. Metalworkers and comb-makers seem to have been strongly represented among the inhabitants of the areas that have been investigated around Christ Church cathedral, at the centre of what was to become the walled town of medieval Dublin. Viking Dublin had its own defences: an early earthen rampart, which was replaced with a stone wall long before the Anglo-Norman conquest of 1170.

Although Dublin was by far the most successful and important of the towns that the Vikings gave to Ireland, Limerick and Cork, Wexford and Waterford also have their urban origins in Viking trading centres.

Right This unique 10th-century gaming board of wood was found at Ballinderry – a native Irish settlement. But its ornament, including the ring-chain pattern of the Scandinavian Borre style, suggests that it was made in Viking Dublin. It would have been suitable for the popular Viking game of *hnefatafl*.

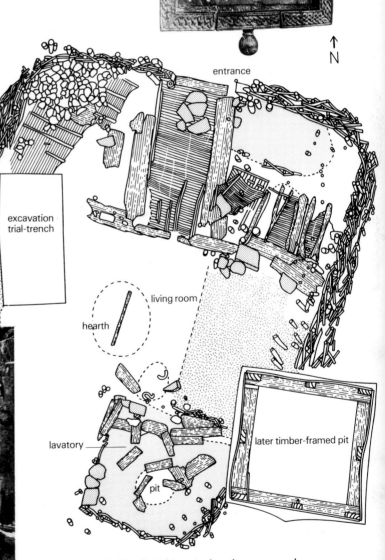

Dublin was founded by the Vikings in the 9th century and grew into a wealthy town in the 10th. It supported many skilled craftsmen who lived typically in small houses built of wattle and daub. The house plan *above* has a single entrance, flanked by small rooms. The living room has a central hearth; the cubicle in the corner may have been a lavatory.

Town crafts & industries

The Viking towns naturally provided centres where craftsmen could congregate and practise their skills. For there merchants would bring the raw materials they required and there they might sell their products to middlemen for distribution through the countryside. There too would be found newly rich traders: men from the north who had just sold their cargoes of furs, or men returned from the East with bags heavy with silver – people with money to burn who might wish to commission some new brooches, or purchase a necklace of glass beads for their wives left at home.

The crafts practised in the Viking towns covered the entire range; everyone from the blacksmith to the potter, the horn- and antler-worker to the bead-maker. Excavations and surface collections in the fields at Hedeby have shown, however, that most of these activities were carried on throughout the town, which was not divided into specialized craft 'quarters', as was once thought. Although, as with all timber settlements, there was a tendency for blacksmiths to be placed near the edge of the town because of the fire-risk from their furnaces.

Bead-making

Glass bead-makers imported their rough glass from Western Europe in lumps or small cubes intended for mosaics; broken drinking vessels were another source of raw material. Simple beads were made in single colours, but more sophisticated ones were decorated with coloured trails, or were completely multi-coloured. These last were produced by making rods of glass, combining them into bundles and then drawing them out to make new rods of multicoloured glass. These were then sliced and the pieces fused together to make composite coloured beads of remarkable complexity.

To form glass beads rough glass was melted in crucibles and drawn out into sticks that were then softened and wound round metal rods. Glass sticks of different colours were combined to form more elaborate beads, such as those found at Ribe in Jutland, *right*. Some were also embellished with trails of glass in other colours.

Bead-making was a craft carried out in many Viking towns and small trading centres, such as at Paviken on Gotland where these beads and glass fragments were found. The glass cubes at the top of the picture were imported as raw material, perhaps from northern Italy; scrap glass and waste (centre) were also recycled. This was much easier than having to make glass from scratch.

Amber is fossilized resin from submerged pine forests and has been much prized by man since prehistoric times. It can be found washed up on southern Baltic and North Sea beaches (East Anglia and south-west Jutland). *Left* At Ribe some 4 pounds (2 kilos) of rough amber was discovered, but few worked pieces.

Rough amber was brought to Hedeby for working into a variety of small trinkets, particularly beads and pendants. Those illustrated *below* include unfinished and damaged examples, of which one is leg-shaped. The round objects to its right are playing pieces.

Amber- and jet-working

Amber was a Baltic commodity that had been exported from its Baltic sources for many centuries before the Viking Age. It was used for making small objects such as beads, pendants and gaming pieces, although occasionally it was carved into more elaborate products. As always, it was valued by the Vikings not only for its ornamental qualities but also for its attributed magical properties.

On the other hand, the only source of jet available to the Vikings was in England, at Whitby on the Yorkshire coast. So that the jet used for this carving of gripping beasts would have been imported into Norway probably from York, where there was jet-working during the Viking Age.

Comb-making

Comb-makers used the antlers of red deer, which gave their products strength; these were collected after they had shed naturally. A pair of long plates was cut to form the comb back, then between these was riveted a series of smaller rectangular plates, into which the teeth were cut. Finally the back might be

Some English jet was exported from Yorkshire to Norway during the Viking Age. This carving of a pair of bear-like gripping beasts brings to mind related examples in amber (see page 137).

ornamented with a pattern of incised lines. In some instances combs were provided with cases, also made of antler strips riveted together, so that the combs could be suspended about the person without damage.

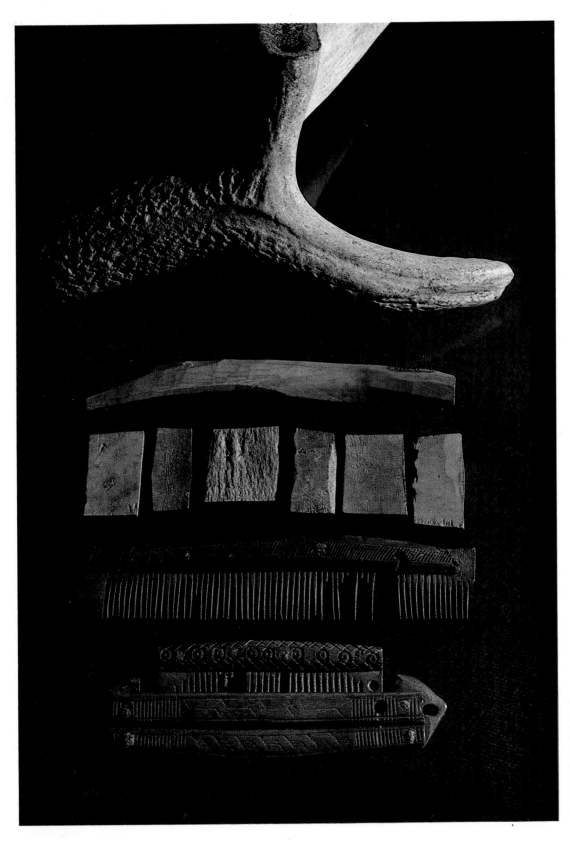

Comb-making using deer antlers was widely practised throughout the Viking world. The methods were the same from Dublin (where these examples were found) to Staraja Ladoga, blanks being cut and assembled before the teeth were sawn.

Above Antler moulds could be used without damage for casting in pewter, and were thus suitable for the mass-production of cheap brooches in towns such as Hedeby.

Casting

Bronze-casting was carried out in all Scandinavian markets and towns by specialist craftsmen-jewellers capable of creating individual objects of some beauty, or of mass-producing cheap brooches for the less wealthy. The bronze (it had to be imported) was melted in clay crucibles on a charcoal hearth, with the heat raised by bellows, the nozzle of which had to be protected by a small furnace stone. A clay mould for an elaborate object was made from at least two pieces, which were built around a wax model of the object to be cast. The mould was then heated so that the wax could be poured off before the bronze was poured in. Clay moulds had to be broken to release the casting; but simple objects were mass-produced by impressing them directly into clay to form a series of moulds. Alternatively, moulds of stone and bone could be re-used repeatedly for casting in pewter. Rough castings had to be finished by tooling and polishing. There might be a pin to be fixed, or further embellishments, such as gilding, to be added before the final product could be offered in the market.

Clay moulds for casting bronze ornaments, such as brooches, were generally produced from wax or clay models, although simple moulds could be made by pressing an object directly into clay.

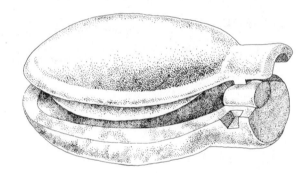

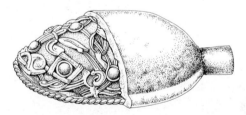

The upper part of the two-part mould was formed by pressing clay over the model of the brooch to be cast, a plug being fitted at one end to establish a hole through which the molten metal would later be poured.

More clay was pressed into the cloth-lined part to form the back of the mould. When this had dried the two parts were separated and the cloth removed, leaving a narrow gap within the mould (when the parts were reunited) into which the bronze was poured. Such moulds had to be broken to release the finished casting.

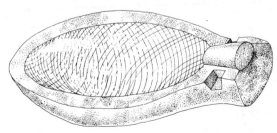

Once the clay had dried the model was removed (if a wax model had been used, the mould was heated and the wax poured off). The newly impressed mould was baked to harden it. A layer of clay-impregnated cloth was then inserted inside it, over the impressed face, as a means of determining the thickness of the casting.

Left A clay mould for an Urnes-style brooch (a cheaper version of the one from Lindholm Høje on page 151), and, *below*, an unfinished bronze casting from such a mould. Both were found discarded in an early 12th-century workshop in Lund.

Left This set of blacksmith's tools formed part of the grave-goods of a wealthy Norwegian Viking – demonstrating the high status and rewards enjoyed by a good smith in Viking society. Here, around his anvil, have been grouped tongs, hammers, files, chisels, shears, a wire-drawing plate and a tool for making nails.

Below Soapstone was quarried and carved into cooking and storage pots, wherever it occurred naturally in the Viking world. In Norway it had even replaced the use of pottery.

Soapstone

The quarrying of soapstone and manufacture of soapstone vessels became major industries in the Viking Age, particularly in Norway where soapstone was used as a substitute for pottery. It was exported to Iceland and to Jutland, as far south as Hedeby.

Whetstones

Another Norwegian export, both to Jutland and to the British Isles, was superior schist of the type favoured for whetstones, essential for sharpening weapons, tools and knives. Stone from the well-known quarries at Eidsborg, Telemark, in southern Norway, has been found at several sites in England, including York. A ship that sank at Klåstad on the coast of Vestfold had some whetstones among its cargo. It may have been bound for Kaupang whence Norwegian schist was exported.

The eastern routes

Scandinavian merchants travelling south to Byzantium gathered each year in Kiev, on the west bank of the river Dnieper, while they waited for the spring flood waters to subside. The city is overlooked in this view by a statue of Prince Vladimir, of Scandinavian descent, who consolidated the city-state of Kiev. He was converted to Christianity in 988.

o reach the Black Sea and the Caspian, and so to tap the wealth of Byzantium or the Eastern Caliphate of the Arab Empire, Scandinavian merchants had to follow river routes, not always through friendly territory, and often involving overland portages to transfer from one river to another, or to bypass rapids. Wide though such rivers as the Dnieper and the Volga are, such difficulties would have made it necessary to use smaller craft than the North Sea trading vessels. But the vital trading commodities of slaves and furs would not necessarily have been carried from Scandinavia; they might equally have been acquired forcibly, or otherwise, on the way.

The Russian *Primary Chronicle* describes the route that Scandinavian merchants would have followed on their return from the Byzantine Empire (the 'Greeks'):

Starting from the Greeks, this route proceeds along the Dnieper, above which a portage leads to the Lovat. By following the Lovat, the great Lake Ilmen is reached. The river Volkhov which flows out of this lake enters the great Lake Nevo [Ladoga]. The mouth of this lake [river Neva] opens out into the Varangian Sea [the Baltic].

The southern part of this route is described in greater detail by the Byzantine Emperor Constantine Porphyrogenitus. He wrote that in the tenth century the Rus (as the Scandinavians in Russia were called, and after whom Russia came to be named) took at least six weeks to make the journey down the Dnieper, for there were rapids to be negotiated, and hostile tribes to be fought off.

Seen from the other end, the Scandinavian merchant setting out from the Baltic might have joined this route either by way of the river Dvina, which flows out into the Gulf of Riga, or by the Gulf of Finland and the river Neva, as described above. The town of Staraja (Old) Ladoga, known to the Scandinavians as *Aldeigjuborg*, lies just off Lake Ladoga, eight miles up the river Volkhov. This small site, defended by an earthen rampart, has been excavated; Swedish material was found but its wooden buildings are not Scandinavian, being of a block-house type, built of logs with notched and overlapping ends, so that the ethnic identity of its earliest inhabitants is unknown. The population of the south-east Ladoga area is thought to have been essentially Finnish, but the Viking Age saw intrusions by Scandinavians, Slavs and Balts. The barrow burials in this district demonstrate beyond reasonable doubt that there were Scandinavians, but they were gradually integrated into the local population.

Further down this route is Gnezdovo, where a cemetery has been investigated that belonged to the Viking Age predecessor of Smolensk. Here, as at Kiev, the burials contain a fair amount of Scandinavian material, among much more that is not. Kiev and Novgorod, situated between Gnezdovo and Staraja Ladoga, were the two settlements of greatest importance to the Scandinavians in Russia. However, major excavations in Novgorod, known to the Scandinavians as *Holmgarðr*, have revealed superimposed timber streets lined with block houses. There is little material that is Scandinavian in the areas of the town that have been investigated, but an early Viking settlement might well have been situated on the lower ground on the other side of the river.

Kiev, situated on the steep west bank of the Dnieper, was even more important than Novgorod, becoming the centre of the medieval Russian state. It was ruled by Scandinavian princes – though its population was also mainly Slavonic – and it was here that the Scandinavian merchants gathered each year before setting out in June for Byzantium, when the spring floodwaters had subsided sufficiently to allow them a safe passage. At the mouth of the Dnieper, they stopped at the island of Berezany, then sailed on across the Black Sea to reach their goal.

Not all the Vikings who travelled the Russian rivers were bent on peaceful purposes. Byzantium was attacked by fleets from Kiev on at least two occasions. Raiders were also active on the Caspian Sea between 910 and 912, and again in the middle of the century. These later raiders will have travelled along the second of the great eastern routes.

This route from the Baltic to the Caspian was joined either by way of Staraja Ladoga and Novgorod, or by way of Lake Onega, to bring one down the Volga to Bulgar at its bend. This was the market-place of the Bulgars, to which the fur-traders came from the Perm forests in the east, to which Arabic silver came by caravan from Khiva to the south of the Aral Sea, and which served as one terminus for the caravans of the silk-route from China. From Bulgar, merchants or raiders might voyage on to Itil, the capital of the Khazars, and thus reach the Caspian, with the possibility of travelling on to Baghdad by camel-train from Gorgan. Alternatively, they might join the trans-European land route to Mainz, Kiev, Cracow and Prague.

This bronze brazier was found in Sweden in 1943, hidden beneath a rock. It was probably made in Baghdad about the year 800 and thus may have travelled the Volga route in the hands of a Viking merchant.

The silver trade

Over 60,000 Arabic coins have been found in Scandinavia from the Viking Age. These are sometimes called Kufic coins because the script they bear is named after the city of Kufah in Mesopotamia. Their legends are particularly useful since they generally record the name of the mint and date of issue.

While the Scandinavians may have exercised some control over the Dnieper route to Byzantium, on the Volga they had to pay tribute to both the Bulgars and the Khazars; but the rewards were rich, for the journey was less difficult and it led straight to the silver supplies of the Eastern Caliphate. It was on the Volga that Scandinavian merchants met Arabs, such as Ibn Fadlan, who have left descriptions of their wares and their ways. Furs, honey, wax, weapons and slaves were, we learn, the stock-in-trade of the silver-hungry Scandinavian merchants.

In the late tenth century there was a shift away from this Eastern route, for reasons that are not altogether clear. There might have been political problems, but the change in trading pattern might equally have been caused by practical commercial considerations – the great silver mines of the Eastern Caliphate were rapidly being exhausted, while new sources were being exploited much nearer home, in the Harz mountains of central Germany.

While it lasted, the volume of trade with the East must have been enormous. Over 60,000 Arab coins have been found in Scandinavia; Samarkand, Tashkent and Baghdad are all mints that are strongly represented. But the Arabic silver that reached Scandinavia was rarely kept as coins.

Viking traders were equipped with a small pair of scales for weighing out the silver needed for a deal. These were ingeniously designed to fold up and fit into a small box.

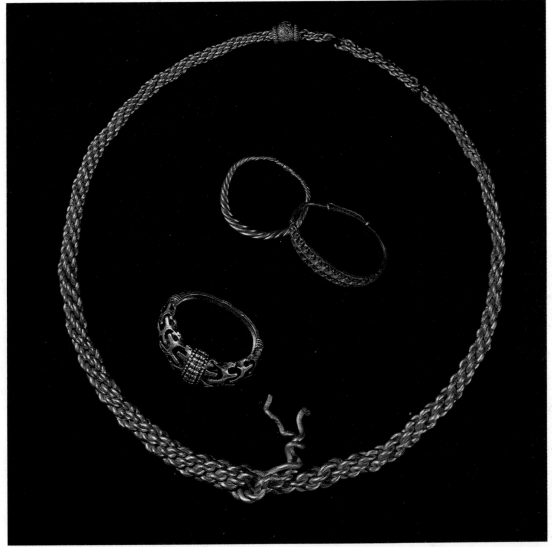

Use of precious metals

Throughout the Viking Age most of Scandinavia was without a coin-using economy; silver and gold were treated as bullion, to be weighed out as required by a merchant in his portable (and ingeniously folding) scales. Under such circumstances there was no point in keeping precious metal in the form of coins. It would have been melted down and cast into ingots, for more compact storage and ease of handling, or, most often, made into jewellery, thus providing the owner with an opportunity for conspicuous display of his wealth. Both ingots and jewellery could be cut up at a later date if small change was required.

Viking silver hoards, buried for safe-keeping in the ground by owners who were never able to return for them, thus consist of a great variety of objects: coins and ingots, brooches, pendants, neck-rings, arm-rings, finger-rings, both complete objects and their fragments (or so-called 'hack silver'). Well over a thousand hoards of silver and a few of gold have been found in Viking Age Scandinavia, when there were no native sources of these metals being worked. Faced with such evidence, we can entertain no doubts as to the success of the Vikings in accumulating wealth in large quantities, whether by fair means or foul.

Home Life

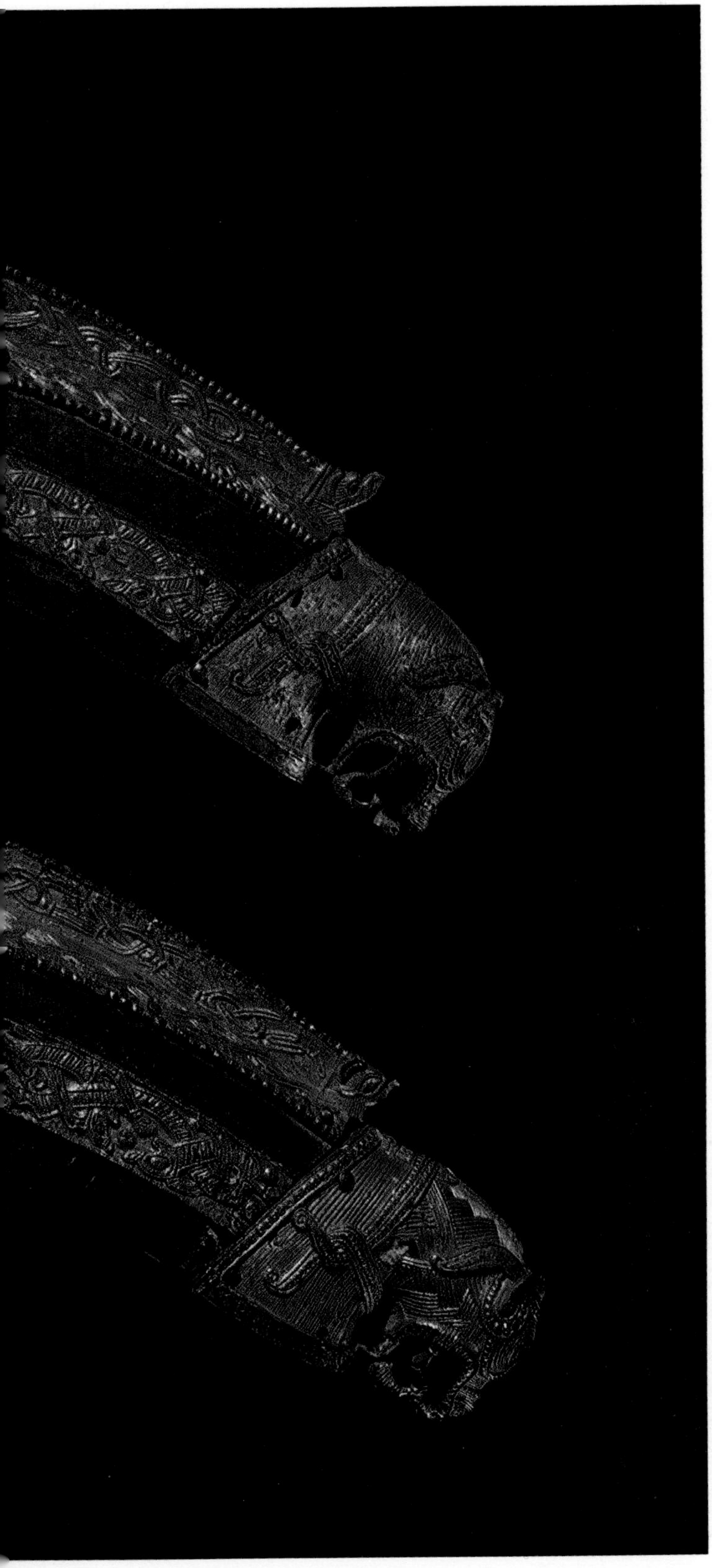

Horse-drawn carts and wagons provided an important form of land transport in the Viking Age. Wooden harness-bows were placed across the horses' backs, with metal mounts through which the reins could be more easily controlled. This matched pair of bows, found at Mammen in Jutland, is richly ornamented with gilt-bronze, although the wood is modern.

Clothing & jewellery

Human figures are rare in Viking art and always stylized, but the few known examples provide direct evidence of contemporary styles of dress. This Viking woman (a Swedish pendant) wears a trailing dress and shawl with a festoon of beads hanging probably from a brooch on each shoulder. Her hair falls loosely from a knot behind her head.

ur knowledge of dress in the Viking Age is derived from three quite different sources of evidence, all of which suffer from severe limitations and must be treated with caution. Firstly, there are contemporary representations, such as the figure pendants or the people of the Gotlandic picture-stones or the Oseberg tapestry. Since there existed no tradition of naturalism in Viking art, these figures are somewhat stylized and lacking in detail, but on a general level they provide direct evidence for the cut of clothes of which we would otherwise be ignorant. Secondly, there are mentions of dress in the literary sources. Given that most of these date from the later medieval period we cannot be sure that in such details they are not drawing more on current fashions than on memories from several generations before. But *Rígspula*, a poem that was perhaps composed in the tenth century (although preserved in an Icelandic manuscript from about 1350), describes a farmer's wife as wearing some kind of a smock, with shoulder-brooches, a necker-

An impressed gold foil from Norway (here much enlarged), depicts embracing figures. The man wears an arm-ring and a long cloak typically fastened with a large brooch on the right shoulder, thus leaving the sword arm free.

chief and a head-dress. Such details as neckerchiefs or underwear mentioned in the literary sources are of particular interest since of their nature they do not appear on picture-stones or tapestries and do not survive burial. Lastly, and most tangible, there are the excavated remains of cloth and clothing, and of the brooches that held it together.

Archaeological evidence for textiles is confined to scraps, for under normal burial conditions they rot away rapidly in the ground. But there are important fragments from graves that have been preserved through contact with brooches or other metal objects – reserved in their corrosion products or impregnated with metal salts – and also finds from waterlogged Viking Age deposits, as at Lund and York, that can tell us much about the quality and variety of available cloth. The arrangement of brooches on a fully clothed corpse is a matter of vital concern to the archaeologist. Brooches were first and foremost dress-fasteners; it is thus possible to deduce something about the number and nature of the clothes in use from the number and disposition of the brooches needed to hold them all together. Unfortunately for the study of dress, this important source of information dries up during the later Viking Age, with the adoption of Christianity and the abandonment of the practice of burying the body fully clothed and equipped. The result is that comparatively speaking we know a great deal about dress in the ninth and tenth centuries and virtually nothing about fashions in the eleventh.

The Viking woman

The figure representations make it clear that the basic costume of a Viking woman consisted of a long chemise over which the dress was worn; either or both might be so long as to trail behind her. A shawl, cloak or jacket would complete the basic ensemble, and aprons were also sometimes worn. Archaeological evidence demonstrates that the chemise was of wool or linen, the latter sometimes pleated, with short sleeves or no sleeves at all. The dress was woollen and was worn suspended from shoulder-straps, in the form of paired loops held together by a pair of brooches.

Brooches

Given the necessity for wearing brooches as fasteners, the opportunity was naturally taken to turn them into objects of adornment and display – according to the means of the wearer. Fashion played a part here. New types and shapes of brooches were developed from time to time, several of them inspired by Western European fashions, and their ornament was continually being modified to reflect the developing styles of Viking Art.

Brooches survive that are individual masterpieces of the gold- and silversmith's craft, clearly produced on commission for wealthy patrons; there are also plenty from the other end of the scale, which were produced in standard series made of base metals for the poorer members of the community. Typically the cheaper brooches were coarse copies of the finer specimens, imitation often being carried to the extent of gilding or tinning bronze brooches to give them the appearance of gold and silver. Any bronze brooch would in fact have commanded some price, for such metal had to be imported into Scandinavia during the Viking Age. No doubt old or broken brooches were part-exchanged for new so that the jeweller might melt them down in his crucibles to cast again into the latest models.

During the ninth and tenth centuries the shoulder-brooches used by Scandinavian women to fasten their dresses were almost all of a type that was domed and oval in shape, somewhat resembling the shell of a tortoise. This has led to their becoming known, rather misleadingly, as 'tortoise brooches', a usage best abandoned. Such oval brooches were cast in bronze in one or more pieces, and with ornament of a greater or lesser degree of elaboration depending on the customer's

means; the pin and catch are concealed from sight within the dome.

Oval brooches were produced in pairs, as the dress style dictated. Nearly all such brooches are covered with stylized animal ornament, of varying degrees of complexity and coherence; in addition some were gilt, or were embellished with bosses and twisted silver wires. Some types were literally mass-produced, one brooch being used as the model for many others. About 1,000 copies of the commonest variety are known, and have been found from Iceland in the west to Kiev in the

Brooches were both essential fasteners and decorative ornaments. These four are basic types that any Scandinavian woman might have owned. The pair of large oval brooches were worn one on each shoulder to hold up the dress, while a smaller brooch – often trefoil-shaped or 'equal-armed' – fastened the shawl or cloak. Similar brooches are found in women's graves throughout the Viking world.

Styles in shawl brooches varied with the fashions. *Above* A round gold brooch imitating an imported coin – a *solidus* of Charlemagne's son, Louis the Pious. *Right* Tenth-century equal-armed brooches from Birka. The larger one at the top is very ornate and was no doubt specially commissioned.

This Danish penannular or ring-brooch, with terminals in the form of moustached Vikings' heads, probably fastened a man's cloak. The style was adapted from a Scottish or Irish type of dress-fastening.

east. Many of the most recent oval brooches are the crudest of the whole sequence; this might well be because the wearing of a shawl had become such an established fashion that the brooches were nearly always covered in use, so that their surface appearance was no longer so important. No new types of oval brooch were created in the late Viking Age and they fell out of use in Scandinavia.

Only in the island of Gotland did Scandinavian women of the Viking Age eschew the fashion for oval shoulder-brooches. They preferred instead a pair of smaller bronze brooches resembling animal heads, with squared-off snouts and projecting ears. With these they also wore their own distinctive forms of additional brooches, pins and necklaces.

The Viking woman's shawl or cloak was fastened by a third brooch, which she wore on her chest between her oval brooches. This took a variety of forms. During the early Viking Age, particularly in Norway, it was fashionable to wear brooches adapted from pieces of metalwork brought back by raiders from Britain and Ireland. More usual were brooches with two or three arms, trefoil brooches being inspired by West European strap-mounts. Other styles were modelled on

brooches that Viking settlers found being worn in Scotland and Ireland.

During the tenth century large round brooches for cloaks and shawls, often elaborately ornamented with gold or silver filigree, became increasingly popular. They were produced in various patterns and styles, some even being based on coins. This brooch type continued to be made and used in the late Viking Age, and after. Small round brooches worn at the neck, to fasten the opening of the chemise, were also in use during the tenth century; this is usually the only type of brooch found in a child's grave.

Thus, in the middle of the Viking Age, a wealthy woman might have displayed four brooches, to which she would have added a necklace of beads, with maybe some pendants, and quite possibly a ring or two as well.

Beads and necklaces

In many cases beads were worn as festoons strung between the oval brooches, but complete necklaces are also found. Once again the nature and variety of such ornaments would have depended on the family's wealth, for the beads might include imported cornelians and crystals, although they were more usually of amber or glass. The latter were certainly

Left Beads were often suspended between the oval shoulder-brooches, but necklaces were also worn. These two rare and expensive examples come from the Baltic. The outer one is Slav; its beads are decorated with minute silver granules in finer workmanship than could be achieved by Scandinavian craftsmen of the time. The inner necklace, with crystal pendants set in silver, is influenced by Slav designs, but was probably made on Gotland.

An elaborate silver cloak-pin from Birka was fastened by a cord tied to the small ring.

being produced in Scandinavia from imported raw glass, although some of the finest multicoloured specimens may have come from the Rhineland and elsewhere in Western Europe. On Gotland several strings of small beads might be worn together, held apart by spacer-plates; elaborate collars were also fashionable there, formed by threading to-gether a series of matching mitre-shaped pendants. The Gotlandic silver hoards con-tain a number of splendid necklaces made up of filigree-ornamented beads with pendants of silver-mounted crystals, in the style of Slav jewellers of the eastern Baltic. Another Slav fashion adopted by a very few was for wearing elaborate earrings, also skilfully

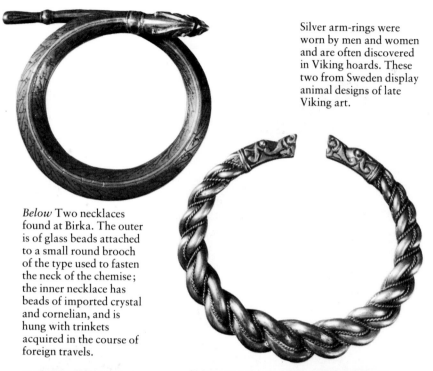

Silver arm-rings were worn by men and women and are often discovered in Viking hoards. These two from Sweden display animal designs of late Viking art.

Below Two necklaces found at Birka. The outer is of glass beads attached to a small round brooch of the type used to fasten the neck of the chemise; the inner necklace has beads of imported crystal and cornelian, and is hung with trinkets acquired in the course of foreign travels.

embellished with silver filigree to a degree of precision never quite mastered by Scandinavian jewellers.

Neck-rings and arm-rings

Although earrings were rare in Viking Age Scandinavia, rings of other kinds were worn by both men and women. Rods of gold or silver were twisted or plaited together to form neck-rings and arm-rings, while miniaturized versions were used for finger-rings. Other types of massive ring were cast and ornamented with complex stamped patterns. The purpose of many such rings would have been the display of wealth. This attitude to ornaments is brought out well by the tenth-century Arab writer Ibn Fadlan, describing the appearance of the women with a party of northern merchants whom he met travelling on the river Volga:

> Round her neck she wears gold or silver rings; when a man amasses 10,000 *dirhems* he makes his wife one gold ring; when he has 20,000 he makes two; and so the woman gets a new ring for every 10,000 *dirhems* her husband acquires, and often a woman has many of these rings.

Silver rings were certainly much commoner than gold, for the *dirhems* were the silver Arabic coins that provided the raw material for their manufacture. But then, what was the use of a bag full of silver coins in an economy that was not coin-using? It might be buried in the ground for safekeeping, but if the silver was only going to be weighed out when needed for some transaction, the coins might as well be melted down and turned into ornaments. These could always be cut up later if small change was needed; meanwhile they could be displayed for the prestige they would bring.

The Viking man

Apart from such rings, male jewellery was essentially confined to brooches and pins for fastening the cloak, although pendants on chains (such as Thor's hammers) might be worn by either sex. Furs, hides, and shaggy woollen cloaks were all worn by men and would have required a massive brooch or pin to accommodate such heavy material, when they were not simply tied in place with thongs. The Vikings rapidly adopted and adapted the large pins and ring-brooches that were used for such purposes in Britain and Ireland. Smaller cloaks were worn fastened with simpler pins of bronze or bone on the right shoulder, so that the sword arm could be kept free for any emergency.

Men's clothing was basically simple, consisting of a shirt and trousers or breeches, with a simple tunic over all. The representations of male figures suggest that there was considerable scope for choice over the cut of one's trousers. Although in the West they seem to have been cut both broad and narrow, some worn in the Baltic were baggy, even billowing, following Eastern fashions. Cloaks and tunics could be brightly coloured and edged with tablet-woven braids, perhaps even including the use of gold threads. A single bead was sometimes used as a button to close the shirt opening at the neck. A knife, as maybe a purse, would be hung from a belt, or on a cord around the neck. Similarly a woman of status would hang such objects as keys and toilet implements from a brooch.

Slaves, we learn from *Rígspula*, were more simply dressed in cloth of undyed wool. One imagines a poncho-like garment, tied around with a cord or thong. No doubt children were dressed in a similar simple manner, although little is known about their clothing.

Shoes, gloves and hats

Footwear was of calf- or goatskin, laced around the ankle. Boots and shoes have only occasionally been found, but then again their preservation normally depends on damp soil conditions. Recent excavations in towns such as Lund, Hedeby, York and Dublin have all produced much debris left by shoemakers and cobblers – including wooden lasts from both York and Hedeby, the latter being child-sized.

Gloves and hats of wool or leather would have completed the outfits of both men and women when the weather so dictated. Both sexes might hold their hair back with a band of ornamented silk or linen, although married women appear to have kept their hair covered with a scarf or head-dress.

Personal appearance

Many of the female representations often depict women's hair worn long, but knotted at the back of the head. That men might take great care of their beards and moustaches can be seen from the carving of the Sigtuna warrior. If the Arab merchant Al-Tartushi is to be believed, and he did visit Hedeby about the year 950, then its inhabitants prepared 'an artificial make-up for the eyes; when they use it their beauty never fades, on the contrary it increases in both men and women.'

Saturday was bath-day; baths might take the form of a sauna in a small bath house like that at Jarlshof. But what one is to believe about the cleanliness of the Vikings depends at first sight on which source one chooses to consult. If you pick Ibn Fadlan, then you learn that they were 'the filthiest of God's creatures', because to his mind they did not wash often enough and when they did they all shared the same bowl of water. In England, on the other hand, it was observed that the Danes combed their hair, bathed and changed so often that they were particularly successful with the ladies. Obviously in such a personal matter standards varied enormously; in any case one would not expect them to have been the same for a party of ship-borne merchants far from home, as for a young man about town with an eye for the girls. But cleanliness does seem to have been expected. A collection of poems of Viking Age origin, known as *Hávamál* (*High One's Speech*, meaning the words of Odin), says that a guest is met by his host at the table 'with water, a towel, and a hearty welcome', and goes on to advise that one should always be 'freshly washed' when setting off for the Thing.

Unlike the popular image of a Viking raider, this warrior of carved elk-horn, found at Sigtuna in Sweden, has no horns on his helmet. He wears his moustache and beard neatly trimmed.

Weaving & cloth designs

Spinning and weaving were the year-round tasks of Viking women, both to clothe their families and to produce cloth for other essential purposes, such as the sails for Viking ships. Special combs with long iron teeth were used to card the roughly cleaned wool. It was then attached to a distaff – a wooden stick held in the left hand or the crook of the arm – and fibres teased from it were fastened to a spindle, weighted at the bottom with a spindle-whorl of clay or stone. The spindle was set turning and, as it dropped to the ground, drew out the wool into a thread. This was then wound into a ball, or a skein if it was intended for dyeing. Skeins were made with the aid of a reel – a handle with a curved bar at either end, on to which the wool was wound crosswise from corner to corner. The finished wool was woven on a warp-weighted loom – an upright loom leant against the wall of the house. A weaver's other tools consisted of a sword-like weaving-batten of wood, whalebone or iron, and small pointed pin-beaters of wood or bone, used to make detailed adjustments to the threads.

Plain (or tabby) weave and twill were the main weaves used in Viking Age Scandinavia. Plain weave is the simpler: single weft threads are passed alternately over and under the warp threads. In twill, *above*, the weft threads pass over one warp thread, then under two or more others, producing a diagonal effect.

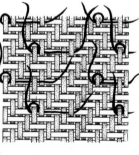

Shaggy woollen cloaks were a major export from Iceland (where this example was found). The tufted cloth was produced by inserting short lengths of wool into the warp during weaving.

1 crossbeam
2 rest
3 upright
4 heddle-bar
5 rest
6 lower warp thread
7 upper warp thread
8 beam dividing the warp
9 weight of baked clay or stone

No Viking Age warp-weighted loom survives, but it may be reconstructed on the basis of those still used in primitive communities. In such looms the warp (vertical threads) is held taut by weights and divided into two layers by a beam near the bottom. The upper warp threads hang in front of the beam at the same angle as the loom, while the lower threads hang vertically. Working from the top down, the weaver passes the weft (horizontal threads) through the gap in the warp, then beats it upwards with a weaving-batten. The lower warp threads are tied to a heddle-bar, supported on two rests. By pulling this out to the end of its rests (as in the drawing *above*), the weaver draws the lower threads through the upper, thus changing their position before the weft is passed back in the opposite direction.

THE OSEBERG TEXTILES

In the royal burial-chamber of the Oseberg ship were found fragments of wall-hangings with pictorial designs – unique survivals of perhaps a widespread art of woven tapestry among Viking women. These narrow bands may have adorned the chamber as once they had hung in a royal hall. What the scenes represent is unknown. Riders and horse-drawn carts move in procession from right to left, between borders patterned with geometric motifs. Yellow, red and black predominate, the contours being emphasized by threads of other colours. The drawing, *right,* is a reconstruction of one tapestry, of which the photograph, *below,* shows a portion.

Below Five design motifs of varying complexity reconstructed from the textiles in the Oseberg royal grave.

Right: Tablet-woven braid (enlarged) from Birka in Sweden; several examples have been preserved by their use of gold and silver threads. In tablet-weaving the warp threads are passed through holes at the four corners of a number of rectangular plaques of wood or antler. These are twisted a quarter-turn at a time to alter the position of the warp threads, so producing the intricate patterns. Such braids were used to edge cloaks and tunics or to tie back the hair. In the Oseberg grave fifty-two tablets were found, set ready for weaving.

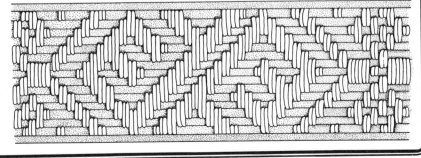

Household activities

The main occupation of Viking women, aside from the preparation of food, will have been clothing the family. Even in those households that could afford to purchase the finest woollen cloth imported from Frisia, or silks from Byzantium, spinning and weaving would have occupied several hours of the day, although for such ladies many of the chores would have been done by slaves. For this lengthy task begins with the combing of the plucked or shorn wool, which then needs to be spun; the yarn might be dyed before being woven (in which case vegetable dyes had to be prepared, or even mineral ones, as noted at Stöng). The woven cloth would be finished by being shrunk in water to close up the gaps and possibly by being fulled, that is soaked in an alkaline of detergent property, such as cow urine, to reduce its oil and dirt content.

The cloth was cut to shape with small textile-shears, which would have been kept carefully for that purpose in a casket, or even in their own specially shaped box. Needles too needed protection and were sometimes carried in a small cylindrical container, made from a hollow bird bone, suspended from a brooch. But cloth was required for many other purposes than just clothing; there were tents and wagon covers to be made and, above all, the sails for the Viking ships. Those ladies with time to spare might devote themselves to tablet-weaving ornamental braid, or even to embroidery.

In southern Scandinavia flax was grown, and its preparation for making linen would have been another time-consuming task. Certain glass bun-shaped objects are usually thought to have been used for smoothing seams in linen garments. The use of a number of finely ornamented plaques of whalebone, occasionally found in wealthy women's graves (where there might also be a weaving sword, for instance), is less obvious. It has been suggested that they were used as smoothing boards, but in only one instance has such a plaque been found together with a glass smoother. It could be that they were used in mangling washing, or for pleating linen by winding folded strips of wet cloth around them and leaving these to dry.

Food and drink

All these household tasks would have had to be fitted around the preparation of the twice-daily meals, served morning and evening. It is hard to generalize about diet, for it would have varied considerably from one part of the Viking world to another, depending on the resources available in each region. Certain foods were traded, both locally and over long distances. A fish factory was operating in York; a find of rye at Fyrkat is presumed to have been imported (probably from Russia); and a walnut in the Oseberg ship burial must have come from farther south. In fact the royal lady of Oseberg was well provided with food in her grave (not to mention her entire kitchen – and an aged retainer to do the dirty work). There were two oxen, some wheat and oats, cress, wild apples and hazelnuts, and even herbs and spices, cumin, mustard and horseradish. Other wild fruits, including

Carved whalebone plaques have sometimes been excavated from the graves of rich Viking women, particularly in Norway; they were possibly boards for mangling, smoothing or pleating cloth. The bun-shaped glass smoother is of a type also found in women's graves and may have been used for pressing seams in linen.

cherries, plums, sloes, elderberries, black-berries, raspberries and strawberries, have been found at Hedeby.

Cabbages, peas and onions, including garlic, were the most common vegetables grown. Some Swedish bread that has been analysed was found to consist of dried peas and pine bark; scarcely a delicacy, this was probably a poor man's substitute for grain. A lot of grit had become incorporated in it, as was the case in another Swedish find of bread, which was shown to be made of coarsely ground barley flour. This grit came from the coarse stone of the hand querns, which crumbled into the flour as the grain was ground. With such a quantity of grit in their bread it is scarcely surprising that the Vikings' teeth were gradually worn down. *Rígspula* refers to 'thin loaves, white, of wheat', so the rich at any rate were able to afford fine wheat flour rather than the usual barley bread.

The dough was kneaded in wooden troughs, like those among the Oseberg kitchen equipment, and then baked on the embers on the long-handled iron pans known from several women's graves. The grinding and baking would have been a daily chore, for this unleavened barley bread needed to be eaten at once while it was still hot, before it became rock hard. Bread ovens have been excavated in both Hedeby and Lund, so perhaps in the larger Viking towns there were already men who baked for their living.

Mutton and lamb, beef and veal, pig, goat and horse were all eaten by the Vikings, although such domestic animals were bred for a variety of uses: for their wool and hides, for their dairy products, for riding and for traction. In addition there were many others that were hunted: elk, deer, wild boar and bear, and in the north also reindeer, whales and seals. Smaller game such as hares, and birds such as ducks, were trapped or shot to add variety to the menu. In the Atlantic islands seabirds and their eggs provided an essential addition to the diet of the Viking settlers. Chickens and geese were kept about the farmstead (as were dogs and cats).

Nets, hooks, floats and sinkers from many Viking settlements show the importance of fishing in both seawater and fresh waters. The Baltic herring was clearly as much enjoyed as it is today. Fish seems to have been particularly important in helping to feed the concentration of mouths in urban centres, such as Hedeby, Birka, Lund and York, all of which have produced evidence that substantial quantities of fish were being consumed. Cod, haddock and herring were the principal fish brought to York by North Sea fishermen, but locally caught fish, especially eels, were also available.

Meat and fish were both preserved to provide food for the winter, or for provisioning boats. Slaves would be put to boiling seawater to obtain salt for such purposes. But these vital supplies were also pickled in brine or whey, wind-dried and possibly smoked. Fresh food was eaten raw or cooked in a number of different ways, both indoors and out. A great cooking pit was discovered outside the hall at Hofstadir, no doubt to cater for the feasts. Some farmsteads, like that at Jarlshof, appear to have had separate kitchens but in most the cooking would have taken place on the long-hearth in the hall.

Cauldrons of iron or soapstone, and occasionally pottery, were suspended over the

Kitchen utensils of iron and wood. *Below* A long-handled roasting-fork and baking-plate; *below left,* a cheese-making drainaway with a bowl and spoon from Lund.

flames from a tripod or hung on chains or thongs from a roof-beam; other clay pots and soapstone bowls would be placed among the embers on the stone-lined hearths. In them would have been prepared substantial meat stews, broths or porridge. Meat and fish might also be baked in the ground or in ovens heated with warm stones; that at Jarlshof seems to have been used for fish – ling, saithe and cod. Meat was certainly roasted on spits or long-handled forks; such would have been the 'meat well browned, and fully cooked birds' served by the noble lady in *Rígspula*, on silver-mounted dishes brought to a linen-draped table.

Milk was drunk or made into butter and cheese – the separated whey being used in pickling. Great vats, like those set in the dairy at Stöng, were used for storage and their contents ladled out into buckets for service at table into wooden cups and bowls. The women also brewed beer for the feasts and parties that accompanied the pagan festivals and that helped to pass the winter months, with their long northern nights. Honey was used as the base for sweet, fermented mead; beer was made from malted barley and hops might be added for flavour (they have been found at Hedeby). Fruit wines would have provided the strongest alcoholic drinks known to the Vikings, for the secret of distillation had not then reached Scandinavia. Many a drunken party is recalled in the sagas, but the voice of experience speaks to us still from *Hávamál*. The observation that 'beer is not so good for men as it is said to be; the more a man drinks the less control he has of his thoughts', is followed later by the warning to 'be cautious but not over cautious; be most cautious with beer and another man's wife.'

Beer and mead were drunk from the horns of cattle, some of which were elaborately ornamented with metal mounts around the rim. Drinking from horns is an art to be mastered, for otherwise the first trickle becomes a sudden tidal wave; another problem is that they cannot be put down until

Making bread was a daily chore for Viking women, as the flat loaves of unleavened barley bread quickly became hard and inedible. Rotary hand querns were used for grinding the coarse flour. The dough was kneaded in a wooden trough and then baked on a long-handled iron plate among the embers of an open fire.

Board games were much enjoyed by the Vikings. *Above* A whalebone 'king' from an Icelandic gaming set; *below*, Birka playing pieces of coloured glass; *bottom*, two men seated at a board, from a Swedish rune-stone.

emptied, so unless they are being circulated a man must drink the contents in one. All of which would certainly have led to 'a rapid breakdown of reserve, a jovial relaxation of defences, a mutual revelation of the same human instincts and needs', which one modern commentator believes was central to the purpose of the cult feast.

Small silver cups, like that from Jelling, may have been used for fruit wine, for they have no other obvious purpose. True wine was imported, particularly from the Rhineland, but it would only have been served at the tables of the richest. It travelled in barrels of the type seen on the Bayeux Tapestry, being loaded by William's army, for such have been found at Hedeby. There, once the contents had been sold or consumed, the bottoms of some were knocked out and the casks sunk

vertically into the ground to serve as pre-fabricated linings for wells (as the water table was high they were just the right size). Pottery jugs and glass vessels were also imported from the Rhineland to serve the wine from, but silver bowls, which are sometimes found in sets, were probably made for the same purpose. Food was usually served in wooden bowls from which it was eaten with spoons of wood or antler. But meat would have been eaten in the fingers, off a flat wooden trencher, with the help of one's personal knife; forks were certainly not in use.

Hospitality and entertainment

Liberality with food is one of the qualities praised in the epitaphs on the Swedish rune-stones. Generosity in a man was certainly admired by the Vikings, and the provision of hospitality was thought essential. As the *Hávamál* advises, 'When a guest arrives chilled to the very knees from his journey through the mountains, he needs fire, food, and dry clothes.' Besides, one never knew when one might be dependent on others for hospitality oneself. It was not uncommon to be delayed for weeks by bad weather on a journey, or even to be forced to over-winter away from home if on a long voyage.

Winter evenings would have been passed not only in eating and drinking. There were poems to be recited, verses to be composed and the family sagas to be retold so that they would continue to be passed on down the generations (until eventually written down many years later). There would also have been singing and dancing. Board games were played by firelight, or else by the light of simple oil lamps. Pieces of bone or glass were moved over wooden boards, in a variety of games similar to draughts and fox-and-geese. In some sets of playing pieces there is an obvious 'king' who would have had to be protected by his men against an attacking force, in a game called *hnefatafl*. Chess would not, however, have been known in Scandinavia until the end of the Viking Age.

The farmer & smith

With the coming of spring, those Vikings who were planning to depart for a summer's raiding or trading would have needed not only to prepare their ships and gear – forging new weapons and tools in their own smithies from bog iron, dug up and smelted locally – but also to see to the ploughing and sowing of the fields for harvest when they returned to their farmsteads in the autumn.

Agriculture

Small or steep fields would have been cultivated by picks and hoes with iron blades on wooden shafts, or dug with simple wooden spades. Larger fields were ploughed with an ard, the simplest form of plough, consisting of a point dragged through the ground by one or more animals, while being guided by a man. Since the ard merely produces a groove and does not turn a proper furrow, the ground was sometimes cross-ploughed. Not many instances of Viking ploughing have been excavated, though parts of fields have recently been discovered under the Danish towns of Ribe and Viborg. In quite another context, the grooves left by the ploughshare can be seen in ninth-century levels of the Viking settlement in the Udal in the Hebrides, where dark midden material has been ploughed down into the white sand. Dunging fields was a job done by slaves, who also herded the beasts and did heavy work like digging peat for fuel or bog iron ore; they would also have provided materials and labour for building.

The proper plough, with a coulter or iron blade fixed in front of the ploughshare to slice the ground so that the pointed share can undercut it, and with a mould-board to turn the furrow, appears to have been known in Scandinavia at least in the later Viking Age. Such a plough may have been used to create the best-known Viking field, at Lindholm Høje, which was inundated with sand while the tracks of the last cart to cross it still showed clearly over the furrows.

Grain was harvested with a sickle, both men and women joining in. It was also important to ensure an adequate supply of food for as many cattle as possible for the duration of the snowy winters. Here of course there was a wide variation in practice, between say southern Denmark and Iceland, because of the climatic differences. In Denmark there was plenty of pasture for most animals, but in Iceland the cattle needed to be sheltered in byres and provided with about 5,500lb (2,500kg) of hay each for the winter, so the weaker beasts would be killed off beforehand and the meat preserved, as described above. Sheep and goats would survive outdoors, except during prolonged storms. All this hay was cut with scythes; it was supplemented when necessary with foliage cut down with broad-bladed tools rather like billhooks.

It was during the Viking Age that the practice developed of driving both cattle and sheep up into the mountains during the summer months to exploit untouched pastures. This meant of course that more ground could be cultivated and more hay cut around the farmsteads while the hungry beasts were elsewhere. This was particularly a Norwegian mountain phenomenon, to be contrasted once again with the flat and extensive pastures of southern Jutland where herds of cattle could

A Danish field of the late Viking Age was found at Lindholm Høje in the mid-1950s. The excavators stripped off a deep layer of blown sand to reveal the furrows left from its final cultivation, still traversed by Viking cart-tracks.

easily be reared, sufficient even for export. It is thus impossible to generalize about the agricultural economy of the Vikings, apart from observing that it was mixed – part arable, part pastoral, part based on hunting and fishing. The balance depended on what part of the Viking world one lived in and its available natural resources.

Ironworking

Iron-smelting and ironsmithing were basic tasks carried out on many, if not all, farms to provide everything from weapons and tools to boat rivets and nails. We have seen, for instance, that both Jarlshof and Stöng were provided with their own smithies for working iron smelted from bog ore. Higher-quality iron was traded in the form of bars.

Such smithies would have to have been provided with a basic tool kit, including bellows and protective furnace stone; tongs and hammers were needed for handling and shaping the hot iron, with an anvil to beat it upon. Shears were required for cutting sheet metal. Chisels and files were essential, and nail-making was done with a special perforated iron tool to help finish the head.

There were also travelling smiths who could have been specialists in certain work, like making weapons, or who might have had a line in bronze-casting and jewellery-making. Some appear to have been jacks of all trades; the man whose tool chest has been recovered from the bog at Mästermyr on Gotland was a carpenter and smith, for his tools included a saw, axes, adzes, augers, gouges and rasps.

The decorated body of the wagon found in the Oseberg ship burial rests on a pair of cradles that terminate in human heads. Similar wagons can be seen in use on the Oseberg tapestry on page 121; their bodies could be lifted from the wheels and, in southern Scandinavia, were sometimes used as coffins for wealthy women.

The royal lady of Oseberg was provided with four sledges for use over snow in winter and grass in summer. One of these horse-drawn sledges was an ordinary workaday model, but the other three were richly carved.

It is possible that the Mästermyr smith lost his chest during the winter while crossing the ice; perhaps it fell from his sledge. Several such sledges were buried at Oseberg, some of them most ornately carved. Simple sledges would doubtless have been used all the year round, but they would have been particularly useful in the winter. In fact in some parts of Scandinavia it was easier to get about by travelling on the lakes and rivers once they had frozen fast, and since furs are at their best in winter, this may well have been one of the busy periods for a trading centre such as Birka. Skates made of horse and cow bones are sufficiently common finds to show the importance of this form of transport; the skater propelled himself with a pole. Skis have also been found. Horses' hoofs were fitted with small iron spikes for walking over ice.

As can be seen on the Oseberg tapestry and the Gotlandic picture-stones, horseback was the normal form of transport, with heavy loads being carried on pack-horses or in carts and wagons. This is amply borne out by the many finds of riding gear and harness equipment, although not of saddles, which would have been of wood and leather. The use of stirrups was only gradually becoming widespread during the Viking Age. Most remarkable of all is the survival of the wagon in the Oseberg ship burial, although it was crushed flat on discovery and has needed to be patiently pieced together. Its richly carved body befits its royal ownership, but such wagons in simpler forms were common enough in southern Scandinavia for their removable bodies to have served as coffins in a number of female burials.

No one can deny that the Vikings were great travellers. But it is almost as if the Oseberg lady was expecting to be in perpetual motion. Not only was she buried in a ship; she was provided with the wagon and four sledges, with at least ten horses to cover her needs on dry land; not to mention her wooden saddle, her two tents and the travelling bed for camping on the way!

Skating over frozen rivers and lakes was a common way of travelling in winter. *Below* A leather ankle-boot found in the York excavations rests on a skate of animal bone. The skater propelled himself with the aid of a pole.

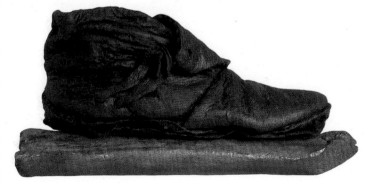

Viking Art

A grotesque animal head bares its fangs on the end of a wooden harness-bow, from Søllested in Denmark, in the tradition of Scandinavian art, which was based on stylized animals. The skills of Viking artists and craftsmen are clear from the superb quality of this three-dimensional, richly gilt bronze casting. Viking art is non-representational, for with few exceptions it did not seek to tell a story or to record people and things, but (as here) consists of the elaborate embellishment of functional objects used by the Vikings in their daily life.

Art & ornament

Broa/Oseberg

800

Borre

850

Jellinge

900

Mammen

950

Ringerike

1000

Urnes

1050

1100

The six main Viking Art styles are summarized here in tabular form, giving a general idea of their respective durations; it is impossible to give them absolute dates.

The vigour and vitality that the Vikings displayed in all their exploits spilled over into their art. Viking art often has a restless quality, much of it being characterized by seething masses of surface ornament created from the bodies of stylized animals. Contorted and distorted animals had formed the basis of Scandinavian art from the fifth century AD, and so it continued throughout the Viking Age. The art of the Vikings was thus rooted in a centuries-old tradition. At the same time it was open to new impulses: it was a confident art able to draw on inspiration from outside, absorbing new motifs borrowed from Western Europe and adapting them according to its own conventions, without slavish imitation. This process continued until, with the waning of the energy that had characterized the Viking Age, the native art developed a decadent quality. Then, as Scandinavia was drawn into the brotherhood of Christian nation-states, it succumbed to the new Romanesque art that was sweeping Europe.

There is little in Viking Age Scandinavia that we can recognize as fine art. Nearly all Viking art is applied art, the decoration of functional objects. But the Vikings had a love of ornament, so their woodcarvers and metalworkers were given the fullest scope to practise their skills in the production of objects and jewellery that would bring flash and colour to daily life.

Our sources for the study of Viking art are limited because of the small number of objects that survive. We know all too little of the textile arts, although the Oseberg tapestry alerts us to what we must be missing; similarly most woodcarving has perished, and we have only traces of painted decoration on wood. The skald Bragi describes in his poem *Ragnarsdrápa* a shield painted with scenes including Thor fishing for the world-serpent, though none such survives. Most of our ornamented objects from the ninth and tenth centuries are ones that were originally placed in the pagan graves – such as weapons, brooches, horse-harness, and other objects of everyday importance for the Vikings. The richest among them, like the royal lady buried at Oseberg, who could afford to patronize skilled craftsmen, would even have had their ships, wagons and bedsteads carved in the style of the moment. This source of information dries up in the later Viking Age with the decline of pagan burial practices. We have instead to turn to fine silver objects buried in hoards, and finds from the developing towns such as Trondheim and Lund. But additionally, there is a whole new range of artifacts associated with the Christian religion. Stone sculpture, for instance, was virtually unknown in Scandinavia outside the island of Gotland before the second half of the tenth century. Then, under Christian influence, there developed the range of rune-incised and ornamented stones set up to commemorate good deeds and dead men.

The first style: Broa and Oseberg

The animals used by Scandinavian artists at the beginning of the Viking Age were curvaceous creatures, zoologically quite unidentifiable because of the advanced degree of their stylization, although birds are numbered among them. The two main finds of ornamented objects in the first Viking art style are quite contrasted: the royal burial at Oseberg, with its unparalleled wealth of woodcarving, and a grave at Broa on Gotland, where a man was buried with a bridle ornamented with a set of twenty-two metal mounts.

The Broa mounts of cast bronze, heavily gilt, are the work of a master craftsman with a gift for design. He made full use of the curvaceous animals, with their small heads, frond-like feet, and multitude of tendrils, which formed the essential part of his Scandinavian artistic heritage. But on a few of the mounts there appears a new motif consisting of a much chunkier animal with paws that grip the frame around it – the so-called 'gripping beast'.

The earliest Viking art style is displayed on these gilt-bronze mounts from a bridle, found in a man's grave at Broa on Gotland. Sinuous animals cover each of the mounts, but that at the bottom right has a chunkier 'gripping beast' at its centre. These two types of animal form the main motifs of what we may call the Broa/Oseberg style. It was from this first Viking style that the others developed.

The Oseberg carvings

he Oseberg woodcarvings – the ornament of the ship, wagon, sledges, bedsteads, and animal-head posts – represent the work of a royal 'school' of Norwegian carvers in Vestfold. The designs include what may be described as the work of traditionalist master carvers, alongside that of their more experimental apprentices. As on the Broa mounts, the traditional sinuous animals predominate, but 'gripping beasts' make their appearance on a number of pieces. One of the animal-head posts is covered with a writhing mass of them; other carvers chose to ignore them completely. One of the most conservative pieces, the post carved by a man who has been nicknamed the 'Academician', because of his meticulous style, is considered to be the finest carving from the burial.

The purpose of these animal-head posts is unknown, but their fearsome aspect, with open jaws, suggests that they were intended to ward off evil spirits. The animal-head posts are the most sculptural of the Oseberg carvings in their concept and execution. The detail of the workmanship is extraordinary but the Vikings' love of extravagant ornament did not rest at elaborately carved surfaces, for some of the Oseberg pieces are further embellished with silver-headed rivets.

The ornament of the great wagon includes a remarkable series of designs, for the most part unparalleled among the other carvings. These range from the naturalistic human heads of the trestles to the interlacing snake-like creatures down its sides. On either end there are scenes with figures that bring to mind those of the Oseberg tapestry. There is a man entangled with snakes – perhaps the legendary hero Gunnar, who was thrown into a snake pit – and an enigmatic scene between a woman, a man and a horseman.

The splendour of the Oseberg carvings and the skill of their workmanship remind us how much of the best Viking art we must be missing, given the small amount of Viking Age woodwork that has survived.

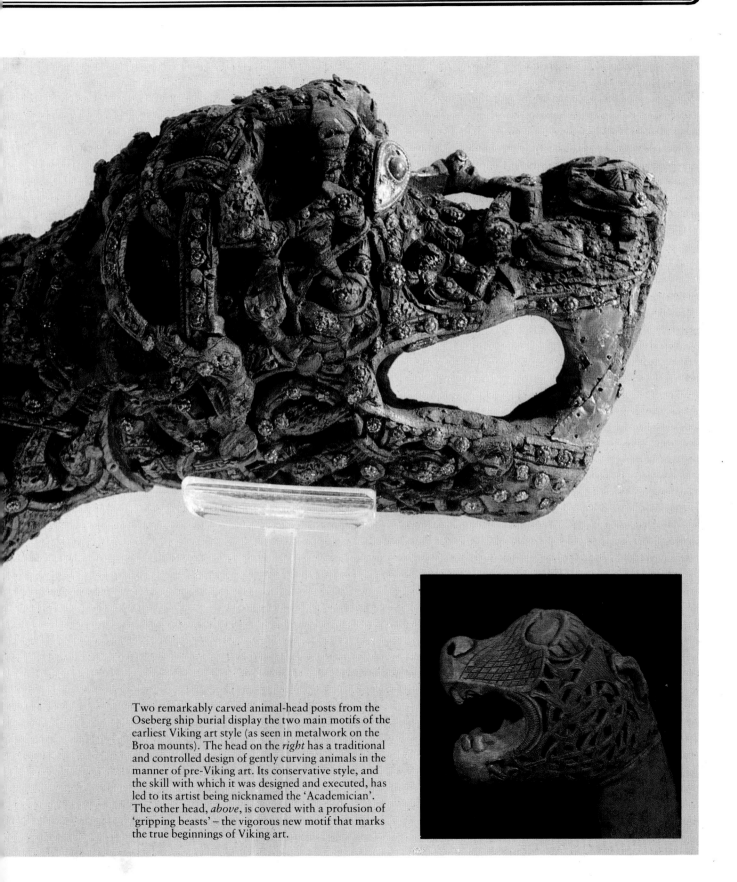

Two remarkably carved animal-head posts from the Oseberg ship burial display the two main motifs of the earliest Viking art style (as seen in metalwork on the Broa mounts). The head on the *right* has a traditional and controlled design of gently curving animals in the manner of pre-Viking art. Its conservative style, and the skill with which it was designed and executed, has led to its artist being nicknamed the 'Academician'. The other head, *above*, is covered with a profusion of 'gripping beasts' – the vigorous new motif that marks the true beginnings of Viking art.

The 'gripping-beast' motif

Rugged, forceful and spirited, the 'gripping beast' is an apt symbol for the Vikings, for its first appearance is what most clearly distinguishes the earliest Viking art from that which had gone before. Such was its appeal to Viking taste that it remained a hallmark of much Viking art for a century and a half. Even after that it did not quite disappear for it re-emerged as a motif in Scandinavian art in later centuries.

As its name implies, the chief features of the gripping beast are its paws that clutch the borders around it, parts of its own anatomy, or neighbouring animals. Its pedigree is obscure but it occurs in a somewhat tentative manner on the Broa mounts, and on some of the carvings from the Oseberg burial it is used with abandon to form dense scrummages of interlocking animals. Such was the invention of the Oseberg school of carvers that it is found there in many guises, even in human form on part of the ship's ornament.

Some of the most splendid of the early gripping beasts are those that decorate a pair of oval brooches from Lisbjerg in Jutland, one of which is illustrated below. A geometrical framework surrounds each animal, which is carefully executed in all its details. The head is shown full face with a grin like a Cheshire cat's; it has a long curling pigtail. Emphasis is

placed on its fore- and hindquarters, which are linked by the slimmest of bodies. The legs are short in comparison with the massive paws that grip its own body and the border. A few carvings in jet and amber of similar beasts have been discovered in Scandinavia.

Having once invented the gripping beast it is not surprising that Viking artists wished to experiment with this figure, for it made an original and lively motif, and moreover the parts of its body were easily rearranged to fit whatever space was available on the object to be decorated. The gripping beast was thus refined to form one of the two principal motifs of the Borre style (the art style that followed Broa, named after the ornament on bronze bridle-mounts placed in another Norwegian ship burial, at Borre in Vestfold).

A Swedish find, a pendant from the Vårby hoard that was buried about 940, shows in simple form the characteristics of the Borre-style gripping beast. The centre of this pendant is formed from a single beast with its body arranged in a pose typical of this style. The ribbon-shaped body is placed in an arc beneath the mask-like head, which has a pair of protruding 'Mickey Mouse' ears. As before, emphasis is placed on the fore- and hindquarters, and the ever-gripping paws. Although enclosed within a circle, this design is essentially triangular in shape.

Right Cheerfully throttling himself, a gripping beast grins from the top of one of a pair of 9th-century Danish brooches. The family of gripping beasts consists of a variety of such contorted animals, with paws that clasp their own bodies, each other, or the framework around them.

Above Artifacts found in the Oseberg ship burial show some of the earliest known gripping beasts, carved in wood. Among them are unusual human versions, as shown, *left*, on a panel from the ship itself.

Two gilt-silver pendants from a hoard hidden at Vårby, Sweden, in about 940, illustrate the gripping beast in different, though contemporary, forms. *Above* A single animal appears in a characteristic Borre-style pose – mask-like head looking towards us over an arched body. *Below* A pair of animals in the Jellinge style have heads in profile, pigtails and ribbon-shaped bodies, but also gripping paws, which reveal their mixed breeding.

A pair of tenth-century Swedish brooches show the new-style gripping beast in all its glory. One, a quatrefoil brooch on a chain, has its surface divided by a cross, with an animal mask at the end of each arm. Within each quadrant can be seen an example of the Borre-style beast, arranged as on the Vårby pendant except that the head looks in towards the centre of the brooch. The other, a silver filigree-ornamented brooch in the form of a disc, omits the dividing cross so that the snouts of the four animals touch at its centre. The bodies have become more ribbon-like than ever, being made from silver wires, their expanded hips filled with tiny granules; the paws are reduced to U-shaped elements.

The Borre style was for much of its currency contemporary with the Jellinge style, named after a find from a royal burial. The Jellinge style proper makes no use of the gripping beast, preferring ribbon-shaped animals seen in profile. But the two styles are often found together even on the same object. Not surprisingly, mating of the animals sometimes took place, resulting in interesting Borre/Jellinge hybrids. A second pendant from the Vårby hoard well illustrates this cross-breeding; it consists of a pair of backward-looking Jellinge-style beasts, with pigtailed heads in profile and thin, hatched bodies, that grip themselves frenetically in the manner of their Borre-style cousins.

Below Amber gripping beasts from Norway show this motif adapted to the round.

Woodcarving & painting

The quality of the Oseberg carvings, from the beginning of the 9th century, can be appreciated from this detail of a sledge, on which a seemingly haphazard jumble of ornament turns out to be a carefully controlled pattern of animals.

The natural abundance of timber in Scandinavia has always provided its inhabitants with wood as their principal raw material. Every farmer in the Viking Age will have been his own carpenter – indeed every man will have carried a knife and there must have been many who whittled away at a stick or a log of an evening and

The 11th-century portal of the church at Urnes in western Norway is deeply carved with an ambitious composition of continuously curving lines – all of which belong to the bodies of animals and snakes that are biting one another.

fancied themselves as carvers. There can be little doubt that the portals, gables and interiors of the houses were often decorated with both carvings and paintings, but wood does not survive well and little remains of the typical ornament that must have formed part of the everyday experience of the Vikings.

Professional carvers

The ornament of the ninth-century Oseberg finds and the eleventh-century Urnes church in Norway is not everyday carving but the work of professionals – and supremely gifted ones at that. Thus despite the fact that wood rots away so rapidly under normal burial conditions, we are fortunate to have from the beginning and end of the Viking Age some remarkable examples of elaborate ornamental carving to demonstrate the Viking sculptor's ambitions and achievements. We have already seen the quality of some of the Oseberg ornament; however, this was carving on a domestic scale, and therefore hard to compare directly with the monumental decoration on the Urnes church. The Urnes designs are nevertheless still based on traditional stylized animals, though now with curved bodies of almost greyhound-like proportions, intertwined with snakes. Two techniques were used: firstly, a low flat relief on the gables, and secondly, a high, rounded carving on the portal and wall itself.

The use of colour

A piece of wood excavated at Hørning church in Denmark is carved with a snake whose body is elegantly looped in the manner of those of the Urnes church. Its eye is painted red and the background is black. Red, blue, brown, black and white seem to have been the common colours in painted decoration. They are found also on rune-stones, as is demonstrated by finds from the island of Öland and the Viking stone at St Paul's in London. Yellow was also used, as on some of the shield boards from the Gokstad ship burial, and on the wooden fragments found in

the Danish royal burial mound at Jelling.

These Jelling fragments are in the style of the ornament on Harald Bluetooth's stone, also at Jelling. One is an openwork tendril pattern, but the other (shown here) is in the form of a bearded man, although only his head and trunk survive; across his waist run bands, bound with a ring, in the manner of the interlace that surrounds the body of Christ on the stone itself.

House furnishings and ornamentation

Recent excavations of the damp deposits of the medieval town of Nidaros, beneath the modern Norwegian city of Trondheim, have produced a couple of planks with animal ornament in the eleventh-century Urnes style. The finer plank lost its end when a sewer trench was dug in 1914 but the animal's head is to be seen at the centre of the fragment, with an almond-shaped eye (point forwards), surrounded by and intertwined with narrow

tendrils. These planks probably formed part of a piece of household furniture.

We also know that houses were themselves ornamented with carving, both within and without. The animal heads that project from the ends of the house-shaped Cammin casket (see page 207) suggest that such houses may have had their gable ends decorated in this manner. A late tenth-century poem, composed in Iceland, describes the scenes carved on the wall panels of a chieftain's hall, and it is from Iceland that we can get at least an idea of what such planks may have looked like. For some eleventh-century carved planks were re-used to from a ceiling in a farm at Flatatunga in the north (see page 191). Below a foliage pattern is a row of saints, so it seems likely that these were salvaged from a church rather than taken from an earlier hall.

Fine though such masterpieces are, the accidents of survival have left us without woodcarving of significance from much of the ninth and tenth centuries. To follow the development of Viking art, we must therefore turn to the products of the metalworker.

Few pieces of Viking woodcarving survive and traces of original painting are even rarer, although it may have been normal to colour all forms of sculpture, as these examples suggest. *Above left* A single Urnes-style snake carved on a beam from Hørning church in Denmark was painted red to stand out against its black background.

Above A plank from Trondheim, ornamented in the Urnes style, may well have formed part of a piece of furniture – perhaps a chair or a chest.

Right The stylized red and yellow figure of a bound man, found in the royal burial mound at Jelling in Denmark

Metalworkers of the Borre style

Ornamented with gripping beasts in filigree, Danish gold and silver brooches demonstrate that the Borre style is seen at its best on fine metalwork.

Below 'Gaut made this and all in Man' boasts the runic inscription on this cross-slab from Kirk Michael on the Isle of Man. Gaut is the first Viking artist whom we can recognize by his own name. Among his favourite patterns was the ring-chain motif – a hall-mark of the Borre style. It is seen here running up the shaft of the cross.

The ornaments produced by jewellers provide our main source of evidence for the history of Viking art. The development of 'fashionable' styles may be traced through the products of the gold- and silversmiths who worked to order for rich patrons, or sold their work to customers looking for means for ostentatious display of their wealth and rank. The cheaper bronze metalwork often found in graves is not as useful: much of it is flashy and vulgar, and generally its ornament cannot be fitted readily into the mainstream styles.

Filigree and granulation

The bronze bridle-mounts after which the Borre style is named, though representative of their style, are themselves imitative of finer pieces and therefore do not show the originality of design or quality of workmanship of for example the earlier mounts from Broa.

But the skill with which the Borre-style artist could handle the techniques of filigree and granulation is very evident from such master-pieces as the Værne Kloster gold spur and two Danish disc brooches illustrated here. Filigree consists of beaded wires. To make them, plain wires were first drawn through holes of decreasing size (this part of the technique is the same today). They were then given the appearance of rows of tiny beads by being impressed between grooved surfaces. Alternatively, the indentations might be made more crudely by crosshatching with a knife. The tiny gold or silver grains used in clusters, to produce what is known as granulation, were made by cutting short pieces of wire and placing them on a bed of charcoal; when heated they melted and took on a spherical form. The beaded wires were often combined with plain and twisted wires to build up elaborate lines and borders, and the grains or granules were used to fill in areas of the pattern. Both were soldered to a base-plate of the same metal (whether gold or silver), which was sometimes already impressed in relief with the main outlines of the pattern to be created.

A feature of Borre-style metalwork in cast bronze is that the contours of the ornament normally have nicked edges; this was an attempt to imitate filigree for the mass market. When possible the object was also gilded, to carry the imitation a stage further.

The Borre-style motifs

The Danish disc brooches show well the Borre-style gripping beast, as already identified on brooches from Sweden (on page 137). The heads are, as on the Swedish brooches, at the centre, although on the smaller brooch (from the Vester Vedsted hoard, deposited about 925) they are placed in an unusual position below rather than above the arched bodies.

The second main motif in the Borre style is an interlace pattern, known as the 'ring-chain'. It may be seen here on a Viking cross-slab from the Isle of Man, carved by a man named Gaut, who used only interlace in his work in patterns that are very similar to those found in the sculpture of north-west England, where he may have learnt his craft. Interlace also appears running round the outside of the Værne Kloster spur, although in this case it is further embellished with animal heads, in profile. These profiled heads belong more properly to the beasts of the Jellinge style; it is the mask-like animal heads, also occurring on the spur, that are characteristic of the Borre style.

The Borre style was popular for the best part of 150 years. Not unnaturally, over this period it spread throughout the Viking world, including Russia. The ring-chain motif was the aspect of it that became particularly popular in Britain and Ireland. It may be seen, for instance, on a gaming board found at Ballinderry (page 101), on several Manx stones, and on the Gosforth cross in Cumbria (page 74).

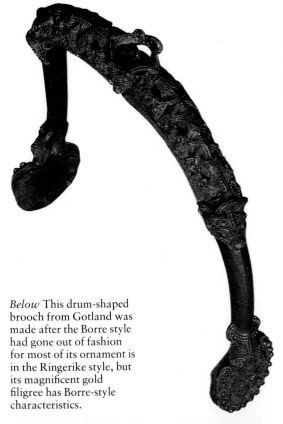

The unique gold spur from Værne Kloster in Norway is a masterpiece of filigree work, combining the Borre-style ring-chain with animal heads in an original and unusual design.

Below This drum-shaped brooch from Gotland was made after the Borre style had gone out of fashion for most of its ornament is in the Ringerike style, but its magnificent gold filigree has Borre-style characteristics.

The Jellinge style

he Jellinge style takes its name from the ornament on a silver cup found, together with the wooden fragments already described on page 139, in the north mound of the Danish royal site at Jelling, in the burial chamber thought to be that of King Gorm and Queen Thyri. This small cup stands on a pedestal foot and is decorated only around its bowl, where a pair of interlocked animals are to be found.

These s-shaped creatures are typical Jellinge-style beasts. Their bodies resemble ornamental ribbons – of constant width and with a ladder pattern running along them. The head is shown in profile, with open jaws and a characteristic curlicue or fold to the upper lip. The long pigtail and spiral hip joint are also characteristic of Jellinge-style animals. Such curvaceous creatures are clearly descendants of those of the Broa style, by

way of Borre. It is in effect a more coherent species of the same genus, which seems to have evolved during the ninth century, remaining in fashion for most of the tenth.

Scandinavian settlers introduced the Jellinge style into Britain, where it was preferred to the Borre style, except for the Borre ring-chain. It was used by the Anglo-Scandinavian carvers of Yorkshire, but generally in rather a debased version (as on the back of the Middleton cross). On the Isle of Man there were sculptors in the mainstream of the style and it might well have been there that the finely ornamented brooches were made that came to be buried at Skaill, on Orkney, around 950 or a little after. Incised on these silver brooches are animals with all the characteristics of those on the Jelling cup, but with the addition of tendril-like offshoots from their bodies – signs of metamorphosis into the beasts of the ensuing Mammen style.

Right and below With heads in profile, spiral hips, pigtails and curling upper lips, the pair of interlaced ribbon-like animals encircling the Jelling cup embody the characteristics of the style that bears its name. *Far right* A more developed version of the Jellinge style is displayed by animals with tendril-like offshoots, which decorate a silver brooch found at Skaill on Orkney. The bird at the bottom is to be compared to that on the Mammen axe.

The Jellinge style had in fact developed these florid tendencies in Scandinavia as well as in Britain, as can be seen from the ornament of a Danish harness-bow, one of a pair found at Søllested on Fyn. It is evident from this bow that Jellinge-style metalworkers followed the Borre-style practice of making cast ornaments imitate filigree work.

True filigree work in the Jellinge style is also found, as on a disc brooch from Tråen in Norway, from a silver hoard concealed about the year 1000. As Swedish and Danish filigree-ornamented brooches in the Borre style have already been examined (see pages 137 and 140), with this Tråen brooch we have the opportunity of making a direct comparison between objects of identical form and technique ornamented with the same composition in two different styles. The Tråen brooch has three animals laid out in the same way as on the earlier brooches, with their heads at the centre, but the pattern can only be understood in detail by reference to the Borre brooches, for at first appearance it looks chaotic.

As is to be expected, in the Jellinge style, the heads are shown in profile, with a curled upper

The Søllested harness-bow on pages 130–1 is superbly ornamented in the Jellinge style. On its central mount, *above*, back-to-back animals support a small panel containing two facing human figures.

This filigree brooch from Norway, *left*, is a Jellinge-style reinterpretation of a familiar Borre-style type.

lip and a long pigtail; the three large granules that form the eyes of the three animals are the clearest guide to the locations of the heads. In the manner of the Borre-style brooches from Sweden, the heads are placed above the arched bodies, forequarters to the right and hindquarters to the left; elongated tails complicate the intertwined pattern even further. There are no gripping paws, however, but simply U-shaped feet.

The Mammen style

he Mammen-style animal grew imperceptibly out of that of the Jellinge style. The two can be difficult to tell apart and indeed during the transitional period it would be a mistake to try to separate them. Gradually the animal's body becomes more substantial, taking on more naturalistic proportions than those of its emaciated predecessors, and its spiral hip joints are increased in size. To match this body growth, there is an increase in the patterning needed to fill it: on the slender body of a Jellinge-style animal there had been no room for more than a single row of bars or beading.

Important though these developments are they do not really break new ground, and one might be tempted to dismiss the Mammen style as little more than a transitional phase linking the Jellinge style with the subsequent Ringerike style. Certainly the Mammen style does not seem to have been in fashion for more than a couple of generations. However, it is marked out as innovatory in the history of Viking art in one important respect.

Throughout the Broa and Borre styles there was no detectable interest in the use of plants, or of their leaves or tendrils, as a basis for ornamental motifs: animals and abstract interlace sufficed. In the Jellinge style there was a suggestion of stubby tendrils providing decorative appendages to the animals' bodies. In the Mammen style there appears for the first time the full use of foliate patterns.

There need be no surprise at this development, for elaborate foliate patterns based on vine scrolls and on acanthus leaves were commonly used in Western Europe during the ninth and tenth centuries. The great gold mount from the Hon hoard (see page 33) gives evidence that Carolingian acanthus-leaf patterns were reaching Scandinavia from the ninth century. At that early stage a small amount of imitation was attempted, but it came to very little. In the later tenth century the time was apparently ripe for a step in this new direction, for one side of the Mammen axe, to which the style owes its name, is entirely given up to a straggly foliate pattern.

This splendid iron battle-axe found at Mammen in Jutland is inlaid with silver wires on both sides: one with a foliate pattern, and the other with a bird. The bird has a spotted body and a massive spiral hip; its wings and tail are drawn out into elongated, curving tendrils. At the very top of the axe is a pair of round eyes above a large nose, beneath which are moustaches and a spiral-marked beard. The same human mask stares out at us from the catch of one of the Mammen-style masterpieces: the Bamberg casket.

The Mammen style with its tremendous use of detail was particularly well suited for carving, as can be seen from the walrus-ivory panels of this casket. Tradition has it that this was the jewel box of Kunigunde, the wife of the German Emperor Henry II.

Above The best work in The Mammen style is to be seen in carved ornament, of which there is no finer example than the Bamberg casket. *Right* A Mammen-style human mask decorates a sword-mount from Sigtuna in Sweden.

The Mammen style is named after the designs on an axe found in the grave of a Danish Viking. On one side is a ragged pattern of tendrils; the other displays a human mask and a bird design (illustrated here). The bird's head is thrown back over its body and its outspread wings are of interlacing tendrils.

Stone sculpture

At the beginning of the Viking Age, the carving of stone monuments was already an old tradition on Gotland, but it was rarely practised in Sweden and was unknown in Norway and Denmark. In the ninth and tenth centuries even the erecting of rune-stones was uncommon. But with the spread of Christianity all this changed and by the eleventh century stone monuments were common throughout Scandinavia. By

Above A pair of Urnes-style beasts frame a human figure on a rune-stone from Ardre on Gotland.

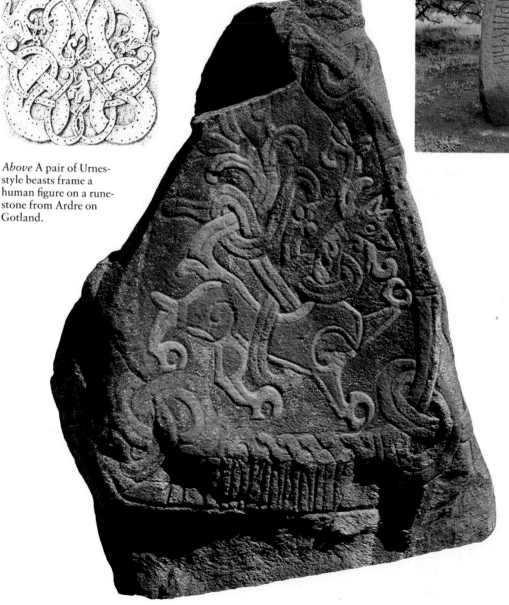

The fashion for erecting stone monuments in Scandinavia was perhaps established by King Harald's memorial to his parents at Jelling, *left*. One side of this massive stone depicts a proud beast fighting a snake that is coiled around its neck and body. Its tail and pigtail are treated as tendrils in the manner of those on the Mammen axe, ultimately borrowed from Western European art. The rune-stone from Skårby, *above*, also has an animal at its centre. But this seated figure of the lion-like 'great beast' is a pale imitation of that at Jelling. The paint on both stones is modern.

then new fashions had been set, and the majority of ornamented stones are decorated in the Ringerike and Urnes styles; often an animal's ribbon-shaped body is used to carry a runic inscription.

The Jelling stone

Harald Bluetooth's memorial stone at Jelling is important not only for its runic inscription and depiction of the Crucifixion, but also for the 'great beast' that occupies its third face. Here we see an animal in the Mammen style, big-bodied and with a foliate crest and tail, engaged in a struggle with a snake that is entwined around its body. Where royalty leads, noblemen follow suit. Such a massive boulder as Harald's, in the largely stone-free Danish landscape, would have been a source of wonder and admiration, and it soon had its imitations. An example from Skårby in southern Sweden is illustrated.

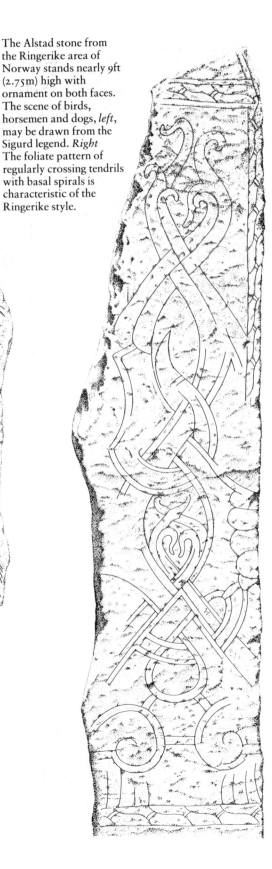

The Alstad stone from the Ringerike area of Norway stands nearly 9ft (2.75m) high with ornament on both faces. The scene of birds, horsemen and dogs, *left*, may be drawn from the Sigurd legend. *Right* The foliate pattern of regularly crossing tendrils with basal spirals is characteristic of the Ringerike style.

Left An 11th-century rune-stone from Lingsberg, in Uppland, Sweden, bears a cross, marking it out as a Christian memorial. The bodies of two Urnes-style animals carry the runic inscription, while an effete version of the 'great beast' occupies the centre of the stone.

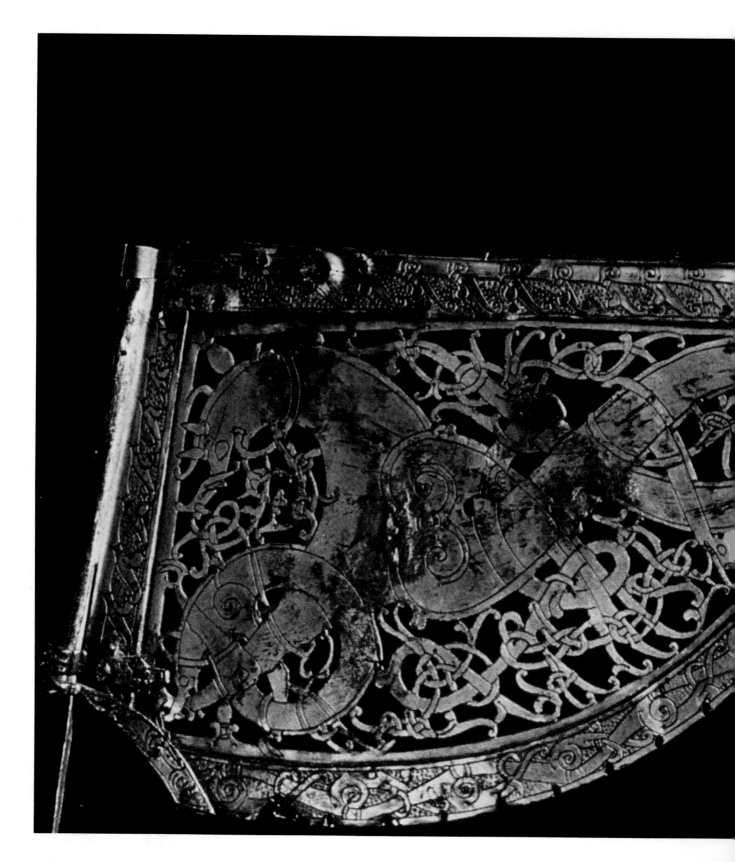

 he Ringerike style, which grew naturally out of the Mammen style during the first half of the eleventh century, emerged at a time when the custom of erecting stone monuments was spreading. It is in fact named after the carved slabs of a rich district of Norway to the north of Oslo, of which the Alstad stone illustrated on page 147 is one. The heavy spirals at the base of the foliate design on this stone have their origins in the spiral hips of the Mammen style; the tendrils themselves have become elongated, and cross each other regularly as they curl gracefully upwards. The gradual development of foliate patterns that took place in the Mammen style has become the principal feature of Ringerike. The Jellinge great beast however, was far from forgotten, as is clear from the Söderala vane.

This gilt-bronze vane from Söderala in Sweden will once have swung from the prow of an eleventh-century Viking ship. There is a 'great beast' mounted on top to keep watch ahead, while the holes along its curved edge were for the attachment of jangling chains or for streamers to act as wind indicators. Vanes of this type are shown in use on a thirteenth-century carving from Bergen. Its subsequent use was as the ornament on a church spire, as was the case with two similar vanes from the same period, from Norway and Gotland.

The three writhing animals in the central openwork panel of the vane continue the tradition of a combat motif, first established in Scandinavia by the sculptor of Harald's stone at Jelling. Something rather similar ornaments the end of the stone monument in St Paul's churchyard in London (see page 161). As on the vane, a lesser animal is looped around the front legs of a great beast, although the two do not appear to be engaged in actual conflict. The St Paul's stone is one of the finest monuments in the Scandinavian Ringerike style and shows how, under Cnut, England was once again introduced to the mainstream of Viking art.

The Söderala vane is a fine example of Ringerike style. The frame surrounding its openwork central panel is ornamented with incised patterns against a background of stamped dots. At the centre of the vane, among the dense undergrowth of tendrils, is a large dragon-like animal, with its foreleg extending into the bottom corner. Around this leg is looped a smaller animal with its jaws clamped firmly to the foot. Harder to spot is the third animal that completes this swirling composition. Its snout touches the curved edge just below the main animal's looped hindquarters; its snaky body tapers away into a series of tendrils.

The Urnes style

The sculptor of the first wooden church at Urnes used three animal motifs to build up his curving composition. A greyhound-like quadruped is seen here biting the neck of a lesser beast with only a single foreleg and hindleg. Around them thin ribbons (with occasional animal heads) snake their way through the looping design.

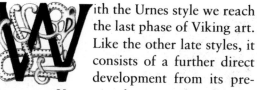

ith the Urnes style we reach the last phase of Viking art. Like the other late styles, it consists of a further direct development from its predecessor; Urnes is thus a refinement of Ringerike. It depends for its effects on an interplay of gracefully curving lines of different widths – sometimes swelling, sometimes tapering, but always on a curve. The tendril clusters so beloved of the Ringerike artist are abandoned; indeed foliate patterns have altogether had their day.

The Urnes style must have developed shortly before the middle of the eleventh century, for the animal ornament on a fluted silver bowl from a hoard at Lilla Valla in Gotland, buried about 1050, displays all its principal characteristics. This elegant bowl is an exceptionally fine masterpiece of the silversmith's craft; moreover, its design shows a restraint that is unusual in Viking art and it may thus appeal to modern eyes more than the crowded surfaces appreciated by the patrons of the day. It was hammered into shape from a flat sheet of silver and then the thirty-two grooves of its fluted body were beaten out; a ring was also raised from beneath the base to form a roundel in its interior, which is ornamented with an interlaced animal. The other ornament is confined to a band below the rim, around which eight elongated animals in confronted pairs are linked together into one continuous row by palmettes – bud-like devices that represent the sole survivals of the Ringerike foliate patterns. The ornament was incised and its surface left plain against a stippled background; finally, both the ornamented areas were lightly gilded.

The Urnes style takes its name from the woodcarving at the little church of Urnes in western Norway. This building is a stave-church (that is, it is built of tree trunks split vertically in two) dating from the twelfth century, but incorporated into its fabric are re-used portions of its predecessor, including the eleventh-century carvings. These carvings were described on page 138; however, it will be useful at this point to look more closely at the motifs.

Basically, the artist has created a new design based on the old combat motif, for the animals and snakes are all biting their neighbours. But see what has happened to the Ringerike great beast. Given the new Urnes look, he has become an effete and disdainful creature; every detail has been attenuated. Nevertheless, he is possessed of a certain elegance, and this becomes even more evident when he takes on a life of his own (with a single snake looped around his feet), as on an openwork brooch from Lindholm Høje.

The carvings at Urnes are a unique survival, but such would have been the style adopted for many of the first churches in Scandinavia. The wooden fragment from the church at Hørning in Denmark (see page 139) indicates that the style was widespread during its century of popularity. In Sweden it is common on rune-stones, while on Gotland there developed a particularly lively variant.

To a great extent the Urnes style will have been disseminated from the towns that were then developing apace over much of Scandinavia. Excavations at Trondheim in Norway show how the fully developed Urnes style was

A small silver brooch found at Lindholm Høje displays the true elegance of the Urnes style.

in use to ornament major pieces of household furnishing (see page 139), but also that its popularity was such that it was adapted at an everyday level for use on objects such as pins and spoons. And at the late Viking town of Lund there has been excavated the workshop of a jeweller who was casting bronze versions of the Lindholm Høje brooch during the early part of the twelfth century.

Although unusually restrained in its ornament for a piece of Viking art, this fluted silver bowl from a Gotlandic hoard at Lilla Valla carries a band of Urnes-style animals around its gilded rim.

Late Viking art in England & Ireland

An 11th-century English manuscript has an initial letter 'd' in the form of a Ringerike-style snake, showing how Anglo-Saxon art became influenced by that of Scandinavia under the Danish King Cnut.

The St Paul's stone in London is evidence that England was introduced to the Ringerike style while the Danish King Cnut was on the throne. Anglo-Saxon art of the time used foliate patterns in abundance, drawn originally from the art of the Frankish Empire, so it was compatible with the Ringerike style favoured by the followers of Cnut, and the two were on occasion successfully blended.

A late Anglo-Saxon manuscript preserved in the Cambridge University Library contains an initial 'd' in the form of a snake, which is quite as fine as the snake-like creature around the legs of the 'great beast' of the St Paul's stone (see page 161). The manuscript may have been written and ornamented in Gloucestershire, where a rather crude slab from Bibury shows that the style was certainly

known. On the other hand the Bibury slab cannot compare with one from Otley in West Yorkshire, which has excellent Ringerike-style tendrils of a quality nearer to that of the St Paul's stone.

The Urnes style never enjoyed the same popularity as Ringerike in England, but there is a small series of openwork brooches and mounts (such as that recently found in Lincoln) to show that there were Viking settlers who still wished to follow their native styles. It is rather more surprising to find it firmly established in sculpture outside the old area of Scandinavian settlement. The animals at the feet of a figure of Christ carved in the East Sussex church of Jevington have typically Urnes-style features.

More remarkable still is the popularity of the Ringerike and Urnes styles in Ireland, for until the later eleventh century native Irish art had remained virtually untouched by that of the Viking inhabitants of the new towns in their midst. We know, however, that in Dublin during the tenth and eleventh centuries there were artists trying out designs in both Scandinavian and Irish styles. Perhaps the skill and success of these metropolitan metalworkers led to their receiving commissions for work to be sent all over Ireland, so popularizing the Ringerike and Urnes styles.

In fact the final flowering of the Urnes style took place in Ireland, and under its influence some of the very finest pieces of Irish metalwork ever to be made were produced in the late eleventh and twelfth centuries. Among these pieces is the Cross of Cong, a processional cross made as a reliquary for a fragment of the True Cross, as its inscription records; it was commissioned by the King of Connacht, about 1123.

Romanesque

Although Viking art remained true to its traditions for three centuries, despite borrowings from other cultures, by the twelfth century the vitality had gone out of it. So there was no resistance in Scandinavia to the impact of the new Romanesque art. Romanesque art, with its robust qualities and occasional grotesqueries, in fact had much that appealed to Scandinavian taste; while at the same time it is hardly surprising that elements of the Urnes style occasionally found their way into the Romanesque of Scandinavia, Ireland and England.

Indeed in the remoter valleys and fjords of Scandinavia the motifs of Viking art lived on. A Norwegian wooden harness-bow of the twelfth century or later is covered with a gripping-beast motif; the Borre ring-chain continued to turn up all over the place in Scandinavian folk art.

But Viking art itself faded as the Viking Age faded. In this as in so many other ways it was a reflection of its period; by its study we can approach closer to the Viking people and appreciate their self-assurance, their extrovert nature and their technical skills. The fact that their art may be beyond our immediate comprehension should not lead us to neglect its study.

The Urnes-style Cross of Cong, from the early 12th century, is one of the finest pieces ever fashioned by Irish metalworkers.

Evidence that Viking styles lingered on in Scandinavian folk art after the Viking Age was over is provided by this 12th-century Norwegian harness-bow, which is decorated with gripping beasts.

Rune-masters & Skalds

The rock-carving at Ramsund, Södermanland, Sweden, shows the hero Sigurd stabbing the dragon Fafnir through the belly. The outlines of the dragon's body frame a runic inscription made by a woman called Sigrid in memory of her husband Holmger.

The Viking script

It is often thought that the Vikings were illiterate until they became good Catholics and learned the Roman alphabet, but to make this assumption is to take a simplified view of literacy, thinking of it only as the type of reading and writing we do today. From the second century AD – and perhaps earlier – the northern nations had had a script, as indeed had many of the other Germanic peoples. It was not intended for writing in ink or parchment, but rather was designed for cutting on wood with a knife-point. The English language retains a memory of this, for the word 'write' originally meant 'to score with a sharp tool'.

The advantages of the ancient northern method of recording over that used by Christian scribes are obvious when you think of the practical considerations. A medieval man wishing to write a manuscript had first to prepare the parchment from animal skin, then make the ink from oak galls and metallic salts, then the pen from a goose quill, and finally rule the surface with a sharp implement, before he was ready to begin. A Viking carried a knife and could pick up a twig anywhere. He shaved the twig until he had produced one or more smooth sides on which he could incise his letters from one end to the other. If he made a mistake he could easily cut it away. Of course, there were disadvantages in recording a message in this way. You could not write a very long one, for that would need one or more long pieces of wood, which would not be easy to manipulate or store. But for short texts it was ideal.

Runes on wood, metal, bone and stone

The alphabet the Vikings used is called 'runic', each letter known as a 'rune'. Later medieval Norse sources often mention runic messages cut on sticks, but unfortunately wood does not preserve well over the centuries, and until recently few runic wooden objects from early times had been found. Then, from the excavations of medieval Bergen, came a great collection of pieces of wood with runes on them, a few of them letters on business, personal or political subjects. Further finds of this sort have appeared elsewhere, even occasional ones from the Viking Age, which suggests that many of the Vikings may have used this form of correspondence.

Nobody knows exactly when or where the runic characters were invented. It was several centuries before the Viking period and probably somewhere near the Roman Empire, since many of the letters of the early inscriptions resemble those of the Roman alphabet; although, because they were developed for cutting on wood, they have their own characteristic shapes. Curves were avoided because they were hard to cut, and so were horizontal lines that might coincide with the wood grain and be difficult to make out. Consequently, the earliest runes consisted largely of vertical stems that were cut against the grain, and sloping lines that would stand out clearly from it. By the beginning of the

The damaged rune-stone from Tu, Jæren, Norway, dates from the late 10th century. Its inscription tells that 'Helgi raised this stone in memory of his brother Ketil.'

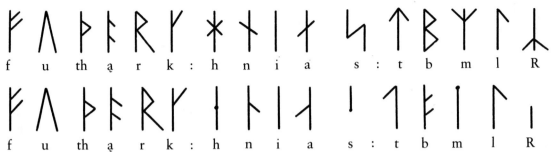

f u th ạ r k : h n i a s : t b m l R

f u th ạ r k : h n i a s : t b m l R

Viking Age the Scandinavian rune-masters had developed an alphabet quite distinct from those of other Germanic peoples, such as the Anglo-Saxons, the Frisians and the Continental Germans. It had sixteen letters, and from the values of its first six characters is called the *futhark*. Even within Scandinavia there was no standard form of the letters, and the different inscriptions vary a good deal. The Vikings used two main types of runes, with numbers of lesser or local variants. One type is called the Common or Danish *futhark* (although it also occurs outside Denmark), and the other is the short-twig or Swedo-Norwegian *futhark* (although again it is not confined to those countries).

A quick glance at these two alphabets will show that they are not very efficient. They need more letters, and they need them better distributed over the sounds of the language. For instance, although there are characters for *t*, *k* and *b*, there are none for *d*, *g* and *p*. Although there are two symbols for different types of *a*, there are none for *e* and *o*. In the post-Viking Age the rune-masters invented new symbols to fill up these gaps, but the Vikings remained content with sixteen letters. Consequently, the spelling of their runic inscriptions is very peculiar. When the carver wanted to represent *d*, he had to use *t* instead; for *g* he used *k*; for *p* he used *b*; and he had to manage as best he could when it came to vowels. Thus the Danish King Gormr (Gorm) appears on his memorial stone as *kurmR*, and the Danish King Svein (Swein) is *suin*. Moreover, since the spelling practice allowed a rune-master to omit *n* when it came before a consonant, a man called Thormundr appears

in runic spelling as *thurmutR*. From this it will be seen that runic inscriptions are not easy to read, and there is a good deal of dispute about the meanings of some of them.

Though the runic characters were originally designed for cutting on wood, they were soon adapted for other materials, many of them more durable. Consequently, there survive a lot of runic inscriptions on metal, bone and stone. Here the carvers could use different techniques for cutting the letters, since they were no longer dealing with a fibrous material and did not have to worry about the direction of grain. Cutting curves was less of a problem on stone, and so the loops of letters like *th*, *b* and *r* were rounded. Different stones required different tools. The fairly soft slates of the Isle of Man were probably incised with a heavy knife. Danish inscriptions were often picked out with the point of a small axe. At Bridekirk, Cumbria,

The font at Bridekirk, Cumbria, has a line of Norse runes near its base giving an English text. The carver has portrayed himself in the bottom left corner, chipping away at his work with a mallet and chisel.

Above The runes of the stone from Dynna, Norway, commemorate a girl, Astrid, who was *mær hǫnnurst á Hadalandi*, 'the handiest, [that is, most skilful] girl in Hadeland'. She was apparently a Christian, since the face of the stone has a group of Epiphany scenes carved on it.

Right This piece of a human skull was found at Ribe, Jutland. It dates from *c*. 800, and its inscription shows early letter forms. The text is hard to interpret, but seems to be a charm, invoking Odin and others, to give protection against sickness.

is a rune-incised font that shows the carver chipping away at the stone with a mallet and chisel. On metal, runes could be incised, scratched or punched. Some later Viking kings issued coins, and here the legends would be cut in reverse on dies from which the coins were stamped. Occasionally the die-cutters used runes for their legends, as in issues of the eleventh-century Danish King Svein Estridsson. Altogether in the Viking Age runes were used for quite a wide range of texts: memorials, boundary posts, marker-stones for bridges and roads, owner's or maker's marks, as well as for casual graffiti by Vikings whiling away the time. Runes were also used in magic formulae (although there is a tendency for epigraphists to think that all in-

scriptions that they find hard to interpret are magic), as on the Ribe skull fragment; this has led some to suggest that runes were in origin a magic script, though the theory is now largely discounted. How many Vikings could read or write runes we do not know, nor how they acquired the skills. Nor do we know what sort of man the rune-master – the man who cut the runes – was, how trained, how professional and how highly regarded.

Painted rune-stones

Inevitably, many runic monuments are now hard to read because of the damage, corrosion or weathering they have suffered over the years. The rune-stones have deteriorated in another important respect. In some – perhaps most – cases they were meant to be painted. Nearly all this colouring has worn off with exposure to the weather, but here and there tiny traces remain that encourage reconstruction. The chief colours used were red, brown, blue and black, and the traditional colour for the letters themselves was red. A dragon pattern on a rune-stone in London shows the beasts coloured in dark red and black against a creamy background, the animals' bodies spattered with white spots. Presumably the runes were painted too, but no colouring remains. For evidence of this we

On a painted rune-stone from Köping church, Öland, different parts of the sentence have been picked out in different colours. The subject, 'the brothers' (at the left), is in red; the verb, 'had put up', in white; the object, 'a stone', in red; and so on.

must turn to fragments of painted rune-stones that have been discovered in Sweden, most of them embedded in the walls of medieval churches where their paint was protected. From Köping church, Öland, came about sixty bits of stone, with both incised lines and decorative features coloured. In the texts different words would sometimes be given different colours, which helped the reader to divide up a sequence of letters into its individual words, and in one case the painter used different colours to draw attention to different parts of the sentence, so that the painting assisted the interpretation. Any errors or uncertainty that the carver left in his runes could be amended or clarified in the painting. However, in most cases such aids towards reading inscriptions are now lost.

Significance of runic inscriptions

The runic inscriptions from the Viking Age are important for three reasons. They record early stages of the Scandinavian tongues, and so tell us something of the language the Vikings spoke. Their distribution throughout the world is some indication of the geographical areas the Vikings visited. Their content shows us aspects of the Viking Age that are not recorded elsewhere; from them we know how the Vikings saw themselves.

Runic finds in Scandinavia & overseas

Below One of two major stones at Lingsberg, Uppland. Three men set them up to mark a causeway over a marsh, and this one commemorates Ulfrik 'who took two payments of geld in England'.

Below right The carved boulder at Sjusta, Uppland, is a memorial to a man who died at Novgorod.

The scatter of their runic inscriptions plots the voyages of the Vikings. Here, of course, the runic stones are the most important since they are the least portable. An inscribed weapon or jewel could pass from hand to hand, be sold or stolen, and end up far from its place of origin, so that the site of its discovery may have little to do with the Vikings; but few would think of lugging a heavy chunk of inscribed stone from one place to another. Thus the distribution of the rune-stones (and of Viking inscriptions on standing monuments) should tell us what lands the Vikings travelled in and settled. Of course, the evidence is not as simple as this, for the use of runes was spread unevenly through the various peoples and through their different social classes. Denmark has some two hundred Viking Age rune-stones, distributed fairly evenly over the country. Norway has only about forty, less evenly scattered, with something of a concentration in the south-west province of Jæren. Sweden's rune-stones number thousands, with particular groupings in Uppland, Västergötland and Östergötland, as well as the islands of Gotland and Öland.

Overseas, too, the distribution was inexplicably uneven. We know from written sources that Iceland was settled largely by Vikings of Norwegian stock in the years 870–930, but that island has as yet yielded no Viking Age runic inscriptions, although the script was used there in the later Middle Ages. Normandy, a Danish colony, has no runic texts at all. From the Faeroes, also occupied by Norsemen, only a couple of rune-stones are known. From Ireland, where the Vikings kept a strong presence for centuries, there are only three or four rune-stones, although there is also a rune-inscribed sword-fitting and the recent Dublin excavations have produced informal scratchings on bone and wood. In

ᚠᚱᚴᛒ:ᚠᛅᚦᛏᛏ:ᚠᛁᛏᚱᛁ:ᛄᛅᚱᚠᛅᛋᛏᚱ

England, the Danelaw and the Norwegian settlements of the north-west left behind a handful of rune-stones, mostly battered and fragmentary, though important among these are the early eleventh-century gravestone from St Paul's churchyard, London, and a fragment of a stone found at Cnut's capital, Winchester, while from Lincoln comes a bone comb-case that boasts in runes that 'Thorfast made a good comb.' Mainland Scotland and the Hebrides show a small scatter of rune-stones, as do the Shetlands and the Orkneys (the Orkneys were to produce many more inscriptions in the post-Viking period). In contrast to this sparsity is the remarkable case of the Isle of Man, which has nearly thirty runic stones and crosses whose characters show similarities with those of Jæren in the south-west of Norway.

Runes in the New World?

Further west are the settlements on Greenland (whose runes are mainly post-Viking) and the American continent. Americans, particularly those of Scandinavian descent, have long yearned to find runic confirmation of their ancestors' exploits in the New World to parallel the authentic archaeological discovery of a Viking site in Newfoundland. This has sometimes led them to interpret as runes marks on standing stones, or even on early buildings, that are accidental, weathering, or graffiti of some other origin. However, no expert runologist has yet accepted any American inscription as genuine. A famous fake is the Kensington stone from Minnesota, whose text claims that a group of Swedes and Norwegians visited there on a voyage of discovery in 1362 (or according to some 1462). After decades of publicity and a good deal of controversy, the Minnesota historian Theodore C. Blegen finally exposed the imposture in a book written in 1968.

Three views of a Viking rune-stone found in St Paul's churchyard, London, in 1852. The middle picture shows the remaining vestiges of Viking Age paint, while that at the top is a reconstruction of how the colouring may have originally appeared. The runes are cut in two lines on the edge of the stone, and tell that 'Ginna and Toki had this stone set up.'

Eastern discoveries

From the East the finds, although sparser, are in some ways more exciting. There are a couple of casual discoveries of inscribed bones at trading posts at Lübeck and Kamien Pomorski on the south Baltic coast and four known inscriptions from Russia. The most northerly of the Russian finds is a wooden stick from an occupation level at Staraja Ladoga. Cut on it is a verse inscription, presumably Swedish, dated to the early Viking Age. Since such an object has no intrinsic value, it is unlikely to have been brought into Ladoga from outside, and so was probably cut there by a Scandinavian speaker for Scandinavian readers; which suggests that a Swedish community lived in this Russian market town. Further south, in Novgorod, an eleventh-century Swedish visitor used a piece of bone, perhaps from his dinner, on which to cut a *futhark*, although why we do not know. The most important of the Russian inscriptions is on a memorial stone found on the island of Berezany at the mouth of the river Dnieper. It records the death of one of a pair of trading partners

('Brand made this stone coffin for his partner Karl ...') and is something of a legal announcement recording that Brand had taken over the business and was responsible to Karl's heirs for his share of the profits. Further south again, at Piraeus near Athens, a

In 1687 the Venetians carried home a marble lion from Piraeus, Athens, as a prize of war. While still on its Greek site it had been seen by a visiting Swede who carved on it a runic text. Part of the badly worn inscription can still be traced.

travelling Viking came upon the marble figure of a lion, and cut on it a serpentine band enclosing a runic text. The lion is now in Venice, but the figure is so badly worn and weathered that its letters are practically illegible, although their identification as runes is not in doubt. Perhaps the most evocative of these Eastern inscriptions is a casual graffito on the marble ledge of a gallery of the great church of Hagia Sophia in Istanbul. A series of rough scratches, it is only partly legible, but the name 'Halfdan' has been read.

A view of the great church of Hagia Sophia, Istanbul, from the gallery on which a Viking scratched his name. The runes can be seen on the balustrade at the bottom of the picture.

Runes recording Viking activities

The rune-stones of Scandinavia confirm this picture of widespread activity, and show the Vikings in their various capacities of pirates, professional soldiers, merchants, and farmers who brought home the profits of their expeditions to invest in land and stock. A silver neck-ring from a hoard found in Senja, Troms, northern Norway, carries a verse runic text that looks as thought it probably records the source of the hoarder's wealth.

Fórum drengia Fríslands á vit
ok vígs fǫtum vér skiptum.

We went to meet the lads of Frisia
and we it was who split the spoils of war.

Both Norwegians and Swedes were among the mercenaries who joined Cnut's army to plunder England in the early eleventh century. In Galteland, Aust-Agder, south Norway, a stone, now broken into fragments, was put up by Arnstein in memory of his son Bjor 'who met his death in the army when Cnut attacked England'. A man called Ali of Väsby, Uppland, Sweden, was luckier: he survived to erect a stone in his own honour, recording as a memorable fact that he 'took a payment of danegeld from Cnut in England.' Another Uppland stone, from Yttergärde, is in memory of a man called Ulf who 'took three payments of geld in England. The first was the one that Tosti paid, then Thorkel, then Cnut.' Here he names in turn three leading Viking commanders. Although he was a professional killer, Ulf was a Christian, or at any rate those who commemorated him were, for they ask that 'God and God's mother help his soul.' At Valleberga, Skåne (now in Sweden, but in Viking times part of Denmark), is a stone that two men put up 'in memory of Manni and Sveni: God help their souls, but they lie in London' – as presumably did the unknown man after whom Ginna and Toki put up their dragon-carved stone in St Paul's churchyard in that city.

In memoriam for Eastern adventurers

Many Swedish rune-stones record exploits in the East, supplementing the meagre written sources in this field. At Veda, Uppland, is a stone in memory of Irenmund who 'bought this farm, and he made his money *í Gǫrðum.*' The last phrase means literally 'in the towns', and is the common expression for the Scandinavian trading strongholds of western Russia. At Mervalla, Södermanland, is a monument to the skipper of a trading vessel; it breaks into verse as it records his fame:

Hann oft siglt til Simgala
dýrum knerri um Domisnes.

He often sailed to Semgallen
round Domesnäs in his fine ship.

Domesnäs is the point of Courland, and this Swede made a regular journey into the Gulf of Finland, where the great river Dvina affords an entry into Russia. More adventurous were

The rune-stone that Ali put up in his own honour at Väsby. He was one of the Swedes who took part in the attacks on England in the early 11th century, and here he records how he 'took Cnut's geld in England.'

those who made the perilous journey through Russia and across the Black Sea to Byzantium (which the Vikings called *Mikligarðr*, the Great City), or who penetrated far into the East in search of wealth. At Ed, Uppland, is a stone whose runes were commissioned by a man, Rognvald, who says that 'in Greece he was captain of the host.' By 'Greece' the Vikings meant the Eastern Roman Empire, and since Byzantium had a force of Viking Imperial Guards in the eleventh century, it is likely that Rognvald was one of their officers. A group of nearly thirty rune-stones from the region of Lake Mälar stresses the dangers of these expeditions. From them we learn that in the first half of the eleventh century a major expedition set out to seek fortune in the East, under the command of a man called Ingvar. Few – perhaps none – returned, and the stones commemorate the young lads of wealthy families who perished far from their homes. One example is at Svinnegarn, Uppland, where a group of stones was put up in memory of Banki, 'who had a ship of his own, and steered it east in Ingvar's host'. Another stone, at Lundby, Södermanland, tells of Skardi, 'who went from here east with Ingvar; son of Eyvind, he lies in Serkland.' *Serkland* is not a very precise place-name, but it is used to mean the land of dark-skinned peoples round the Mediterranean and in the Middle East, and here probably refers to part of the Arab dominions. Most impressive of these Ingvar inscriptions is the one from Gripsholm, Södermanland, put up in memory of Ingvar's brother Harald by his mother Tola. Following the memorial text there is a verse inscription:

þeir fóru drengila fiarri at gulli
ok austarla erni gáfu
dóu sunnarla á Serklandi.

Like men they journeyed far for gold
and in the east they fed the eagle,
in the south they died, in Serkland.
The poet sees the adventure romantically. These young men travelled in search of gold.

They feasted the eagles on the enemies they killed in battle. And they died in the south far from their homeland.

Rights and virtues

Not all inscriptions describe this active Viking life. Some reveal its more peaceful and domestic aspects; such a one is the stone at Dynna, Norway, put up in memory of Astrid who was 'the most skilful girl in Hadeland'. Or an inscription may record a man's possessions and his contribution to the amenities of his neighbourhood. An example is a group of stones in Uppland, Sweden, erected by a local magnate, Jarlabanki; at Täby, still beside the road that it com-

The Gripsholm stone, Södermanland, in memory of Harald, who died on his brother Ingvar's ill-fated Eastern expedition. The runic band is in the form of a snake, the text beginning at its head. At the top right begins the verse section, its first word set outside the band.

Right The runic face of the greater Jelling stone, dating from the 10th century. King Harald Bluetooth set it up for his parents. *Below* One of Jarlabanki's stones at Täby. The inscription begins at bottom centre and curls round to the left (*iarlabaki lit raisa stain thisa atsik kuikuan*), continuing from the bottom round to the right. *Below right* The runes on the Hunterston brooch give the undivided text, *malbrithaastilk*, 'Melbrigda owns this brooch', followed by arbitrary forms to fill in the rest of the space available.

memorates, is one that reads 'Jarlabanki put up this stone in his own lifetime, and made this causeway for his soul, and he alone possessed the whole of Täby: may God help his soul.' The great inscription at Jelling, Jutland, glorifies a royal dynasty: 'King Harald had this monument made in memory of his father Gorm and his mother Thyri: this was the Harald who won for himself all Denmark and Norway, and made the Danes Christians.' A stone may also act as a legal document, as does the Berezany text. A similar case is an inscription at Nora, Uppland, Sweden, which asserts a claim to land: 'Bjorn, Finnvid's son, had this rock carved in memory of his brother Olaf. He was treacherously killed on Finnveden. God help his soul. This farm is the rightful estate and the family inheritance of the sons of Finnvid at Älgesta.' As well as these formal texts cut in runes, there are homely ones, inscriptions naming the maker of an object – as on the Lincoln comb-case – or its owner. A splendid Celtic-style brooch found at Hunterston, Strathclyde, has on it inscribed in runes 'Melbrigda owns this brooch.' Though the possessor had a Celtic name, the language is Scandinavian, and this may give a hint as to the way the Norsemen were integrated into the communities of west Scotland.

A cultural record

So much for the Vikings' activities. Equally important to the historian is to know something of the temper of the Viking Age, the sort of behaviour that the Vikings admired; and this, too, the runic memorials tell us. They describe a society that knew it was aristocratic and heroic, its members bound together by the ties of family relationship or by the duties that were expected, on either side, by lord and man. They praise the heroic virtues of valour, endurance, generosity, loyalty, respect for honour and truth to one's word. Not of course that Vikings always held to these virtues. A fragment of a runic cross at Braddan, Isle of Man, has preserved for ever the name of a man who behaved villainously, and there is no doubt that the carver intended, not only to cut the name (now lost) of the dead man, but to publicize this shameful behaviour: '. . . but Hrosketil betrayed under trust a man bound to him by oaths.' Inevitably, however, it was those who did their Viking duty whose fame was most often recorded. A king might recognize the loyalty of a retainer, as on one of the stones from Hedeby, north Germany: 'King Svein set up this stone in memory of his retainer Skardi, who had taken part in an expedition westwards, but now met his death at Hedeby.' Often the thought of these heroic virtues inspired the inscriber to poetry. A stone at Turinge, Södermanland, keeps the memory of Thorstein, one of a pair of brothers well respected in the neighbourhood. Among those who subscribed to the monument were the *húskarlar*, the household retinue. The verse of praise reads:

Brœðr váru þeir beztra manna
á landi ok í liði úti,
heldu sína húskarla vel.
Hann fell í orrostu austr í Gǫrðum,
liðs foryngi landmanna beztr.

These brothers were the best of men
at home and abroad on expedition.
They maintained their retinue well.
Thorstein fell in battle east in Russia,
army leader, best of landmen.

The remaining runes on the face of the cross at Braddan, Isle of Man. The text begins abruptly at the left of the lower line: *nroskitil:uilti:i: triku*, then continues on the upper line: *aithsoara: siin*. In standard Old Norse this becomes [e]*n Hrossketill vélti í tryggu eiðsvara siin*: literally, 'and Hrosketil deceived under trust his oathsworn [friend].'

Presumably what pleased the *húskarlar* was that Thorstein was a generous lord, supplying his men with plenty of good things. On the other hand, a Viking might win respect by fighting to the death and refusing to surrender, like the man commemorated at Sjörup, Skåne. This inscription begins simply, 'Saxi put up this stone in memory of his comrade Asbjorn, Toki's son', and then goes on to a short verse that explains why Asbjorn both needed and deserved commemoration:

Sá fló eigi at Upsǫlum
en vá meðan (hann) vápn hafði.

He did not flee at Uppsala,
but fought while he could hold weapons.

Skaldic verse
The poems quoted so far are in a fairly simple verse form that relies heavily on alliteration for its effect. However, there are some runic monuments that record a more complex form

of verse, of the type known as skaldic. 'Skaldic' derives from the Icelandic word *skåld*, poet, though that word is used in English to mean a Norse court poet, or a writer who composed a similar sort of elaborate verse. A runic example of skaldic poetry is cut on the late Viking memorial stone at Karlevi on the Swedish island of Öland. After a simple commemorative inscription in prose, the text breaks into a verse in praise of the dead man. It is given here in normalized spelling and in literal translation:

> Fólginn liggr hinns fylgðu
> – flestr vissi þat – mestar
> dæðir dolga Þrúðar
> draugr í þeimsi haugi.
> Munat reið-Viðurr ráða
> rógstarkr í Danmarku
> Endils iǫrmungrundar
> ǫrgrandari landi.

> Hidden lies he whom followed
> – most have known that – the greatest
> virtues, of the Thrud of battles
> the tree, in this mound.
> No chariot-Odin will rule
> battle-strong in Denmark
> of Endil's spacious ground,
> more free from fault, land.

Read straight through, the translation does not make much sense, for two good reasons. Each half-stanza has two or three phrases mixed up together, and the reader has to disentangle them; the poet, instead of using everyday language, has employed elaborate images, known as 'kennings', which the reader has to be taught to understand. If we rearrange the wording of this stanza we get the following statements: 'Hidden in this mound lies the tree of the Thrud of battles whom – as most people knew – the greatest virtues followed. No chariot-Odin of Endil's spacious ground, strong in battle, more free from fault, will rule land in Denmark.'

So much for the reordering, but what about the meaning of the kennings? Thrud is the name of Thor's daughter, a minor deity. The

Thrud of battles is therefore a war goddess or valkyrie. The tree of the valkyrie is a warrior, who stands firm in battle like a tree rooted to the ground. Endil is a sea king, so his spacious ground is the ocean, and the ocean's chariot is a ship. The Odin, god, who controls the ship is its captain. If we substitute these explanations for the kennings we get a simple set of comments: 'Hidden in this mound lies the warrior whom – as most people knew – the greatest virtues followed. No ship's captain, strong in battle, more free from fault, will rule land in Denmark.'

As a historical statement this is not much, though it does tell us that a Viking sea warrior who was buried with ceremony on a Swedish island was a landowner in Denmark, and from that we might conclude that the various Viking countries were no more separate entities than are their modern counterparts. But the inscription does reveal an important piece of cultural information. The elaborate verse with its intricate word-order and its complex images was meant to be read and understood, otherwise there was no point in cutting it. That means there must have been a literate audience who had been educated to understand verse as difficult as this. However, we have still not seen just how difficult this verse form is. Examine the stanza in detail and you will see its complexity. It is a typical example of a commonly used metrical pattern called *dróttkvætt*, which means something like 'court metre'. The stanza has eight lines. Each line has six syllables, and three of them are stressed and three unstressed, although the stress patterns vary from line to line. In each even line there are two syllables that rhyme (*flestr*/*mest-*; *draugr*/*haug-*; *-starkr*/*-mark-*; *-grand-*/*land-*). In each odd line there are two stressed syllables with part-rhyme, that is the syllables end with the same consonant but contain different vowels (*fólg-*/*fylg-*; *dæð-*/*Þrúð-*; *reið-*/*ráð-*; *End-*/*grund-*). Moreover, in each odd line there are two stressed syllables that begin with the same sound, and these alliterate with the first syllable of the following even line (*fólg-*/*fylg-*/*flestr*; *dæð-*/*dolg-*/ *draugr*; and so on). To get all this detail into a taut stanza form requires a skilled and trained poet. Indeed, it requires a school of poets, and also an audience that knows what to look for in a verse; from which we may conclude that the Vikings were not just a crowd of axe-happy hooligans, as they are so often portrayed, but people with a literature that demanded sophistication and culture.

A single verse was hard enough, but a complete long poem might have twenty or forty such stanzas divided into an introductory section, a concluding section and a number of groups in between, each with its own refrain. It would be too long to record in runes, and had to be preserved in the poet's memory. Indeed, the elaborate rhyming and alliteration were conventional devices to help the composer to memorize his poem.

The skald and his poetry

Skaldic poetry was in the main occasional poetry. It showed the poet's reaction to current events, to something that had just happened to him, or to a prince he was visiting. Many poems consist of a single verse – the Karlevi stone gives an example – and very often these verses have been preserved in manuscript texts of a rather later date. In particular they are found in the Icelandic prose narratives called sagas, which were written in the thirteenth or fourteenth centuries. The sagas suggest that a skilled poet could compose one of these *dróttkvætt* stanzas on the spur of the moment, to record his instant reaction to some notable experience. Nearly all we know of the life-style of the skald derives from these later sagas. Although they cannot be relied upon as history, we can probably believe something of what they tell us about skalds. For most of the Viking Age skaldic poetry seems to have been an Icelandic speciality. The poet was a young man of good family in Iceland travelling abroad for fun, experience, adventure,

money, to make important connections or to win a reputation. If he could compose good verse he was welcome at any of the great courts of northern Europe, with the Viking kings of Norway or of Sweden, Denmark, Dublin or York, or the great earl of the Orkneys. He would be made a member of the prince's retinue, and would serve in return as recorder of his lord's great deeds, as public entertainer or as private counsellor. At some time or other he would be expected to produce a poem in his lord's honour, a long poem with a pattern of refrains known as a *drápa*, if it were for a king, or perhaps a shorter poem without refrain, a *flokkr*, for someone of lesser importance. A poem might praise a living king, or be a funeral ode recording his exploits for his children, and it is these poems that supply much of the historical fact known about Viking kings. Poems such as this have often survived only by being quoted in Icelandic sagas, and especially in those called *konunga sǫgur*, the sagas of kings. The thirteenth-century Icelander Snorri Sturluson, author of the most famous collection of these sagas, *Heimskringla*, recounted in his introduction his sources of knowledge of the early kings of Norway. The most important evidence, he thought, was:

> . . . what is said in those poems that were declaimed in front of the princes themselves or their sons. We accept as true all that those poems tell about their travels and battles. For it is the practice of skalds to praise most the man whose presence they are in, and nobody would dare to tell the man himself about deeds which everybody who heard – even the man himself – knew to be lies and deceit. That would be scorn, not praise.

Nobody who has sat through after-dinner speeches in honour of public men will be much convinced by this argument, but even if the poems do not tell the truth about the kings they praise, and certainly not the whole truth, at least they show what qualities Viking poets thought a king should be praised for.

The memorial stone of the Viking chief Sibbi the Good, at Karlevi, Öland. Its long and detailed inscription begins with a prose passage naming the dead man, and then goes on to a strophe of skaldic poetry in his praise.

Odes and praise poems

Sometimes the saga-writer cited a long section of the poem, perhaps even all of it. An example is *Hákonarmál*, a funeral ode to the tenth-century Norwegian King Hakon, and quoted in his various sagas. Hakon was brought up at the court of King Athelstan of Wessex, and so was, at least in name, a Christian: hence his title 'the Good'. Despite this, when he died of wounds after one of those inter-Scandinavian skirmishes that were so common in the Viking Age, his skald wrote a pagan poem about him. The skald's name was Eyvind, and he was nicknamed 'Despoiler of Skalds' because, having few ideas of his own, he pinched those of others, and this ode on Hakon is one of his thefts, for it bears a marked resemblance to a rather earlier poem commemorating King Eirik, nicknamed 'Bloodaxe'. Eyvind's poem shows Hakon in his last battle. Odin, god of war, sends out two valkyries to choose from the warriors on show someone valiant enough to come and live in his hall at Valholl. They pick Hakon, and direct the battle so that he holds the field and puts his enemies to flight. Then they summon him to join Odin (the poet's way of saying that he dies from the effects of the fight). Hakon tries to refuse, and complains that Odin should not seize him in his moment of triumph, but in the end his wrath is turned away and the gods welcome the mighty soldier. The ode ends with verses glorifying Hakon as a king without equal:

> Mun óbundinn
> a ýta sjǫt
> Fenrisulfr of fara
> áðr jafngóðr
> á auða trǫð
> konungmaðr komi.

> Freed from his bonds
> to the home of men
> the wolf Fenrir will run
> before there comes so good
> a man of royal birth
> to the desolate fields.

In two ways Eyvind's poem is not a typical skaldic praise poem. It is in simpler form than the common *dróttkvætt*, and it tells a story. Most skaldic poems are not strict narrative. Instead of describing events, they allude to them, and these allusions are often tantalizing. The skald assumed his audience knew what he was talking about because they knew their prince's history, so he would describe a battle or a voyage conventionally and with a minimum of detail. Here in literal translation is a single verse from a poem that Ottar the Black composed about Olaf Haraldsson of Norway (St Olaf):

> Prince, I learned that heavy
> your army far from ships,
> reddened Ringmere Heath,
> piled up a heap of slain, with blood.
> Fell before you, before it ceased,
> people of the land, in the shields' clashing,
> the army of the English, to the earth,
> frantic, and many in flight.

Sorted into sentences (and there are slightly different ways of doing this), this becomes:

> Prince I learned that your army, far
> from their ships, piled up a heavy heap
> of slain and reddened Ringmere Heath
> with blood. Before it ceased, the people
> of the land, the army of the English,
> frantic, fell to the earth before you in
> the shields' clashing, and many in flight.

All of which says little more than that Olaf Haraldsson beat the English at Ringmere Heath in Norfolk.

Another skald, Sigvat, also wrote a poem to Olaf and included a verse on the same battle. In straightforward prose this says:

> Once more Olaf, for the seventh time,
> set up a sword-meeting in Ulfcetel's
> land, as I shall tell. All the English stood
> arrayed at Ringmere Heath as Harald's
> son stirred up trouble. Men fell there.

Equally conventional, this adds another bit of information, that Ringmere was in Ulfcetel's land. Anglo-Saxon historians know Ulfcetel well, for he was the East Anglian commander who fought bravely against marauding

The top part of this incised stone from a grave-field near Stenkyrka, Gotland, shows a mounted warrior and before him a woman, perhaps a valkyrie, offering a drinking horn.

Vikings in the early eleventh century. No contemporary English source locates a battle at Ringmere, but the twelfth-century chronicler Florence of Worcester names it, and this is the battle of the *Anglo-Saxon Chronicle* entry for 1010 in which the Vikings routed an entire English army except for the Cambridgeshire levy, which stood firm. The *Chronicle* calls the Viking army a Danish one, but these verses show that there was a contingent of Norwegians fighting under their future king. By probing the skaldic poems in this way we can find out a lot of detail about the Viking Age that is not recorded elsewhere, though it has to be disentangled from turgid tributes to the valour of the princes who paid the poets.

Skald and lord

A skald's poems were not always sycophantic, for he had a certain freedom of speech with his lord, and courtiers would sometimes use him to break unpalatable news or give advice that would be ill received from anyone else. Magnus, son of the royal martyr Olaf, took control of Norway in 1035 on the death of Cnut of Denmark. According to his saga he began by taking revenge on those who had opposed his father, stripping them of their goods and honours in defiance of the law. Not surprisingly, he became widely unpopular and there was danger of revolt. The King's friends chose his skald Sigvat to tell the King that his behaviour was impolitic, and he did it in a series of verses called *Bersǫglisvísur* (*Plain-speaking Verses*). From them we get a clear picture of the state of the kingdom in the 1030s, and the relationship between monarch and people. Sigvat began by asserting his loyalty to Magnus, and his willingness to fight for him. He listed the kings who had preceded Magnus, showing that they were respected because they had kept the legal contract with their subjects and protected them from exploitation. Then, asking forgiveness for his bluntness, he told him how the landowners were complaining that Magnus had broken the law he had vowed, as King of Norway, to keep:

> Great prince, who is urging you to go back on your promises? . . . A king who will hold his people must stick to his word. It is unseemly, lord, for you to break your oaths. Who, king, is urging you to slaughter your servants' cattle? It is unjust for a ruler to behave like this in his own country. Never before has a young king been so advised. Your men are getting weary of this robbery. The people are angry, prince. . . . There is one thing that everybody is saying, 'My lord is taking the rightful property of his servants.' The noble landowners are rising in wrath.

Sigvat criticized his king fearlessly, but it was in a poem that asserted the positive values on which the Norse kingdom was built: a contractual relationship of mutual help between lord and people, a respect for laws and promises within a Viking community (whatever you might do to people outside it), and a recognition of the importance of the family and the continuity of its estates.

Skaldic verse as poetry

Of course it is unfair to treat skaldic verse in this way, simply as a source of historical knowledge. It was intended as literature, and no literal translation can give the original's richness of texture and its poetic quality. To find something of the poetry we must turn to a version made by a modern poet, further from the detail of the Old Norse but getting its general sense and feeling. Here is how John Lucas translates a vigorous Viking verse by the great tenth-century Icelandic poet Egil Skallagrimsson:

> I've been with sword and spear
> slippery with bright blood
> where kites wheeled. And how well
> we violent vikings clashed!
> Red flames ate up men's roofs,
> raging we killed and killed;
> and skewered bodies sprawled
> sleepy in town gate-ways.

From Odin to Christ

Among the Viking Age burials at Lindholm Høje in Jutland, Denmark, are about 200 marked by stones set in the form of a ship – symbolizing the idea of death as a voyage into the unknown.

Paganism

At the start of the Viking Age virtually everyone in the Scandinavian countries was still pagan; there having been very little contact with Christianity. Through the following centuries knowledge of Christian belief came to these countries in a variety of ways. Raiders who plundered and killed in church and monastery looted artifacts of Christian significance such as crosses and chalices. These were usually melted down for the value of the metal, but some fine objects were brought home as souvenirs. Christian men and women were among those captured and taken back as slaves; their religion may have had little influence on their captors, but must have added something to the general knowledge. The Viking traders met and had peaceable dealings with Christian merchants abroad, in both the Roman West and the Greek Byzantine East. Viking mercenaries served in the armies of Christian leaders, and were sometimes required to undergo provisional baptismal ceremonies. Finally, Christian missionaries came to Scandinavia, and their teaching was carried on to Scandinavia's Atlantic colonies, the Faeroe Islands, Iceland and Greenland. The process was gradual, but by the eleventh century most of Scandinavia had been formally converted, though Sweden remained intermittently pagan almost into the twelfth, and doubtless traces of paganism lingered elsewhere.

Sources of evidence

We need to remain aware that Viking paganism did not exist in total isolation from contemporary Christian Europe, and in fact it is from later Christian Norsemen, specifically from the Icelanders, that we get the fullest information on pagan practice and belief – though sometimes these excellent storytellers may be more concerned with the story than the record. It is not fair to expect from poems and prose tales about the old gods, written down by Christians of the twelfth century or later, the diligent analysis of a trained antiquarian or anthropologist. But these stories and poems give us many merry anecdotes and legends about the nature and activities of gods and goddesses such as Thor and Odin, Frey and Freyja, as well as descriptive accounts of the creation and end of the world according to Norse mythology. Many of our general concepts about Viking belief, about mead-drinking in Valholl, or the valkyries riding the air to choose the slain, derive from this medieval Icelandic literature.

The written observations of foreigners also tell us something about Viking paganism, though we cannot always be sure whether their records are from first-hand observation

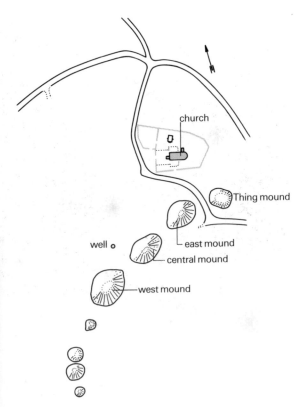

Uppsala was the famous centre of pagan worship in Viking Age Sweden. In place of the original temple a Christian church now stands near the huge 5th- and 6th-century royal burial mounds. *Below* Adam of Bremen's graphic description of Uppsala (based on hearsay) inspired this elaborate imaginary reconstruction by Olaus Magnus in 1555, which shows the temple, bound by golden chains, the sacred evergreen tree and the spring in which a man was drowned as a sacrificial victim.

or travellers' tales. Adam of Bremen, writing in the eleventh century about Swedish paganism, gives detailed accounts of sacrifices at Uppsala, but had not seen these himself. The Arab chronicler Ibn Fadlan, who described a pagan Viking funeral on the Volga, doubtless gave as exact an account as he could. But in this area Viking practices may have been influenced by neighbouring Slav ones, and the Arab's interpretation of what he saw was probably partly hindered by communication problems. For instance, the word for 'Paradise' occurs several times in his account, the place described as 'green and beautiful'. This is scarcely Valholl as described in west Norse sources, and it is doubtful what other

It was common pagan practice to bury men and women with the objects they had needed during their lifetime on earth. The Vikings were no exception and the excavation of their grave sites provides us with considerable evidence of both beliefs and daily activities. The contents of the grassy burial mounds at Birka, *above*, clearly reflect the town's importance as a trading centre; finds have included coins, luxury goods, merchants' scales and warriors' gear.

Norse word 'Paradise' could be translating.

Detailed and precise knowledge comes to us from the archaeologists, for it was common pagan practice to bury men and women with the objects they had needed during their lifetime on earth, presumably in the belief that they would still be needed in the afterlife. The excavation of a burial gives us information on three levels: firstly it shows us what ordinary objects were in daily use in the Viking Age – for many of the artifacts show signs of such use, and were clearly not made specifically for the death-ceremony; secondly it shows us the actual funeral customs operating in specific areas of pagan Viking Scandinavia, the method and manner of the burial; thirdly it demonstrates something about the beliefs of the people who carried out such customs. The use of the ship in burials probably means that death was

thought of as a journey, and even when actual ships were not used, graves were often marked by stones set in the form of a ship.

Excavation of settlements can also turn up artifacts of pagan significance, amulets, for example, and talismans. We find tiny figures of the gods themselves, and miniatures of their more distinctive possessions such as Thor's hammer. Excavation of temple sites is a chancy operation, since where building was in wood remaining evidence is minimal and hard to interpret. But many scholars have tried their hand at drawing reconstructions of the Uppsala temple, though nothing now survives above ground.

Place-name evidence can add to that of archaeology, showing which different gods and goddesses were worshipped and where, or what places were considered sacred. *Helgafell*, the Holy Mountain, is a type of

This plan is of one of the richest female burials excavated at Birka. Along one side of the wooden chamber lay a bronze bowl, a casket (containing a comb and a glass linen-smoother), a wine jug and drinking glass from the Rhineland, and two buckets. In the opposite corner was a whalebone plaque (see also page 122). The woman was buried fully clothed with her brooches and beads in place, including the large equal-armed brooch illustrated at the top of page 116. An iron ring with Thor's hammer pendants was found under the skull and presumably had been placed around the neck of the dead woman.

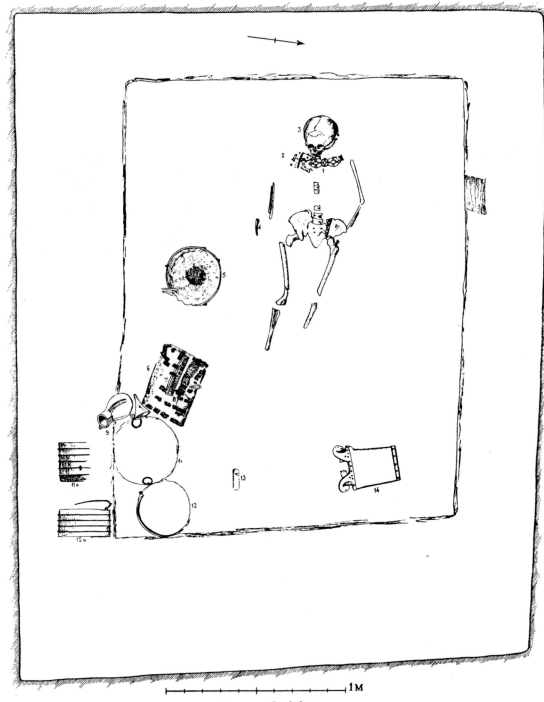

1M

Abb. 274. Grab 854.

name that often recurs, indicating a feature of general sanctity rather than a cult site for one specific deity. There were also sacred groves and islands, pastures and rivers. One useful aspect of the place-name evidence is its distribution pattern. The extent to which Odin names are found in Denmark suggests a dominant Odin cult there, a fact that may have political significance, since Odin was regarded as the god of kings and warriors.

The worship of Odin

Right A metalworker's die from Öland, for impressing foils to ornament a pre-Viking helmet (such as that on page 15), depicts a young man in a horned helmet taking part in a weapon dance for Odin – the warrior's god.

The bronze figure from Lindby in Skåne, *below*, appears to be one-eyed and may thus represent Odin, who is said to have given an eye for understanding.

The source that most clearly defines the position of Odin is the *Prose Edda* of Snorri Sturluson, an Icelander writing at the beginning of the thirteenth century, at a time when Iceland had been Christian for about 200 years, and knowledge of pagan traditions implied no sort of belief in them. Snorri says:

Odin is the highest and oldest of the gods; he rules all things, and however powerful the other gods are they all serve him as children their father .... Odin is called All-father, because he is the father of all the gods; he is also called Valfather because his chosen sons are all those who die in battle. Valholl is for them.

The word *valr*, the first element of Valholl and Valfather (and valkyrie) means 'the slain' and is used of men killed in battle. Snorri also gives a list of names by which Odin is known, drawn from the poem *Grímnismál*. These names include 'god of the hanged', 'helmeted one' and various others connected with battle and death. Odin's birds and animals are those that feed on corpses, the ravens and wolves, though his ravens Huginn and Muninn, Thought and Memory, relate also to his other function as a god of wisdom.

A group of poems known collectively as the *Poetic Edda* (or sometimes *Elder Edda*, since it precedes Snorri who drew heavily on this material), difficult to date, but surviving in a thirteenth-century manuscript a good deal younger than its contents, has many poems centred on Odin's search for wisdom and understanding. *Vafþrúðnismál* describes a contest of knowledge between Odin and the giant Vafthruthnir, who claims to have visited nine worlds and penetrated the depths of Niflhel, the realm of the dead; from him Odin learns many secrets of the world before winning the contest by a disgraceful trick question. *Vǫluspá* records what the sibyl told Odin about the end of the world, the destruction of men and gods and the monsters that will be let loose, the brood of Loki, the wolf Fenrir, the world-serpent Midgardsorm. *Hávamál* (*High One's Speech*), gives what purport to be Odin's own descriptions of his search for and attainment of knowledge: 'I began to grow and to become wise'; 'I took up the runes, shrieking I grasped them.' The poem cites many accomplishments apparently claimed by the High One himself: the ability to blunt the weapons of adversaries, to loosen fetters, to quieten wind and wave. Some are enigmatic, such as the claim to control 'those who ride the homesteads', others less cryptic, such as his statement that 'If I see a corpse hanging on the gallows I can carve and paint such runes that he walks and speaks with me.' A curious source of wisdom, one might think, but Odin is also said to have hung on the 'windswept tree' himself, 'offered to Odin, myself to myself', and on another occasion to have given an eye in exchange for understanding.

Odin's other major function as god of poets and poetry rests on a long and complex story told to us in various forms. Basically in Snorri's lucid version, the story is that dwarfs made a powerful mead drink out of honey and the blood of a murdered man, Kvasir, 'who was so wise there was no question he could not answer'. Those who drink this mead become poets. By stealing the drink Odin made it accessible to gods and men, and poetry is therefore Odin's gift, Odin himself being patron of all poets. Skalds refer frequently to their art in these terms. Egil Skallagrimsson mentions two of Odin's functions in his poem *Hǫfuðlausn* (*Head-Ransom*), which he recited in York to win his life as recompense from Eirik Bloodaxe. Egil claims to have carried Odin's mead (that is his poem) to English fields, and, when describing Eirik's victories, he says that Odin watched where the dead (*valr*) lay.

Since so much of our material comes from late and literary Icelandic sources, it is difficult to know how much of what we learn from them can be applied to Odin worship throughout Scandinavia. Fascinating additional evidence comes from the carved stones of Gotland. One friendly detail in Snorri's account of Odin is the description of his grey, eight-legged horse Sleipnir, and the name Sleipnir is also found in several Eddic poems. In *Baldrs Draumar* for example, 'Up rose Odin. . . . And he on Sleipnir laid the saddle.' The ninth-century Gotland picture-stones show a rider on an eight-legged horse, and it is a pleasing conjecture that we have here a Scandinavian depiction of the god himself and his splendid beast.

Obviously related to the figure on the Öland die, is a Viking Age amulet from a woman's grave in Uppland in the form of a warrior with a horned helmet, sword and spears. The horns on these ritual helmets have birds' head terminals.

Carved stones from Gotland, as well as depicting ships, provide evidence of Odin worship and may illustrate aspects of life after death. On this 8th-century stone from Tjängvide, Alskog, the man riding an eight-legged horse may be Odin on Sleipnir, the figures with drinking horn or spear perhaps valkyries, and the building in the background possibly a symbolic representation of Valholl.

179

The worship of Thor

Thor's hammer amulets from 10th-century Sweden, both made of silver. *Above* A splendidly stylized version from Skåne (enlarged), with the glaring eyes associated with Thor in many Eddic tales; *below*, a plain silver pendant from Uppland.

hough Snorri so clearly places Odin as All-father, the highest of the gods, it seems that Odin did not invariably hold this position. The eleventh-century English homilist Ælfric, writing about heathen gods, equates Thor, not Odin, with the chief Roman deity Jupiter, and he is more likely to be basing his statements on the paganism of contemporary Viking invaders than vague recollections of the far-distant pre-Christian past of Anglo-Saxon England. The German chronicler Adam of Bremen, describing the images of the gods in the Uppsala temple, one of which is Odin's, tells us that another is of Thor, the most powerful of the gods. When the poet Egil Skallagrimsson calls on the gods to drive Eirik Bloodaxe out of Norway his use of the term 'land god' twice in separate poems is commonly thought to be an appeal to Thor. There is some evidence for thinking that when the phrase 'the god' is used on its own it is

used of Thor. In a manuscript account of the pagan law at the time of the settlement of Iceland an important and binding oath is cited calling to witness 'Frey, Njord and the almighty god'. Almighty is a term so familiar to us in Christian belief that it is difficult to grasp its significance in the context of a pagan pantheon, but here again the appeal is probably to Thor in his protective role. This protective aspect of Thor is predominant in Snorri's tales in the *Prose Edda*. The gods themselves are vulnerable without Thor, though even Thor is vulnerable without his beloved hammer, Mjollnir. Eddic poems about Odin's search for wisdom tend to be heavy with solemnity, but the poem Þrymskvida, which describes Thor's journey to recover his lost hammer, is a most cheerful comedy. The giants, perennial enemies of the gods, have stolen Mjollnir, and will only return it if Freyja is brought to their lord as bride. Thor's immediate reaction seems to be that this is fair exchange, but Freyja, goddess of love, makes it clear that her desperation for a husband is not yet such that she need look for one among the giants. The solution reached is that Thor, god of physical strength, most masculine of the gods, disguises himself in bridal clothes, puts on Freyja's distinctive and recognizable gold necklace, and drives off to the giants amid the appropriate accompaniment of fire and earthquake. His behaviour on arrival lacks feminine delicacy – at the bridal feast he consumes an ox, eight salmon and three barrels of mead – but eventually the hammer is brought in 'to hallow the bride'. Thor's ensuing destruction of the giants is vigorous and rapid, 'and so Odin's son got his hammer back.'

Whether Thor's hammer was genuinely part of a wedding ritual may be doubted, but memorial stones survive with the runic formula 'May Thor hallow', or with Thor's hammer as part of the design carved on them. The veneration that the Viking pagans accorded this symbol may also be seen in the miniature hammers, usually of silver, that still survive. Some of these amulets were apparently designed to be worn as pendants, most are ornate, but others have no value and can only have been symbolic of their owners' beliefs.

The widespread popularity of Thor is shown in a number of ways. He it was in particular whose name was taken abroad by the Vikings to be honoured in the place-names of their new settlements. Iceland has a range of Thor's harbours and headlands (Thorshofn and Thorsness) and many of the personal names of Norsemen contain the element Thor, as in Thorgrim and Thorstein. That it is not only Icelanders who remember the Thor legends is shown by a range of carvings illustrating Thor in one of his best-remembered fights. According to Snorri he has a number of encounters with the world-serpent Midgardsorm, and at the end of the world and the doom of the gods each will be the death of the other. Eddic prose and poetry recount how Thor went fishing, baited his hook with the head of an ox, and caught the world-serpent on his line. The widespread popularity of the legend is shown by its appearance on carved stones as far apart as Altuna, Sweden, and Gosforth, England.

The legend of how Thor went fishing for the world-serpent Midgardsorm is carved on stones in Sweden and England. *Right* Thor stands in a boat with raised hammer near the bottom of an 11th-century rune-stone from Altuna, put up in memory of two men burnt in their house. From his left hand dangles the ox-head bait, while the serpent coils below.

Left A similar fishing scene is depicted on a stone at Gosforth in Cumbria. Here the second figure in the boat may be the giant Hymir – Snorri's version of the story includes him in this adventure.

Other deities

The bronze figure from Rällinge in Sweden, *left*, must represent the fertility god Frey, who may also be depicted, wooing the giantess Gerd, *above* (enlarged), on gold plaques found at Helgö. *Below* A walrus-ivory, beard-clutching figure from Lund (also enlarged), has been identified variously as Frey or Thor, but may simply be a 'king' for a board game.

here is scarcely space to look at all the gods and goddesses of the Viking pantheon, at Frigg, wife of Odin, at Idun, keeper of those excellent apples that preserve the youth of the gods, at Baldr the beautiful and beloved, for whose death all created things were asked to weep that they might win his release from Hel. Some, like Tyr the one-handed, whom English sources equate with Mars, the war god, seem to be important figures in the early period but to fade a little in the later centuries of the Viking Age. Frey, his sister Freyja and their father Njord form a distinct group connected with fertility and prosperity. Place-name evidence suggests that their cult was particularly strong in Sweden, but there is evidence too that they were worshipped in Norway, and there is much in Icelandic literature about individuals who venerated Frey. One story about the early settlers of Iceland says that snow would not lie on a certain grave because Frey loved the dead man too dearly to let frost come between them. Sagas, like Snorri's *Edda*, are written down by Christians in a period much later than the events they describe, but even where the incidents themselves may be fictional, the writers are more likely to be remembering than inventing traditions about the paganism of their ancestors. In *Egils Saga*, the daughter of Egil, anticipating death, says 'I have not eaten and shall not till I am with Freyja.' Such a comment may be reminiscent of a belief that whereas dead warriors went to Odin's Valholl, women were welcomed by Freyja, but the Eddic poem *Grímnismál* claims more astringently that Freyja shares the spoils of battle with Odin.

The valkyries

In this capacity Freyja may be linked with the valkyries. Their name means 'chooser of the slain', although literature has romanticized and tamed them. The tenth-century poem *Eiríksmál* describes the valkyries as welcoming the heroes with wine and it may be that this feminine occupation of theirs is represented in the carvings and amulets of women carrying drinking horns. But as minor deities of death, they are given as proper names the ordinary words for battle, such as the old Norse word *hildr*, and many a skaldic poet refers to battle as the play or storm of Hild.

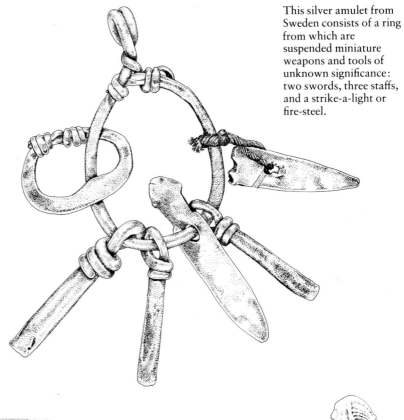

This silver amulet from Sweden consists of a ring from which are suspended miniature weapons and tools of unknown significance: two swords, three staffs, and a strike-a-light or fire-steel.

A Swedish pendant in the form of a woman holding out a drinking vessel may represent a valkyrie welcoming a dead warrior to Valholl.

The moustached face carved on a furnace stone, found on the beach at Snaptun in Jutland, may be that of Loki, who precipitated the last battle by killing Odin's favourite son Baldr. There are lines cut across the closed mouth, and Loki was once punished on losing a wager by having his lips sewn together.

The Sigurd legend & the world's end

Apart of the romanticization process begins with the transformation of valkyries into women involved with mortal heroes. The famous Sigurd legend contains an example of this, for the Brynhild to whom he becomes betrothed both has ordinary human ancestry, and at the same time is one of Odin's valkyries. Icelandic literature explains that Brynhild's long sleep behind a flame-barrier was Odin's punishment because she awarded victory against his instructions. Sigurd himself is a hero of supernatural stature and the full legend cycle surrounding him interweaves tales of prehistory and tales of the gods. The popularity of the legend can be gauged from the fact that whereas approximately half the Eddic poems deal with myths of the gods, nearly all the rest are episodes of the Sigurd cycle.

Sigurd roasts neat steaks of dragon's heart over the flames and licks his burnt thumb, on a 10th-century stone from Kirk Andreas, Isle of Man.

sucking his blistered thumb, and learning thereby to understand the tongue of the birds.

The last battle

Sigurd's father, Sigmund, is named in the poem *Eiriksmál* as the hero who welcomes Eirik to the company in Valholl. Sigmund asks Odin why they are expecting Eirik and gets the enigmatic answer: 'Because of uncertainty: the grey wolf looks at the home of the gods.' The grey wolf Fenrir will be the death of Odin in the last battle of the gods and men against giants and monsters, as a whole range of prophecy in the Eddic prose and poetry tells us, but it is hard to know how much of this

Stone-carvers also delighted in Sigurd, especially in the episode of the dragon fight. Sigurd himself, his horse Grani, the dragon Fafnir and the treacherous smith Regin are found on any number of carved stones throughout the Viking world. A favourite detail for the artist was the standard folklore motif of Sigurd roasting the dragon's heart,

apocalyptic vision is part of genuine Viking Age belief, and how much is subsequent literary creation, partly influenced by Christian thinking about the end of the world and Doomsday. Snorri tells the tale with dramatic relish:

The wolf will swallow the sun . . . then
a second wolf will seize the moon and

he too will do great damage. The stars will disappear from the heavens .... The wolf Fenrir will then be free. The sea will invade the land because Midgardsorm turns in a giant rage intending to come ashore.

Natural violence such as earthquakes will be paralleled by degeneracy among men, wars, slaughter of kin and incest. Nevertheless, Snorri's version, based on *Vafþrúðnismál* and *Völuspá* promises the rising of a new and lovelier world after the destruction of the old. The sun before she was swallowed by the wolf had given birth to a daughter who will travel the skies in her place; two mortals survived the destruction and will people earth again; some of the gods will live, sons of the dead Odin and Thor, and 'They find in the grass the golden playing pieces the gods once owned' – a hopeful evocation of a new era.

It is not clear how much this sophisticated mythology had to do with the beliefs of those buried in ships or mounds or more humble graves throughout the Norse world. But at least some Vikings had playing pieces, if not golden ones, buried with them, and harvesting implements too, as well as weapons, indicating perhaps that their hope of the future life included something other than the continuous fighting and drinking of Valholl.

Another 10th-century Manx stone depicts Odin with his raven and spear, being attacked by the grey wolf Fenrir – who, it is prophesied, will cause his death at the last battle.

Left The dragon-killing episode from the Sigurd legend is told on the Ramsund rock in Sweden (also shown on pages 154–5), Sigurd's adventures being largely contained within the band of runic text that forms the dragon's body. He killed Fafnir, the story tells, by hiding in a pit and stabbing upwards with his sword as the dragon crawled above him. This scene appears at the bottom right of the carving, while to the left, within the runic band, lies the dead Regin, Sigurd's betrayer, with his smith's tools. Beside him Sigurd sits roasting the dead dragon's heart over the forge fire, his burnt thumb to his mouth. 'When the blood from the dragon's heart touched his tongue he knew the language of the birds.' Birds perch in the tree behind to which his horse Grani is tethered.

Pagan to Christian

On the most complete of the crosses at Middleton in Yorkshire, England, is this fine representation of a helmeted Viking warrior surrounded by his weapons. This scene may represent his dead body laid out for burial in the pagan style.

To the Vikings living and travelling in a Europe that was almost entirely Christian, conversion did not come as a single explosive event. If we think of the earlier situation in England, where Christianity obliterated virtually all recorded knowledge of pagan thought and practice, the way in which some Norsemen remained coolly balanced between two religions, examining the merits of both, and in some cases trying to get the protective benefits of both, is a fascinating study. It is presumably one of the results of this detachment, that even after conversion there is still this willingness among the converted to remember and write about paganism rather than discarding it simply as error, idolatry and devil-worship.

The transition period between paganism and Christianity leaves traces in carving, literature and metalwork. Whether Vikings first started to wear a Thor's hammer round their necks because Christians wore pendant crosses and crucifixes, or whether the tradition is independent of Christian influence, cannot now be determined. But certainly there was enough of a market for both for one enterprising smith to leave behind him in Denmark a single soapstone mould for the production of both cross and hammer amulets. Most of the surviving pendants are clearly identifiable as either hammer or cross, but there are examples where the design of the one seems to have influenced the other, even one example where we are not sure which it was meant to be. Whether the canny Viking who wore it intended the ambiguity is not certain. Among saga characters with such ambivalent attitudes, most noticeable is Helgi, one of the early Icelandic settlers, who named his farm *Kristnes*, Christ's Headland, but did not entirely abandon Thor, whom he was accustomed to invoke in serious matters. A Viking poet somewhat sadly renounces the heathen gods in his verse. He confesses that he cannot entirely hate them, 'though Christ I

From hammer to cross: the enterprising 10th-century metalworker at Trendgården in Denmark who made the soapstone mould was clearly ready to cater for clients of both persuasions.

serve now'. This seems to be exactly the attitude of the men who commissioned or carved stone crosses such as those at Gosforth in Cumbria and Middleton in North Yorkshire. Middleton has several crosses and cross fragments of Viking date with characteristic Viking ornamentation. The most impressive shows on one panel a representation of a helmeted man surrounded by his weapons. It is a reasonable supposition that the newly converted took time to adjust to the thought of burial without grave-goods, and that at least on this occasion they demonstrated on the Christian symbol itself the style of furnished burial to which they were accustomed. At Gosforth, though again the cross itself is an indication of Christian belief, carvings on it appear to derive from pagan myth and legend: for example, the portrayal of a woman with a drinking horn, so like her sisters on the Gotland stones, and the figure confronting a serpent, perhaps Sigurd, dragon-killer, perhaps Thor and Midgardsorm.

Snorri sees no difficulty in describing the appropriate nomenclature for Christ alongside that for pagan deities. For example, one section of his work on poetic diction asks how it is proper to name Freyja, and the answer he gives is that 'She may be called daughter of Njord, sister of Frey, wife of Od, mother of Hnoss', and so on. A later section asks how it is proper to name Christ and the answer begins: 'He can be called creator of heaven and of earth, of angels and of the sun, ruler of the world and of the kingdom of heaven and of angels, king of the heavens and of the sun and of angels and of Jerusalem and of Jordan', and so forth. Snorri of course is writing in a Christian environment well after the transition period, but it is interesting that the first poet he quotes of those who refer to Christ is Eilif Gudrunarson, an Icelander living around the period of Iceland's conversion, who is known to have written Þórsdrápa, a poem recounting one of Thor's adventures against the giants, and whose poem referring to Christ, quoted by Snorri, uses imagery from pagan myth.

This Icelandic silver pendant with its fierce animal-head suspension-loop, could be a stylized Thor's hammer or perhaps a barbaric cross.

Christianity

Left Silver crucifixes found in Sweden display a stylized figure of Christ wearing trousers and bound to the cross. The small filigree version is from a grave at Birka, the other from a Gotlandic silver hoard.

Below A gilt brooch from Hedeby also depicts the crucifixion. The first churches at Hedeby and Birka were built by St Ansgar in the 9th century, but little progress was made with conversions until much later in the Viking Age.

 he Vikings who settled in such Christian countries as England, Ireland or Normandy rapidly adopted the religion of the land they lived in. Danes who had settled in northern districts of England during Alfred's reign were thought in the mid-tenth century to need protection against pagan Norwegian invaders, at any rate by the writer of one poem in the *Anglo-Saxon Chronicle*. The poem, entered in the *Chronicle* under the year 942, claims that the Danes were captive in the chains of the heathen, under the Northmen, until King Edmund released them; this maybe reflects the patriotism and religion of these settlers as much as it does the writer's view.

The conversion of Scandinavia, Iceland and Greenland
In the meantime, at home in Denmark, Christianity was also making its impact felt. Harald Bluetooth died in 986 and what Harald believed himself to have achieved in the service of the Christian God is proudly recorded on the great rune-stone at Jelling, where Harald declares that he 'won for himself all Denmark and Norway, and made the Danes Christians.'

It may be noted that though he claims to have 'won' Norway there is nothing in this statement about making the Norwegians Christian. In fact Earl Hakon, who held Norway under Harald, was a firm supporter of pagan cults, but in 995 Hakon was succeeded by Olaf Tryggvason, a vigorous, even an aggressive Christian. One of his poets describes him as a destroyer of heathen sanctuaries, and a reliable twelfth-century Icelandic historian credits him with the conversion of Iceland as well as of Norway. Later Icelandic saga-writers attribute to him the conversion of Greenland as well. His was a short rule, four years or five, and there was undoubtedly much opposition to his imposition of Christianity, especially in the remote areas of Norway where pagan thought had scarcely been challenged. But his achievements in that time must have been considerable, since Olaf Haraldsson – St Olaf – who took over Norway in 1015, was able to consolidate the conversion.

On mainland Scandinavia, if we accept what the sagas say about Olaf Tryggvason and St Olaf, there was inevitable opposition to the introduction of Christianity and some ferocity, even brutality, in establishing it. There was opposition in Iceland too, but the story of the eventual conversion of Iceland brought about so calmly and rationally makes pleasant reading. The twelfth-century historian Ari, a good scholar and a man careful to quote his sources, describes in detail Iceland's conversion in the year 1000. Initially things did not look too good for Iceland or Icelanders, since the first priest sent by Olaf Tryggvason to convert them baptized a number of influential men, 'but when he had been here one year he went away, having killed two or three men who had slandered him.' A turbulent priest! His report to Olaf implied that the conversion of Iceland would be a problem, and Olaf reacted with violence, threatening to kill or maim all Icelanders then in Norway. He was persuaded out of this plan by a couple of admirably clear-headed Icelanders who put their minds to the conversion of their country and the averting of Olaf's anger. They returned to Iceland and planned matters for the next meeting of the Althing, Iceland's national assembly. Here Christian and heathen might have fought,

but the decision was finally put into the hands of the Lawspeaker, who was at that time still heathen himself. 'He lay down and drew his cloak over him and lay there that whole day and the night after, not speaking a word.' By then he had come to a decision. His first thought was that the country must not be split – all must agree to follow one law, for division of law meant breaking of peace and laying waste of land. The 'law' he chose for his countrymen to follow was that of Christianity, and all those in the land who had not yet undergone the baptismal ceremony were to do so. But he also made provision for those who were unwilling to forsake their old ways,

On one face of King Harald's great rune-stone at Jelling in Denmark is this representation of the bound Christ. The figure is again formalized with no attempt at naturalistic detail, the formality being emphasized by the symmetrical ribbon interlace around Christ's body.

and allowed men still to sacrifice to their pagan gods in secret if they so wished.

The building of churches

According to the saga of Erik the Red, the discoverer of Greenland, Eirik's son Leif was sent by Olaf Tryggvason to preach Christianity in Greenland. Eirik did not welcome the new faith, but his wife Thjodhild 'accepted immediately and had a church built, not too near their home. It was called Thjodhild's church.' When archaeologists excavated Brattahlid, Eirik's farm on Greenland, a little way from the main homestead and hidden from it by the lie of the land, the remains of Thjodhild's small turf-walled church and its accompanying cemetery were discovered.

In time the Greenland settlements numbered, in addition to Thjodhild's, approximately seventeen stone-built churches including a cathedral at Gardar. There were

attempts to take Christianity even further west, for the Icelandic annals record that in the early twelfth century one bishop tried to sail to Vinland. Among the stories recorded about the eleventh-century voyages of discovery from Greenland along the North American coast there is a curiously convincing anecdote concerning friction between Christian and heathen. During a food shortage men prayed to God for supplies, but one unpopular character called Thorhall disappeared to make his own private devotions. When a whale was washed ashore Thorhall claimed, 'Wasn't the Redbeard of more use than your Christ? This is my return for the poem I composed for my patron Thor.' The saga-writer says that when the men knew this to be Thor's gift they threw it over the cliff and trusted in God's mercy, but since he has also said that eating it made them ill there may have been a strongly practical element in the gesture. *Eiriks Saga* records how in the

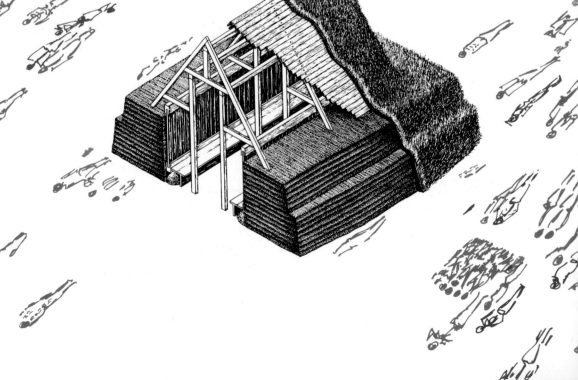

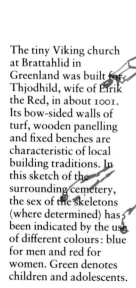

The tiny Viking church at Brattahlid in Greenland was built for Thjodhild, wife of Eirik the Red, in about 1001. Its bow-sided walls of turf, wooden panelling and fixed benches are characteristic of local building traditions. In this sketch of the surrounding cemetery, the sex of the skeletons (where determined) has been indicated by the use of different colours: blue for men and red for women. Green denotes children and adolescents.

The 12th-century tympanum of St Michael's church at Hoveringham in Nottinghamshire, England, shows St Michael fighting a dragon. But the coils of the beast are so much in the Anglo-Scandinavian tradition that it must have been expecting to confront Sigurd or Thor rather than an archangel.

Right Carved wooden panels from the farm at Flatatunga in Iceland may originally have been part of an 11th-century church. Above are interlacing tendrils in the Ringerike style, below, a row of saints' heads.

Greenland colony itself, when the harvest had been poor and food was short, the men asked a pagan prophetess to tell the future for them. What happened next demonstrates again the tolerance that could exist between Christian and pagan. When the prophetess needed someone to sing certain specific songs, Gudrid, the only woman present who knew them, refused, 'for I am a Christian woman'. She was persuaded to do so however by the telling argument that she could both give help 'and be no worse a woman than before'. It is pleasant to note that the prophetess subsequently foretold for Gudrid a splendid future back in Iceland, 'and over your descendants shine brighter rays than I can see with clarity.' Indeed, one of these descendants turned out to be a bishop.

The Eastern influence

The Christianity of Scandinavia and its Atlantic colonies came largely from the West, a considerable part being played by English and German missionaries and teachers. But there was also a strong Viking movement eastward and contacts especially between Sweden and Byzantium. Swedish rune-stones record men who died in *Grikkland* and often have a cross as part of the design as well as the formula 'God help his soul' or 'God and

Above Eastern influence can be seen in the design of this silver reliquary, from Gåtebo on Öland, although its Urnes-style details show that it was in fact made in Scandinavia.

Below 'Resurrection' eggs found in Sweden were made as Christian symbols in the Kiev area.

God's mother help his soul.' Here too are records of those who died on pilgrimage to Jerusalem. One competent woman, Ingerun, had her own memorial stone carved before she left home: 'She intends to go east and out to Jerusalem.' The settlement at Kiev, part Slav and part Viking, was converted to Christianity not from the West but from Byzantium, though at this date there was no formal split between Roman and Greek Orthodox Churches and their differences were of ritual rather than theology. Artifacts of religious significance showing the influence of Byzantine ritual and Byzantine art came back to Sweden by way of trade or gift, or private devout purchase.

The effects of Christianity

As the countries of Scandinavia became Christian there followed the inevitable effects on culture, law codes and conduct. Such effects do not take place immediately, and indeed it seems to have been a good deal more difficult for the Vikings to renounce their code of vengeance, for example, than to renounce their heathen gods. In the Icelandic saga literature we find many examples of people conscious that their honour and that of their family depends on killing someone who has slandered or injured them, and some people conscious also of the tensions between the demands of honour and the demands of their religion. In *Njáls Saga* Flosi, not the most important character, but perhaps the one making the most important decision, says succinctly:

> We have two alternatives, neither of
> them good; the one is to turn back,
> which will result in our deaths; the
> other is to kindle fire and burn them in
> their house, which is a great
> responsibility in the sight of God and
> we are Christians. Now let us kindle
> fire as quickly as possible.

What Christianity would hope to achieve was a modification of the desire for vengeance, a willingness to allow fine and

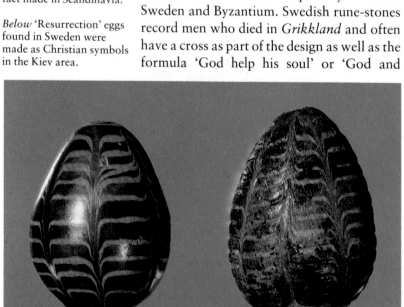

compensation to take the place of killing. Christian saga literature sometimes demonstrates and applauds the greater courage and goodness shown by those willing not to pursue vengeance. The passive courage of the martyr is contrasted with the active courage of the warrior. The Njal of *Njáls Saga*, whose home Flosi is burning, has words of Christian comfort for all his household: 'Believe also this, that God is merciful and he will not let us burn in this world and in the next.' He combines the old heroism and new trust in God, refusing to accept safe exit from his house, 'because I am an old man and unfit to avenge my sons, but I will not live in shame', after which he and his wife lie down in the burning house, cross themselves and commend their souls to God. This is of course the saga-writer's interpretation many years after the event, but the tensions inherent in two sets of values must have been a reality for many in the conversion period and later. The first surviving translation into Norse of the Bible demonstrates how parts of the Old Testament seemed naturally to accord with Viking ethics, and in particular the translation of the Book of Joshua reads as if it might well have fitted into the saga of some Christian warrior king such as Olaf Tryggvason or St Olaf.

Viking saints

The Viking Olaf was not the only one among the first generations of Norse Christians to be awarded the accolade of sainthood, but he was among the earliest and also among the most popular. In pagan times kings had sometimes been raised to divine status after their deaths. In the early Christian period, though missionaries frequently become saints and martyrs, there is some national pride involved in the acquiring of a national and especially of a royal saint. The Norwegian Olaf seems to fulfil the role of patron saint or favourite saint for all newly Christian Scandinavia. His cult, early established in Norway and Iceland, is found also in the British Isles, where many churches of an early date are

dedicated to St Olaf. The *Anglo-Saxon Chronicle* has an entry for 1055 which runs: 'In this year Earl Siward died in York, and he is buried in the minster which he himself had built and consecrated in the name of God and Olaf.' A Swedish rune-stone records of one adventurer that 'He died in Holmgard [Novgorod] in Olaf's church.' Holmgard on the Viking road east reminds us again of Byzantium at the end of that road. Here the Viking mercenaries, the bodyguard of the Byzantine Emperor, were said (admittedly as usual by an Icelandic historian) to have had their own church dedicated to St Olaf, where above the altar hung the sword that Olaf carried in his last battle at Stiklestad in Norway in 1030.

St Olaf, King of Norway, was struck down at the battle of Stiklestad in AD 1030. This event is depicted in an illuminated initial from a folio of the manuscript *Flateyjarbók*, written in Iceland in the 14th century.

Nation-states

The Viking Age republic of Iceland was administered by a system of regional assemblies, or Things, together with a national assembly, the Althing, which met annually for a fortnight each summer at Thingvellir. It was presided over by an elected Lawspeaker who had a special place at the *Lǫgberg*, or Law Rock, indicated here by the white flagstaff.

Government & kings

throughout Scandinavia during the Viking Age the basic unit of government was the Thing, the public assembly of free men of each district that met at regular intervals to consult on matters of importance to the area (including royal elections) and to legislate and administer justice. A plaintiff would bring his complaint to the Thing and it appears that, originally at any rate, the whole assembly was responsible for delivering a verdict. Once this had been given it was then up to the injured party to exact his own redress. Each province or region also had its own Thing, and in time these came to rank higher than the district Things, so that a pyramidal structure developed, with the king at its apex.

In republican Iceland there was a national body, the Althing, the assembly of the whole Icelandic nation, which met annually for a fortnight each summer at Thingvellir. This open-air gathering could be attended by all free men, so that it also served as a fair and a social occasion. In its original form, there existed within the assembly a legislature consisting of thirty-six chieftains under the chairmanship of a Lawspeaker, whom they elected every three years and who had a special place at the *Lǫgberg*, or Law Rock. Justice was administered by a separate 'court' of thirty-six judges, who were also elected by the chieftains.

Things were established elsewhere in the Viking settlements overseas. That for the Faeroes, which met at Thorshavn, is also known to have been presided over by a Lawspeaker. That in the Isle of Man, whose descendant still meets annually on the mound at Tynwald, has already been mentioned, while the Thing mound at Dublin was standing until the seventeenth century. Some have left their traces in place-names, such as Tingwall in both Orkney and Shetland.

Viking kings

In all the Scandinavian countries kingship followed the royal blood, but succession was not automatic, for any candidate for the throne had to be acceptable to the free men assembled at their Things.

Denmark

It seems likely that the kings of Denmark belonged to a single dynasty, established before the beginning of the Viking Age. Denmark appears to have been a more or less united kingdom as early as the reign of Godfred, at the beginning of the ninth century. Godfred's immediate successors, Hemming and Horik, seem also to have been kings of a united Denmark. However, we do not know to what extent this remained the case, or whether any king between Horik, who died 853/4, and Gorm the Old, who came to the throne *c.* 936, was able to hold the country as one kingdom. Of Gorm himself we know little that is not in the realm of folktales. But we do know that he was a king in Denmark, he was a pagan, he raised a family memorial, and he begat a line of powerful kings: Harald Bluetooth, Svein Forkbeard, Cnut the Great, Harthacnut and Svein Estridsson.

Cnut the Great was the most powerful of all the Scandinavian kings to rule during the Viking Age. It has been said of him that he 'came nearer than anybody to establishing a real North Sea Empire.' For he was king not only of Denmark and England but for the last years of his reign of Norway also; that his supremacy was also acknowledged in Sweden is indicated by coins struck at Sigtuna carrying the inscription *Cnut rex Sv[eorum]*. But this great kingdom was a personal creation, without cohesion or unifying organization, so it proved short-lived, disintegrating within a few years of his death in 1035.

Norway

Norway was not united until much later than Denmark. During the ninth century there was a major royal family of Swedish origin ruling around the Oslofjord; we are familiar with

The martyrdom of St Olaf is the subject of this painted wooden panel of the 14th century from Trøndelag in Norway. The royal saint stands in the centre of the panel holding an orb and an axe; the scenes on the left show his death at Stiklestad in 1030 and his later enshrinement.

them archaeologically from the outstandingly rich ship burials of Oseberg and Gokstad. In Trøndelag on the other hand authority was wielded by the earls of Lade. The other areas of Norway also had their chieftains. Towards 900 King Harald Finehair of Vestfold set about becoming the sole ruler of Norway and successfully established his control down its west coast, after which it seems to have been accepted that Norway should have one king. It was said that many men left for Iceland in order to escape the imposition of Harald Finehair's rule, choosing to create in that country a republic.

Olaf Tryggvason, the great-grandson of Harald Finehair, was a fierce Christian who was later credited with the conversion not only of Norway, but also of Orkney, the Faeroes, Iceland and Greenland. In Norway the actual process of conversion was completed by Olaf's successor, Olaf Haraldsson, but religious and political conflict, fostered by Danish claims to the throne, led to a revolt against him. Olaf met his death in 1030 at the battle of Stiklestad in Trøndelag; it was followed by such marvels that a year later his remains were translated to Trondheim and he became the first of the royal martyrs and saints of Scandinavia – to be followed in the late eleventh and twelfth centuries by the two Cnuts of Denmark and Eirik of Sweden (not forgetting Magnus in Orkney).

Notable also in Norway's royal line was Harald Hardrada (the Hard-ruler), who was St Olaf's half-brother. He had escaped wounded from Stiklestad at the age of fifteen, and Germany. Harald's family connections thus reached throughout Europe.

Sweden

Adam of Bremen, writing about 1070, said that the Swedes had kings of ancient lineage, although their authority in most matters was subject to the power of public opinion, except in times of war. We know very little of the kings in Uppsala during the ninth and tenth centuries, or of royal administration, but as elsewhere in Scandinavia they would have been peripatetic, moving round from one royal estate to another. In Sweden we know of over sixty such farms all with the name *Husaby* – the element *hús* means 'building', and presumably refers to the size or number of them required to cater for a royal retinue, or for the storage of local taxes paid in kind to await the king's consumption or distribution. They would also have served as centres for assembling the local levies.

One of the first Swedish kings known to have been active on the international scene was Olaf Sköttkonung, who died about 1022. He was the first to be named king over both the *Svear* and the *Götar*, and his overlordship appears to have been recognized in eastern Norway. His daughters were married to King Yaroslav and St Olaf of Norway. During his reign Christianity obtained a permanent footing in Sweden, with the establishment of a missionary bishop at Skara.

Coinage

The first royal coinages of Viking kings were struck towards the end of the ninth century in England, where Scandinavian settlers took over Anglo-Saxon mints. Viking merchants will have learned to use coins as counted money in their dealings overseas, even if for much of the Viking Age they continued among themselves to treat them as no more than lumps of bullion. So it is not surprising that the first native coinage of Scandinavia was struck at Hedeby, with designs based on coins of the Frisian merchants with whom the

An 11th-century wall-painting from the church of St Sophia in Kiev depicts Elizabeth, daughter of Yaroslav and grand-daughter of Vladimir, who had converted the people of Kiev to Christianity. She married Harald Hardrada of Norway – the last great Viking king.

fleeing to Novgorod. From there he went on to join the Varangian Guard, returning to Norway in 1046 to inherit half the kingdom, and succeeding to it all a year later. His further ambitions met with little success, for attacks on Denmark failed to lead to conquest and he met his death at Stamford Bridge in Humberside during an invasion attempt on England. He was without doubt one of the last great figures of the Viking Age. While in Russia Harald had married Elizabeth, a daughter of Yaroslav, King of Novgorod-Kiev, whose wife was Ingigerd, the daughter of King Olaf Sköttkonung of Sweden. Yaroslav's other daughters were also married well – one to King Andrew I of Hungary, and another to King Henry I of France – while four of his sons married into the courts of Byzantium

The first royal coinages of Viking kings were struck in England, where Scandinavian settlers took over Anglo-Saxon mints. *Above* A Thor's hammer, a raven, a bow and arrow, a standard, and a sword decorate coins struck for various 10th-century rulers of York; the coin with the sword reads ERIC REX (King Eirik Bloodaxe). The three 'portraits' are in fact of Anglo-Saxon kings, but have been borrowed for use on coins of Cnut, *centre*, and his sons. All the coins are enlarged.

Below A Frisian trading ship is depicted on this 9th-century coin minted at Hedeby.

Danes had been in contact since the eighth century. The coin workshops at Hedeby appear to have been active from sometime around 825 to the middle of the ninth century. Some coins, based on the Carolingian coinage minted at Dorestad, have shapes imitating the letters of the names CAROLUS (Charlemagne) and DORSTAD (Dorestad), which were placed on either side of the originals. Other Frisian coins of the period bore pictures of animals, masks, temples and ships – designs that were also copied and transformed by the Hedeby craftsmen. After a gap in production, coin workshops were again operating at Hedeby from the end of the ninth century and through much of the tenth. Their products were cruder than before and had no figures, only the patterns based on the letters of CAROLUS and DORSTAD. They were light and thin (with the design struck from one side only), so must have been somewhat impractical in use. However, they proved popular for they are found from north Sweden to south Poland.

Increase in royal authority, together with the growth of trade, led to the establishment of national coinages in Scandinavia at the end of the tenth century, with issues in the names of Olaf Sköttkonung at Sigtuna, of Svein Forkbeard in Denmark and of Olaf Tryggvason in Norway. No coins were struck during the Viking Age in Iceland, nor in the Norse settlements in Scotland, but in Dublin they were first minted for King Sigtrygg about the year 997.

Royal Jelling

Two great mounds dominate the Danish royal necropolis of Jelling in Jutland. Between them stands a medieval stone church, with the two rune-stones before it, now surrounded by the modern graveyard. Massive stones found beneath the south mound have been placed in rows between the mounds to suggest an early sacred enclosure.

he Royal Danish necropolis at Jelling in Jutland is one of the most impressive and fascinating monuments of the Viking Age. At the centre stands a medieval stone church on the site of that built by King Harald Bluetooth in the 960s. Before it are the two rune-stones that tell us much, but by no means all, we need to know about the site and its creation.

The smaller of the two stones has no ornament, but its inscription states that 'King Gorm made this memorial to his wife Thyri, glory [or adornment] of Denmark.' What memorial it was that Gorm raised to the queen who predeceased him is not disclosed.

On either side of the church, dominating the site of Jelling, stand two massive mounds. In that to the north was found a large, low chamber of wood divided by a plank across the middle. There were, however, no bodies in what looks as if it should have been a double grave. The few objects recovered, although of high quality (among them were the carvings and the silver cup described on pages 139 and 142), were scattered finds. The

chamber had clearly been entered in antiquity and its contents removed. But the objects that do survive all point to a mid-tenth-century date for its use; Gorm himself was dead by 950. It therefore seems beyond reasonable doubt that it was Gorm who had the north mound at Jelling built, to provide a tomb for Thyri — and for himself to occupy in due course. So what became of their bodies?

Their son Harald Bluetooth, as king, formally received the Christian faith about 960 and would have been anxious that his parents should be given Christian burial. When his church was built, a large grave was dug at its centre, the north mound was entered and the bodies were transferred to their new Christian resting place. Such we may suppose the events to have been; the details are not yet available of the recent excavations within the church that located the central grave, containing the disarticulated bones of two skeletons together with gold-ornamented fabrics.

There remains to be explained the south mound and a setting of large stones found beneath it. This mound has also been excavated, with the result that we can be sure that it never contained a burial, although there are traces of a post-built structure on top. Other such empty mounds are known elsewhere, so there is little strange about that. They are usually thought to be memorials or cenotaphs. Was it built for such a purpose by Harald himself? For he wished to be buried in his new cathedral church at Roskilde.

The standing stones found beneath the mound formed an open-ended triangle, pointing southwards. It has been suggested that its sides once extended as far as the north mound, so forming a sacred enclosure as part of Thyri's memorial. But there is no satisfactory evidence for this and it would certainly be an enclosure without parallel. It is more probable that what the archaeologists found

King Harald had this monument made in memory of his father Gorm and his mother Thyri: this was the Harald who won for himself all Denmark and Norway, and made the Danes Christians.

Scholars are divided as to the precise dating of the stone. It could perhaps have been set up at the end of Harald's reign after he had 'won for himself all Denmark and Norway'; or it is possible that the stone was erected when he redesigned the complex in the 960s, and the second part of the inscription was added later. Be that as it may, Harald's boast was a true one, even though the unification of Norway with Denmark was to be short-lived. At the back of his claim to glory seems to have been a thorough organization of his own kingdom of Denmark, for the latest research indicates that the great Danish fortresses, and possibly other engineering works, described below, were undertaken during his reign.

The mounds and church at Jelling have all been excavated. The north mound, built over a prehistoric mound, contained a wooden burial chamber. This was empty, the bodies having been transferred to a grave in the first timber church that lies beneath its stone successor. The south mound contained only a light timber framework, but a wooden structure had stood on its top and there were the remains of a stone setting beneath it.

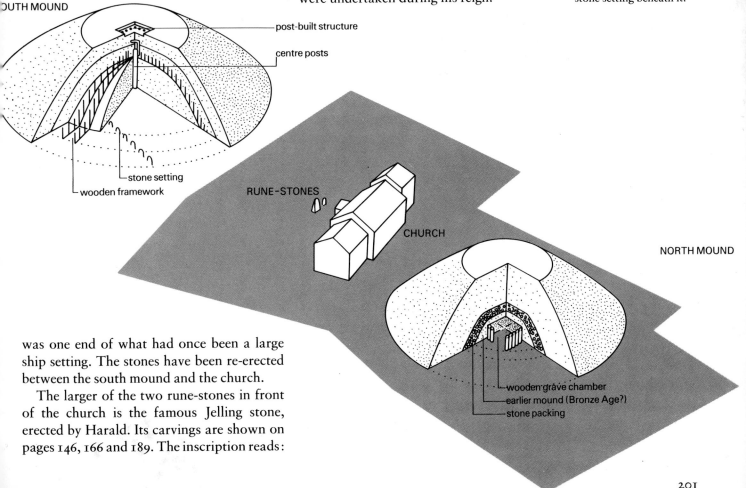

SOUTH MOUND
post-built structure
centre posts
stone setting
wooden framework
RUNE-STONES
CHURCH
NORTH MOUND
wooden grave chamber
earlier mound (Bronze Age?)
stone packing

was one end of what had once been a large ship setting. The stones have been re-erected between the south mound and the church.

The larger of the two rune-stones in front of the church is the famous Jelling stone, erected by Harald. Its carvings are shown on pages 146, 166 and 189. The inscription reads:

The Viking fortresses

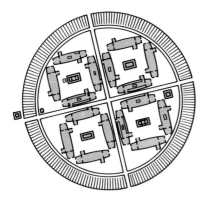

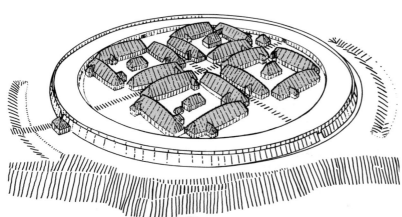

The excavators' plan and reconstruction of Fyrkat demonstrate at a glance the precise and regular layout of the fortress. The identical buildings grouped around court-yards appear to have been used for a variety of functions, evidence that Fyrkat was not simply a military barracks.

Right An aerial view shows the site chosen for the Viking fortress at Fyrkat – on a ridge in a marshy valley. The ramparts, which have been ploughed out, have been reconstructed and the post-holes of the buildings and streets have been marked with concrete. One quadrant of the fortress remains unexcavated.

Fyrkat

The fortress at Fyrkat was built on a ridge in a marshy valley, although the chosen ridge was not large enough to accommodate the preconceived plan without its first having to be levelled and extended. In fact the southern portion of the fortress stands on several feet of built-up soil that would have had to be transported by the cartload across the site. The unit of measurement used in the plan is based on the Roman foot; this was employed in the laying out of all the fortresses, although its exact length varies slightly from site to site (the unit used at Fyrkat measured a little over $11\frac{1}{2}$in, 29.5cm).

The timber-strapped rampart, comprising at least 353,000 cubic feet (10,000 cubic metres) of turf and stone, has an internal diameter of 394ft (120m), that is, 408 Fyrkat feet. At its base it measured 39ft (11.8m) wide, but its original height is unknown; it has been reconstructed to a height of 11ft (3.5m), but may well have been higher originally.

Royal authority must have been behind the planning and construction of the four remarkable circular fortresses built in Denmark during the middle or second half of the tenth century. Although one fortress is on Sjælland, one on Fyn, and the other two in Jutland, they are all slight variations on one basic plan. In this plan the main buildings are surrounded by a timber-laced turf rampart forming a circle, with an external ditch around those parts of the fortress that were not naturally protected by marshy ground or a steep drop. This rampart has four gateways for axial streets, paved with timber. The buildings within each quadrant are arranged in fours to form square courtyards and they are all of the same type. Let us first examine one of the fortresses in detail in an attempt to understand just what was their significance. Of the four, the best and most recently excavated is that at Fyrkat, near Hobro in Jutland.

Presumably it would have had a breastwork in addition; this might have run across the tops of the four gateways, which are set like the points of a compass, dividing the interior into quadrants.

On the outer face of the rampart were laid heavy tongued-and-grooved timbers to prevent attackers from scaling the wall, thus trapping them in an exposed position on the berm – the area between the rampart and the ditch. The ditch was 23ft (7m) wide and 6½ft (2m) deep and surrounded the fortress, except where the land fell away sharply.

Inside the fortress were two crossing main streets paved with wood, and another that ran round the inside face of the rampart. Within each of the quadrants bordered by these streets was placed a block of four large bow-sided buildings around a central court-yard, with a smaller rectangular building standing at its centre.

The buildings that lined the main east-west street all contained central hearths and produced finds of a domestic nature. They have thus been interpreted as dwellings. Two buildings lining the north–south street were possibly workshops; they also had hearths, but these were associated with craftsmen's debris, including that of jewellers, and contained very little domestic rubbish. Two of the buildings facing the rampart were found to have hearths (one quadrant of the fortress has been left unexcavated); again these may have been used as workshops, or smithies. The other bow-sided buildings produced few finds of any sort and had no hearths; they are most likely to have been storehouses and barns. Central planning thus seems to have extended beyond the precise layout of the fortress, even to the use of the buildings within it: decreeing that dwelling houses should face the main east-west street, while service buildings faced the rampart. The houses on the other axial street might well have been planned as dwellings, even if they were then used as workshops.

Outside the north-east part of the rampart was situated the cemetery for the occupants of the fortress. Men, women and children were all represented among the thirty-odd graves that were located by the excavators. Some were buried in coffins, others in cart-bodies, and one even in a chest. All in all, they seem to represent a perfectly ordinary (if well-to-do) Jutlandic community of the middle or later tenth century. There is thus no evidence from either the cemetery or the fortress that Fyrkat was used exclusively as a military barracks, as might be assumed from its plan and defences. The finds from the other fortresses support this observation.

The excavation at Fyrkat also tells us something about the length of its occupation, for no material necessarily of eleventh-century date was found. Moreover, the timber buildings showed no signs of having been repaired at any stage, suggesting that they cannot have had a lifetime of much more than thirty years. The fortress must have quickly rotted; there was then a fire after

The plans of the Viking fortresses of Denmark are so similar that they must be the work of a single authority, no doubt that of the king. Trelleborg, *right*, has the same number of houses within the fortress as Fyrkat, but also has an annexe containing fifteen more. Aggersborg, *below*, is twice the diameter of Fyrkat with three times as many buildings.

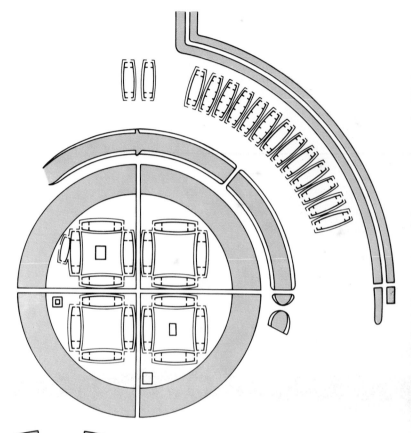

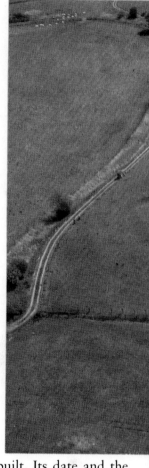

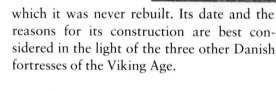

which it was never rebuilt. Its date and the reasons for its construction are best considered in the light of the three other Danish fortresses of the Viking Age.

Aggersborg, Trelleborg and Nonnebakken

Aggersborg, overlooking the Limfjord in northern Jutland, is the largest of the Danish fortresses. This has an internal diameter twice that of Fyrkat, making room for three times as many buildings. Trelleborg, in west Sjælland, contained the same number of houses within the fortress proper as Fyrkat, but it had an annexe with an additional fifteen houses, protected by a rampart concentric with that of the fortress itself, together with a dog-leg in front of the main entrance to accommodate the cemetery. With an internal diameter of 468 Roman feet and a rampart 60 Roman feet thick, Trelleborg is also slightly more massive

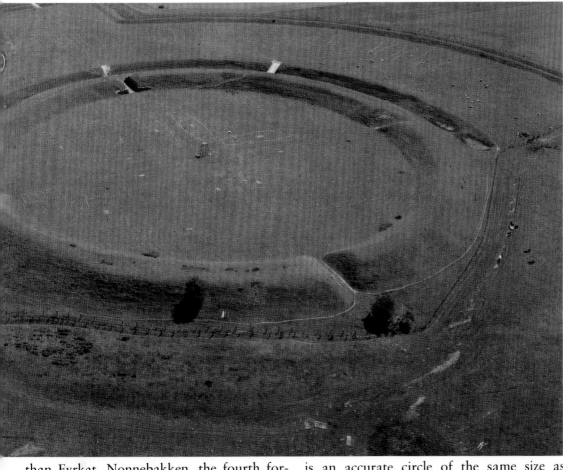

Like Fyrkat the fortress of Trelleborg in western Sjælland was set on a ridge with marshy ground on either side. The annexe, containing additional buildings and also the cemetery, which lay in front of the fortress, can be seen in the background of this photograph.

than Fyrkat. Nonnebakken, the fourth fortress, lies today beneath the suburbs of Odense on Fyn. It is presumed to have been of similar size and type to Fyrkat, but being built over, it has proved difficult to examine its features in any detail.

These great Danish fortresses are without exact parallel in Western Europe and their sudden appearance throughout much of Denmark in the tenth century suggests a common origin for all four under the organization of a central authority. The inspiration for such fortresses is most likely to have come from those of the Slavs and of the Saxons, although they were smaller and lacked the characteristic internal layout of the Danish series. Nearer to them in size is a string of seven forts constructed on the Dutch coast, probably as refuges against Viking attacks. That at Souburg, on the island of Walcheren,

is an accurate circle of the same size as Trelleborg, with the same four gateways, but once again does not have the regularly planned interior.

The precise plan and the fortifications of the Danish fortresses suggest, at first sight, that they were intended purely as military works. Yet, as we have seen at Fyrkat, they were not simply barracks; their function must therefore have been more complex. They clearly could have served as centres where, in times of trouble, armies might be assembled and the local population find refuge. In peacetime they may have served as centres of royal administration where taxes could be gathered, and from which the court could be supplied. For, all things considered, there can be little doubt that these were royal works; and, since the evidence suggests that they were constructed and used within the period

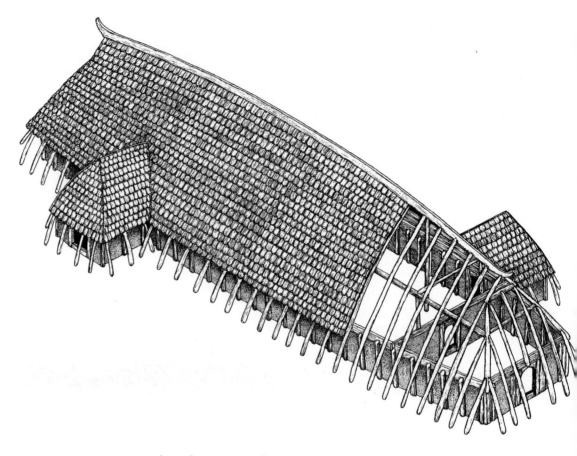

This reconstruction of a so-called Trelleborg type of house is based on the excavations of buildings in the Viking fortress of Fyrkat. These were 96 Roman feet long and built with shingled roofs. The curved roof ridge is a characteristic feature resulting from the use of bow-sided long walls.

Further evidence of the Trelleborg house type is provided by a Hedeby coin, found at Birka, which shows a building with a curved roof and external buttresses. There are also large animal heads carved on the gable ends, similar to those on the Cammin casket.

950 to 1000, it seems that they are to be attributed to Harald Bluetooth, or, less probably, to his son Svein Forkbeard.

The Trelleborg house type

The standardization of the house type found in the Viking fortresses of Denmark has resulted in its being known as the Trelleborg type, after the best known of them. At Trelleborg, a full-size reconstruction was built following the excavations of the post-holes that are almost the sole surviving remains of these timber buildings. Unfortunately, impressive though this reconstruction is, it is now known to be completely misleading in at least one vital respect: the external posts that surround the house inclined inwards and therefore cannot have formed part of an external gallery of the type that has been reconstructed at Trelleborg.

The essential feature of the Trelleborg type of house is its elongated bow-sided form,

which would have produced a distinctively curved roof ridge. A clear impression of the over-all shape of such a building may be gained from a large casket (possibly made as a reliquary) that was long preserved in the treasury of Cammin cathedral in Pomerania, but which was destroyed in the Second World War. Its elk-antler panels have Mammen-style carvings comparable in quality to that of the Bamberg casket (see page 144). The projecting animal heads in gilt-bronze at each end show how the gables of such houses might have been ornamented, bringing to mind the animal-headed finials of the later stave-churches.

Other house-shaped objects can also be used to assist in the reconstruction of the Trelleborg type of house. A fine series of tenth-century tomb-covers from the area of Scandinavian settlement in northern England has proved particularly illuminating. Among these so-called 'hog-backed' tombstones are some that are closely modelled on houses, although their gables are obscured by the bear-like creatures that, by a peculiar convention, clasp their ends. Those at Brompton in North Yorkshire clearly have their roofs covered with shingles (tile-like plates of split wood), of similar type to an example found at Trelleborg. Alternatively, such houses might have been thatched. The long sides of one of the Brompton hog-backs are panelled, with broad plait-ornamented sections divided by plain vertical strips. This is suggestive of the typical wall construction of these houses, which consisted of timber-framed panels of wattle-work. In contrast, the walls of the Trelleborg houses themselves were of stave construction, made of halved tree trunks with the rounded sides set outwards.

At Trelleborg the houses were 100 Roman feet long and were entered by doorways at opposite ends of the long walls (one from the street and the other from the courtyard), which gave direct access to the large central hall. At Fyrkat, all such doorways seem to have been provided with porches. In the gable ends there were further doors that opened into small rooms on either end of the hall.

A coin found at Birka, although struck at Hedeby, shows such a house with its curved ridge, with the addition of inclined posts, or buttresses, on either side. The holes for such outer posts were found around the Trelleborg houses, and it was these that were originally misinterpreted. Further researches (particularly at Fyrkat) demonstrated that the posts set in the outer of the two parallel lines of holes had indeed been set at an angle. Two new interpretations are thus possible: either that they were buttresses to the tops of the walls to help support the weight of the roof; or that they carried sloping roof-posts.

This type of bow-sided house is known in timber throughout Denmark and in southern Sweden (as will be seen below, at Lund). It is also that represented by the turf and stone buildings found in Norse settlements in the Atlantic islands, though without buttresses.

Above The house-shaped Cammin casket has projecting animal heads suggesting that the gable ends of timber houses may have been ornamented in this way. The photograph is of a replica.

'Hog-backed' grave-covers in northern England are shaped like bow-sided houses with shingled roofs and wattle walls.

Defence & communications

A ditch and rampart of the Danevirke still cut across the flat landscape at the base of the Jutland peninsula. This great series of earthworks once protected the Viking Age kingdom of Denmark from southern invaders and cattle-rustlers.

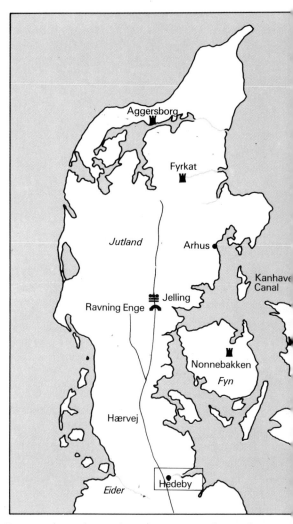

The Danish fortresses are but one aspect of a developing trend for the construction of fortifications in Scandinavia during the later tenth century, as we have already seen represented by the building of ramparts around both Hedeby and Birka. This trend is probably, best understood as a reflection of the growth of centralized authority in the form of royal power. Other towns, such as Århus, in Denmark, are also known to have been defended at this period, while the Skuldelev blockage of sunken ships represents a seaward defence for Roskilde in the late Viking Age. Underwater fortifications in the form of piles were also being built at that time in Denmark and Sweden. However, this is but part of a tradition of sea-defence that seems to go back to before the Viking Age.

Land-defences involving the construction of ramparts also existed well before the tenth century. Hedeby and Birka appear to have had their small hill-forts in the ninth century, while the trading centre of Löddeköpinge in Skåne was defended then with a rampart. More important, the earliest phase of the Danevirke has now been shown to date from the eighth century, before the Viking Age.

The Danevirke
During the Viking Age the southern border of the Danish kingdom was protected against the Germans by a series of linear earthworks

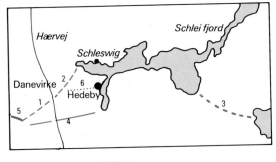

Above The builders of the
Danevirke made full use
of natural obstacles to
complete the barrier
across the neck of the
Jutland peninsula. Recent
studies have grouped its
seven elements into three
main construction phases.

phase I _____
phase II _____
phase III _____

1 Main Wall
2 North Wall
3 East Wall
4 Kovirke
5 Crooked Wall
6 Connecting Wall

⚏ royal necropolis
⚔ fortress
⌒ bridge
Y road

that cross the neck of the Jutland peninsula,
linking natural obstacles; these are known as
the Danevirke. The Danevirke appears first in
the historical record in the Frankish annals,
under the year 808, where it is said that the
Danish King Godfred,

> . . . decided to fortify the border of his
> kingdom against Saxony with a
> rampart, so that a protective bulwark
> would stretch from the eastern bay
> called Østersalt [as far as the western
> sea], along the entire north bank of the
> Eider, broken by a single gate through
> which wagons and horsemen would be
> able to leave and enter.

However, it has been demonstrated by the
study of the tree-rings of the timbers that the

earliest phase of the Danevirke was in fact
constructed very much earlier, about 737.

There are seven distinct elements belonging
to the three main phases of the Danevirke,
which together measure some nineteen miles
in length. The first phase is thought to consist
of the Main Wall, the North Wall, and the
East Wall, which together cut off this Scandinavian peninsula from the rest of Europe.
Secondly, there is the Kovirke (the Cow-
work), which runs to the south of Hedeby.
This is undated, but might be the work of
Godfred referred to in the Frankish annals, for
he would surely have wished to protect the
overland trade of his newly founded port at
Hedeby. The third construction phase took
place after 968 (from tree-rings again), when
two further elements were added: the
Crooked Wall, which is an extension to the
Main Wall, and the Connecting Wall, which
linked Hedeby's new rampart into this
network of defences.

The final result was a formidable barrier
that retained a military significance into the
nineteenth century. Its origins, however, back
in the eighth century, may have had a less ambitious purpose – perhaps it was intended as
an official line of demarcation for the control
of trade and the prevention of cattle-rustling.
The 'single gate' referred to later in the Frankish annals was left for the great *Hærvej*, the
main land route that ran the length of the
Jutland peninsula, as far as Viborg.

Inland waterways

The sea, rivers and lakes remained the normal
arteries of Scandinavian communication and
transport in the Viking Age, but the need for
overland traffic developed apace during these
centuries. Overland portages of ships had
always been a feature of travel (as on the
southern route from Birka), but an unusual
refinement was the construction of a canal,
just over half a mile in length, across the
Danish island of Samsø. This cutting was 36ft
(11m) broad and 4ft (1.25m) deep; for part of
its length its sides had to be lined with oak

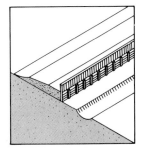

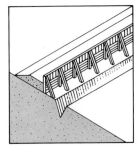

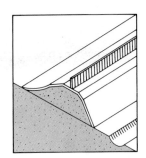

These three diagrams are
reconstructions of the
ramparts and ditches of
each of the main phases
of the Danevirke:

I A timber-faced rampart
with a U-shaped ditch
(Main Wall, North Wall
and East Wall).

II A timber-faced
rampart with buttresses
and a V-shaped ditch
(Kovirke).

III An earthern rampart
with a palisade and a U-
shaped ditch (Crooked
Wall, Connecting Wall
and Hedeby Rampart).

A Viking Age stone causeway under excavation at Risby on Sjælland. Its two sides were linked by a small wooden bridge, beneath which were discovered a simple wooden sledge and a wagon wheel.

planks, which have given a radio-carbon date of 800 ad ± 100, suggesting that it was indeed a Viking Age construction. Its significance can only be guessed at, but its purpose must have been to move ships rapidly, as necessary, from the western to the eastern passages between Jutland and Sjælland. But whether this was a royal project for the defence of the kingdom, or whether it represents private enterprise for piratical purposes, remains an open question.

Roads and bridges

Eleventh-century Scandinavian rune-stones often record the building of bridges as 'good works'. Most of these will have taken the form of causeways across boggy ground, such as

that recently excavated at Risby in Denmark, although this was in fact combined with a small timber bridge across a stream. Such community works had particular Christian significance during the late Viking Age because they would have opened up access to the first few churches and, more importantly at that date, have made it easier for priests to travel between the scattered communities.

Road- and bridge-building was certainly being carried out in Denmark on some scale during the tenth century, for the remains of a true bridge, about half a mile in length, have been discovered at Ravning Enge, not far from Jelling in Jutland and possibly associated with the *Hærvej*. It ran across the marshy valley of the river Vejle, supported on piles set in rows of four, with an angled post at either end to help support the trackway; this will have been 16–20ft (5–6m) wide. The lines of piles were set 8ft (2.4m) apart, so in all some 2,500 posts were required. What is most impressive, however, is the accuracy with which the whole construction was designed and executed. The load-bearing piles were all one Roman foot square in section and the rows had been precisely laid out with the aid of ranging poles, some of which were found in position. It is thus not very surprising to discover that the Ravning Enge bridge is broadly contemporary with the Danish fortresses, for a similar mentality seems to have been at work. Study of the tree-rings has given a date for its construction within a couple of years of 979. Perhaps again we should detect the hand of royal power, for the control and defence of a kingdom depends in great part on the rapidity with which men and instructions may be moved, and thus on the quality of its roadways and bridges.

It appears that Harald Bluetooth may have initiated a whole series of engineering projects, remarkable for their time, that are as much his memorial as Jelling. They do, however, seem to have fallen rapidly out of use – Ravning Enge, like the fortresses, shows no signs of ever having been repaired.

Scandinavian new towns

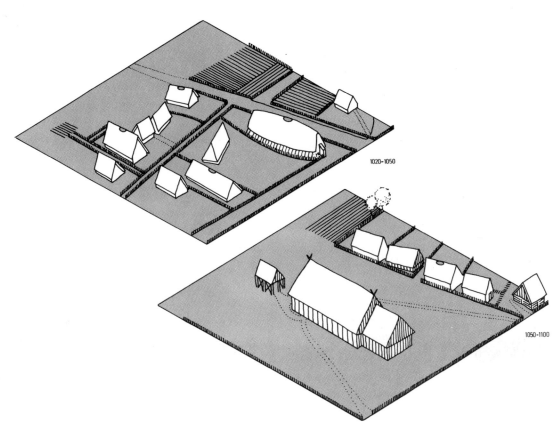

1020-1050

1050-1100

Lund in Skåne was founded as a town by Cnut the Great in about 1020. Large-scale excavations have revealed a small part of its history in the late Viking Age: in one area several buildings (including a large bow-sided house) were cleared away during the 11th century for a stave-church to be built in their place.

Although a king's wealth depended in part on his military successes, his ability to raise taxes whether in cash or in kind provided the means by which he ordinarily maintained the organization and defence of his kingdom. As we have seen, from the beginning of the Viking Age royal interest in trade as a source of income by taxation led to the establishment and protection of towns. The foundation of new towns throughout Scandinavia was a particular feature of the late Viking Age. They were intended not only as markets, but also to serve as religious and administrative centres.

An obvious example in Sweden is Sigtuna, the successor to Birka in terms of its functions as an internal trading and manufacturing centre; for a royal mint was located there, and it also became a bishop's seat. Similarly Hedeby was replaced by Schleswig. Århus,

Viborg, Ålborg and Roskilde, in Denmark, were all established during the Viking Age. In Norway, Bergen, Trondheim (or Nidaros as it was then called) and Oslo are all foundations from the end of the period.

Lund, in southern Sweden (then still within Denmark) is likely to have been typical of these late Viking Age towns in many respects. Here a settlement was turned into a township, functioning as a local market and manufacturing centre, by Cnut the Great in about 1020. It had narrow streets of wattle-and-daub houses, although one larger building of the Trelleborg type has been excavated. This was replaced on the same site, during the eleventh century, by a stave-built church. A great stone cathedral was started about 1080, succeeding another wooden church (that may have served as the first cathedral) of c. 1060. Lund was later chosen as the seat for the first Scandinavian archbishop.

Churches

he earliest churches in Scandinavia would have been built in timber, and archaeological excavations have revealed the traces of a series of eleventh-century buildings in Norway, Sweden, Denmark and England, all of which share a basic similarity in plan and all of which are stave-built. There was of course nothing new or peculiar about the technique of stave construction, for it had been in use, for example at Hedeby and Trelleborg, at an earlier date. The only problem for buildings intended to be permanent was that the lower parts of the planks, being set directly in the ground, rotted away before very long. The result is that the only surviving remains above ground of such eleventh-century churches are where walling was trimmed and re-used at a later date in a church on the same site – as at Urnes in Norway and Greensted in England – for in these later buildings the planks were set in sill-beams and so were raised above ground level to overcome this problem. Of the churches of the first missionaries in the ninth and tenth centuries no traces have yet been discovered, while those built in the Viking settlements overseas (as at Brattahlid) were adapted to local building traditions. The stave-churches are, however, a distinctive group of buildings with their origins in the late Viking Age.

The plans of the eleventh-century churches are simple, consisting of a rectangular nave with an approximately square chancel; in some instances these were both aisled. In the first church at Urnes, there were four central posts in the nave that may have served to heighten the roof; this is certainly the function of the nave posts in its standing twelfth-century successor. Multiple raised roofs were characteristic of the later Norwegian churches, as were elaborate carvings.

The best-preserved and most authentic of these Norwegian churches is that at Borgund, at the inner end of Sognefjord in western Norway; it has an internal structure not very different from that of the second church at

Urnes, so it too probably dates from the twelfth century. But its characteristic profile, with stepped roofs and animal-headed finials, is the result of thirteenth-century additions, although these are a logical outward extension of its internal structure. The eleventh-century carvings from the first church at Urnes suggest that a fully developed tradition of church adornment existed even then.

But in following through the development of the stave-church, we have passed way beyond the Viking Age.

The end of the Viking Age

The formation of true nation-states in Scandinavia, with the growth of royal power and the adoption of Christianity, were the processes that together marked the end of the Viking Age. With the shaping of the three northern Christian kingdoms of Norway, Sweden and Denmark, the Viking movements overseas, for whatever purposes, had gradually petered out, but only after their impact had been felt across a major part of the northern hemisphere – in many cases leaving a permanent imprint. The discovery and exploration of part of North America, the settlement of Greenland, the creation of the Icelandic nation and the peopling of the Faeroes were their distinctive achievements in the far West. In Western Europe, Norse and Danish blood and culture were inextricably mingled to lasting effect with those of Britain, Ireland and Normandy. In the East, during the forging of links with the worlds of Byzantium and Islam, the Vikings, as the Rus, played a vital role in bringing into existence the Slav kingdom that was to perpetuate their name in that of Russia. But the end result for Scandinavia of the establishment of this great network of settlements and contacts that made up the Viking world was to ensure that it was ultimately drawn within the bounds of European Christian civilization, in the process relinquishing most of the pagan barbarian culture that had made the Viking Age such a spectacular phase in northern history.

The stave-churches of
Scandinavia form a
distinctive and original
contribution to European
architecture. They
originated in the Viking
Age, but found their most
elaborate expression in
the 12th and 13th
centuries, as here at
Borgund in Norway.

Bibliography

This list is intended for the general reader and contains no references to the many important papers and excavation reports in learned journals. Only works in English and French are included; many have detailed bibliographies.

GENERAL

Almgren, B. (ed.) *The Viking* (C.A. Watts, London, 1966)

Arbman, H. *The Vikings* (Thames and Hudson, London, 1961, revised 1962; Westview Press, Boulder CO, 1961)

Brøndsted, J. *The Vikings* (Penguin, London and Baltimore, 1960, revised 1965)

Foote, P.G. and Wilson, D.M. *The Viking Achievement* (Sidgwick and Jackson, London, 1970, revised 1979; Praeger, New York, 1970)

Graham-Campbell, J. and Kidd, D. *The Vikings* (British Museum Publications, London, and The Metropolitan Museum of Art, New York, 1980)

Jones, G. *A History of the Vikings* (Oxford University Press, London and New York, 1968)

Kendrick, T.D. *A History of the Vikings* (Methuen, London, and Scribner, New York, 1930)

Musset, L. *Les Peuples Scandinaves au Moyen Age* (Presses Universitaires de France, Paris, 1951)

Musset, L. *Les Invasions: Le second assaut contre l'Europe chrétienne (VIIe–XIe siècles)* (Nouvelle Clio, 12 bis, Paris, 1965)

Sawyer, P.H. *The Age of the Vikings* (Edward Arnold, London, and St Martin's Press, New York, 1962, revised 1971)

Simpson, J. *Everyday Life in the Viking Age* (Batsford, London, 1967; Carousel, London, 1971)

Wilson, D.M. *The Vikings and their Origins* (Thames and Hudson, London, 1970, revised 1980)

ARCHAEOLOGICAL BACKGROUND

Hagen, A. *Norway* (Thames and Hudson, London, 1967)

Kivikoski, E. *Finland* (Thames and Hudson, London, and Praeger, New York, 1967)

Klindt-Jensen, O. *Denmark before the Vikings* (Thames and Hudson, London, and Praeger, New York, 1957)

Stenberger, M. *Sweden* (Thames and Hudson, London, and Praeger, New York, 1963)

LITERARY SOURCES

Campbell, A. *Skaldic Verse and Anglo-Saxon History* (University College, London, 1971)

Dasent, G.W. (trans.) *The Story of Burnt Njal* (Everyman, London, reprinted 1971; E.P. Dutton, New York, 1976)

Fell, C.E. (trans.) *Egils Saga* (Everyman, London, and University of Toronto Press, 1975)

Johnston, G. (trans.) *The Saga of Gisli* (Everyman, London, and University of Toronto Press, 1963)

Jones, G. (trans.) *Eirik the Red and Other Icelandic Sagas* (Oxford University Press, Oxford and New York, 1961)

Magnusson, M. and Pálsson, H. (trans.) *The Vinland Sagas* (Penguin, London and New York, 1965)

Turville-Petre, E.O.G. *Haraldr the Hard-ruler and his Poets* (H.K. Lewis, London, 1966)

Turville-Petre, E.O.G. *Scaldic Poetry* (Oxford University Press, Oxford and New York, 1976)

Young, J.I. *The Prose Edda of Snorri Sturluson* (University of California Press, 1964)

SHIPS

Brøgger, A.W. and Shetelig, H. *The Viking Ships* (Dreyer, Oslo, 1951; C. Hurst, London, and Arthur Vanous, Riveredge NJ, 1971)

Christenson, A.E. *Boats of the North* (Det Norske Samlaget, Oslo, 1968)

Crumlin-Pedersen, O. and Finch, R. *From Viking Ship to Victory* (National Maritime Museum, Greenwich, 1977)

McGrail, S. and McKee, E. *Building and Trials of the Replica of an Ancient Boat: the Gokstad Færing.* National Maritime Museum Monograph No. 11 (Greenwich, 1974)

Olsen, O. and Crumlin-Pedersen, O. *Five Viking Ships from Roskilde Fjord* (Vikingeskibshallen, Roskilde, 1978)

WESTWARD VOYAGES

Ingstad, H. *Westward to Vinland* (Jonathan Cape, London, and St Martin's Press, New York, 1969)

Jones, G. *The Norse Atlantic Saga* (Oxford University Press, Oxford, 1964)

Krogh, K.J. *Viking Greenland* (National Museum, Copenhagen, 1967)

Magnusson, M. *Viking Expansion Westwards* (Bodley Head, London, and Henry Z. Walck, New York, 1973)

see also, above, *Eirik the Red and Other Icelandic Sagas* and *The Vinland Sagas*

ART

Anker, P. *L' Art Scandinave*, Vol. I (Zodiaque, France, 1969). Translated as *The Art of Scandinavia*, Vol. I (Paul Hamlyn, Feltham, 1970)

Wilson, D.M. and Klindt-Jensen, O. *Viking Art* (George Allen and Unwin, London, and Cornell University Press, Ithaca NY, 1966)

RUNES

Elliott, R.W.V. *Runes, an Introduction* (Manchester University Press, 1959)

Jansson, S.B.F. *The Runes of Sweden* Phoenix House, London, and Bedminster Press, Totowa NJ, 1962)

Musset, L. *Introduction à la runologie* (Aubier-Montaigne, Paris, 1965, revised 1976)

Page, R.I. *An Introduction to English Runes* (Methuen, London, and Barnes and Noble, New York, 1973). Mainly on the Anglo-Saxon material, but with a chapter on Norse runes in England.

MYTHOLOGY

Ellis-Davidson, H.R. *Gods and Myths of Northern Europe* (Penguin, London, 1964 and New York, 1965)

Ellis-Davidson, H.R. *Scandinavian Mythology* (Paul Hamlyn, Feltham, 1969)

Turville-Petre, E.O.G. *Myth and Religion of the North* (Weidenfeld and Nicolson, London, 1964; Greenwood Press, Westport CT, 1975)

215

Acknowledgments

The publishers would like to thank the following individuals and organizations for their assistance:
(t = top, b = bottom, l = left, r = right, c = centre)

ARTWORK
Back jacket and page 34 Dave Pugh
11 Eugene Fleury
18 Dave Pugh (after E. Bakka)
23, 27 Eugene Fleury
34, 35, 38 Dave Pugh
40 Venner Artists (after O. Olsen and O. Crumlin-Pedersen)
43 Kevin Maddison (after O. Crumlin-Pedersen)
44–5, 46–7 Venner Artists
48 Kevin Maddison
50 Jenny Smith
52–3 Kevin Maddison (after B. Almgren)
54–7 Venner Artists
66–7 Eugene Fleury
70 Dave Pugh (after J. R. C. Hamilton)
71 Kevin Maddison
75 Dave Pugh (after A. King)
77 Dave Pugh (after S. Dahl)
81 Ian Stewart (after M. Stenberger)
88–9 Eugene Fleury
92 Dave Pugh (after H. Jankuhn)
94–5 Ian Stewart
96 Dave Pugh (after H. Arbman)
101 Dave Pugh (after B. Ó Ríórdáin)
102 Annie Winterbotham
106 Kevin Maddison (after H. Brinch-Madsen)
110, 119 Kevin Maddison
120 (l) Kevin Maddison (after M. Hoffman); (c) Jenny Smith (after E. E. Guðjonsson)
121 (t) Jenny Smith; (r) Jenny Smith (after S. Krafft); (b) Jenny Smith (after A. Geijer)
124–5, 126 Kevin Maddison
132 Eugene Fleury
136 (l) Kevin Maddison (after S. Krafft); (c) Jenny Smith
137, 140 Jenny Smith
142 (l) Jenny Smith (after E. Wilson); (r) Jenny Smith (after J. Graham-Campbell)
146, 147 Jenny Smith
153 Dave Pugh
157 Jenny Smith
159, 160 Dave Pugh
161 Jenny Smith
164 Dave Pugh
167 Jenny Smith
175 Dave Pugh (after S. Lindqvist)
179, 180, 182 Kevin Maddison
183 (t) Kevin Maddison; (r) Jenny Smith
184–5 Dave Pugh
187 Kevin Maddison

190–1 Ian Stewart and Dave Pugh (after K. Krogh)
201 Dave Pugh (after *Skalk* magazine, 1974, ill. J. Kraglund)
202, 204 Dave Pugh (after H. Schmidt)
206 Ian Stewart (after H. Schmidt)
207 Kevin Middleton
208–9 Dave Pugh
209 Dave Pugh (after F. Bau)
211 Dave Pugh (after A. Andrén)

PHOTOGRAPHS
The publishers wish particularly to extend their thanks to Lennart Larsen.

ATA = Antikvarisk Topografiska Arkivet, Stockholm
FLP = Frances Lincoln Publishers
HMB = Historisk Museum, Bergen Universitetet
JHA = John Hillelson Agency
LL = Lennart Larsen
NMC = Nationalmuseet, Copenhagen
NMI = National Museum of Ireland
SGS = Schleswig-Holsteinisches Landesmuseum, Schloss Gottorp, Schleswig
SHM = Statens Historiska Museet, Stockholm
UOO = Universitetets Oldsaksamling, Oslo
WFA = Werner Forman Archive

Front jacket Viking Ship Museum, Bygdøy/UOO
Half-title page Photo Eric Kay
Title page Photo G & P Corrigan/Robert Harding Associates
Contents page Photo Horst Munzig/Susan Griggs Agency
Foreword Photo C. M. Dixon
8–9 Photo Paolo Koch/Vision International
10 Photo LL/SHM/© FLP
12–13 Photo Ted Spiegel/JHA
13 Photo Torkild Balslev
14 (t) Photoresources/Viking Ship Museum, Bygdøy/UOO; (b) Courtesy Prof. B. Almgren, Uppsala/Viking Ship Museum, Bygdøy/UOO
15, 16 Photos LL/Gustavianum, Uppsala/© FLP
17 Photo LL/SHM/© FLP
19 Photo George Gerster/JHA
20–1 Photo C. M. Dixon
22 Photo LL/SHM/© FLP
24 Photoresources/Middleton Church, N. Yorks
25 (l) NMC; (r) Photo LL/Gustavianum, Uppsala/© FLP
26 Photo Axel Poignant/Lindisfarne Priory Museum
28, 30)l) Photos Ann-Mari Olsen/HMB
30 (r) Photo LL/NMC/© FLP
33 UOO
36–7 Photo Wedigo Ferchland/Danish

Tourist Board
38 Royal Norwegian Embassy, London
39 (tl) and (b) UOO; (tr) Photo WFA/Viking Ship Museum, Bygdøy/UOO
41 National Maritime Museum, London
42 By courtesy of the Trustees of the British Museum, London
43 (t) Photo Vikingeskibshallen i Roskilde; (c) National Maritime Museum, London
48–9 Photo Michael Holford
50 National Maritime Museum, London
51–3 Photo Michael Holford
58 (t) Weidenfeld & Nicolson Archive/UOO; (b) Photo LL/Royal Coin Cabinet, Stockholm/© FLP
59 NMI
60 (l) Photo Vikingeskibshallen i Roskilde
60–1, 62–3 Photos Michael Holford
64 Photo WFA
68 Photo Dennis Coutts
69 Photo John Dewar/Scottish Development Dept
70 Photo Aerofilms
72 Photo James Graham-Campbell
73, 74 Photos C. M. Dixon
75 Photo Alan King
76–7 Photo Erich Hartmann/Magnum/JHA
78–9 Photo Sten-M. Rosenlund
79 Photo G. Gestsson/National Museum of Iceland, Reykjavik
80 Photos James Graham-Campbell
83 Photo WFA
84 (t) Photo Parks, Canada; (b) Photo LL/NMC/© FLP
85 © 1965 by Yale University (from *The Vinland Map and the Tartar Relation* by R.A. Skelton, T. E. Marston and G.D. Painter, publ. by Yale University Press)
86–7, 90–1 Photos LL/SHM/© FLP
93 (t) Photo Dr Uwe Muuss; (b) Photo James Graham-Campbell
97 Photo Avddir. B. Ambrosiani/SHM
98–9 Photo Knut Einar Oskarsen, Kodal, Norway
100 (t) Photo Sten-M. Rosenlund; (b) Photo Woodmansterne/Yorkshire Museum, York
101 NMI
103 Courtesy Per Lundström, Statens Sjöhistoriska Museum, Stockholm
104 (tl) Photo Mogens Bencard/Sydjysk Universitetscenter, Esbjerg, Denmark; (r) Photo LL/SGS/© FLP; (bl) Photo Ann-Mari Olsen/HMB
105 Photo Ted Spiegel/JHA/NMI
106 (tl) Photo LL/Kulturen, Lund/© FLP; (br) Photos LL/SGS/© FLP
107 (t) UOO; (b) WFA/NMC
108 Photo Ted Spiegel/JHA
109 Weidenfeld & Nicolson Archive/Gävle Museum, Sweden
110 Photo LL/SHM/© FLP
111, 112–13 Photos LL/NMC

114 (t) Photo LL/SHM/© FLP; (b) Photo Ann-Mari Olsen/HMB
115 Photo LL/UOO/© FLP
116 (t) Photo LL/SGS/© FLP; (tr) Photo LL/SHM/© FLP; (cl) Photoresources/NMC
117, 118 Photos LL/SHM/© FLP
120 (t) Photo Bay Hippisley/Courtesy Kulturen, Lund; (b) National Museum of Iceland, Reykjavik
121 UOO
122 Photo Ann-Mari Olsen/HMB
123 (c) and (b) Photo LL/Kulturen, Lund/© FLP; (r) Photo Ann-Mari Olsen/HMB
126 (c) Photo LL/SHM/© FLP; (b) Photo Sten-M. Rosenlund
127 Ålborg Museum, Denmark
128, 129 (t) Viking Ship Museum, Bygdøy/UOO
129 (b) Photo Mike Duffy/York Archaeological Trust
130 Photo LL/NMC
133 Photo Sören Hallgren/SHM
134–5 Photo WFA/Viking Ship Museum, Bygdøy/UOO
135 Photoresources/UOO
136 Photo LL/NMC
137 (l), (tr) and (cr) Photos LL/SHM/© FLP; (br) Photo LL/UOO/© FLP
138 (t) Courtesy Prof. B. Almgren, Uppsala/Viking Ship Museum, Bygdøy/UOO; (b) Photo WFA
139 (tl) and (b) Photos LL/NMC/© FLP; (tr) Photo LL/Trondheim Museum/© FLP
140 Photo LL/NMC
141 (t) Photo Claus Hansmann/SHM; (b) Photo LL/SHM/© FLP
142, 143 (t) Photos LL/NMC
143 (b) Photo LL/UOO/© FLP
144 (c) Photo Claus Hansmann/Bayer Nationalmuseum, München; (b) ATA/Sigtuna Museum
145 Photo LL/NMC
146 (tr) Photo Claus Hansmann; (b) Photoresources
147 Photo Sten-M. Rosenlund
148–9 Photo LL/NMC
150 Photo Riksantikvaren, Kirkegate 14–18, Oslo
151 (t) Photo LL/Ålborg Museum, Denmark; (b) ATA/SHM
152 Cambridge University Library/Ms Ff.1.23, f.37 verso
153 (t) NMI; (b) Nordiska Museet, Stockholm
154–5 Photo Sten-M. Rosenlund
156 HMB
157 Photo R. I. Page/Bridekirk Church, Cumbria
158 (c) Photo Erik Moltke/Antikvarisk Samling, Ribe
158–9 UOO
160 Photo Sten-M. Rosenlund

161 (t) and (c) Courtesy Eva Wilson; (b) Museum of London
162 ATA
162–3 Photo Ted Spiegel/JHA
165 Photo Gosta Glase
166 (t) Royal Danish Embassy, London; (l) Photo Sten-M. Rosenlund; (r) National Museum of Antiquities of Scotland, Edinburgh
169 ATA
170 Photo Michael Holford
172–3 Photo Ted Spiegel/JHA
174–5 Photo Sten-M. Rosenlund
175 From *Historia de Gentibus Septentrionalis*, Olaus Magnus, 1555
176 Photo James Graham-Campbell
177 From *Birka: Die Graber*, H. Arbman, 1943
178 (t) Photo WFA/SHM; (b) Photo LL/SHM/© FLP
179 Photoresources/SHM
180 Photo LL/SHM/© FLP
181 (l) Photo Axel Poignant/Gosforth Church, Cumbria; (r) Photo Sten-M. Rosenlund
182 (tc) and (tr) Photo LL/SHM/© FLP; (b) Photo LL/Kulturen, Lund/© FLP
183 WFA/Moesgård, Denmark
184, 185 Photos WFA/Manx Museum
186 Photo C. M. Dixon/Middleton Church, N. Yorks
187 Photo LL/NMC
188 (t) and (c) Photo LL/SHM/© FLP; (b) LL/SGS/© FLP
189 Photo Christina Gascoigne/Robert Harding Associates
191 (tl) Photo C. M. Dixon/Hoveringham Church, Notts; (r) National Museum of Iceland, Reykjavik
192 Photos LL/SHM/©FLP
193 Stofnun Arna Magnussonar, Reykjavik
194–5 Photo C. M. Dixon
197 Courtesy Trondheim Cathedral
198 Photo Ted Spiegel/JHA
199 (br) Photo LL/Royal Coin Cabinet, Stockholm/© FLP; 'portrait'-head coins Photos Michael Holford/British Museum, London; others Photos R. A. Gardner/British Museum, London
200, 202–3, 204–5 Photos Torkild Balslev
206 Photo LL/Royal Coin Cabinet, Stockholm/© FLP
207 Photo courtesy *Skalk* magazine
208 Photo Dr Uwe Muuss
210 Photo Mogens Schou Jørgensen, Copenhagen
213 Photo WFA

Lines on back jacket and page 171 Translation by John Lucas (from *Egils Saga*, trans. C. E. Fell, Everyman, 1975)

Index by Douglas Matthews